D0053695

AVON PUBLIC LIBRARY
WITHDRAWN BENCHMARK RD.
AVON, CO 81620

WITHDRAWN

# THE
# INEQUALITY
# PARADOX

ALSO BY DOUGLAS MCWILLIAMS

*The Flat White Economy*

# THE
# INEQUALITY
# PARADOX

### How **CAPITALISM** *Can*
### *Work for* **EVERYONE**

# DOUGLAS
# McWILLIAMS

The Overlook Press
New York, NY

This edition first published in hardcover in the United States in 2018 by
The Overlook Press, an imprint of ABRAMS
195 Broadway, 9th floor
New York, NY 10007
www.overlookpress.com

Abrams books are available at special discounts when purchased in quantity for
premiums and promotions as well as fundraising or educational use.
Special editions can also be created to specification. For details, contact
specialsales@abramsbooks.com or the address above.

Copyright © 2018 by Douglas McWilliams

All rights reserved. No part of this publication may be reproduced or
transmitted in any form or by any means, electronic or mechanical, including
photocopy, recording, or any information storage and retrieval system now
known or to be invented, without permission in writing from the publisher,
except by a reviewer who wishes to quote brief passages in connection with
a review written for inclusion in a magazine, newspaper, or broadcast.

Cataloging-in-Publication Data is available from the Library of Congress

Book design and typeformatting by Bernard Schleifer
Manufactured in the United States of America
FIRST EDITION
1 3 5 7 9 10 8 6 4 2
ISBN 978-1-4683-1498-4

To Andrew Richardson and to all those who have
helped me while I have been writing this book

# CONTENTS

# FOREWORD

OTHER THAN BEING BORN WHITE, MALE AND SCOTTISH AND HAVING wonderful loving parents who did everything possible to stimulate my mind as a kid and who sent me to great schools and a super university, I have had two especially lucky breaks which have done much to influence me as an economist.

I was fortunate enough to get a job as Chief Economist of IBM UK in the mid-1980s. This gave me a chance to see how technology was changing the world at a pace that people outside the industry could hardly imagine. Even now, I find those outside the tech industries and especially those outside the commercial sphere can find it hard to keep up with the pace of change in the key technological sectors and see how they alter economic relationships.

What I learned about this helped me immensely with my last book, *The Flat White Economy*. This describes the cluster of companies that has resulted from the tech sector merging with the creative sector to develop a brand-new economy which now accounts for a whole tenth of UK GDP. It really is important to understand this new economy which works on slightly different rules and, as often happens with emerging (and also intangible) sectors, is badly described in economic measurements in most countries.

But even more important than learning about tech was my good luck in being brought up as an expatriate in both pre-independence Malaya and then emerging Malaysia. I can't defend much that the British did as colonialists, though they did good as well as bad. Malaysians are remarkably tolerant of the former colonials, given what happened in the pre-independence era. But being brought up in a fast-developing economy meant that I was lucky enough to see how economic development takes place at firsthand.

When I went to university and started studying the subject, it seemed that the models most commonly taught in the West of how economic development took place were flawed. These models relied on government investment and state-run industrialisation. Sadly there was little evidence of this approach working well and when it did work at all it did so with great inefficiency.[1]

What actually worked in the Far East was a bit different. The state was heavily involved in providing basic services, sanitation, law and order, health, transport infrastructure and most especially education, but the business investment was carried out by the private sector, with external investors, attracted by tax-free zones and cheap labour, providing capital, expertise and access to export markets. (Chapter 5 describes this period in more detail.)

This mixed model of development worked dramatically well from the mid-1960s in Singapore, Hong Kong, Korea and Taiwan, followed by Thailand and Malaysia, and then about 15 years later in many other parts of the world, including of course China and India. It is important to note, however, that the world is changing and the next phase of development for many emerging economies is likely to be based on a different model, with proportionately more internal and public consumption and less reliance on external investment and exports.

Some have claimed that this success in economic development in the Far East was proof of the triumph of capitalism.[2] My take is more nuanced. Capitalism was certainly involved but could never have succeeded on its own had governments not also helped. I would call the Asian success the triumph of a mixed model, neither exclusively capitalist nor exclusively state-driven. It is worth noting that there are different Asian models, though they tend (when compared with approaches in the West) to have substantial similarities. Hong Kong has been the most free market, China the most interventionist and state-driven. All depend on an entrepreneurialism that fortunately had not been stamped out by either colonialism or communism.

I also concluded that the development of the Asian economies was going to be the driving force behind the world economy in the latter part of the 20th century and much of the 21st. And so it has proved to be.

Some of the most heated debates I have had while writing this book have been with people who still think that the world remains driven by the West alone. The statistics would have supported them in 2000 when so-called 'developing economies' accounted for only 24% of the world economy.[3] But by 2010 the share was up to 40%. On my latest estimates for 2017 (published in Cebr's World Economic League Table 2018[4]) the share is now 46% and set to rise to 56% by 2032.

Even while the share is below half, it is normally the case in any market that the most dynamic and disruptive forces tend to set the terms of trade. It is the East that is driving what happens in the West today and arguably has been doing so for the better part of half a century.

My impression is that this is well understood in Europe but that the rise of the Asian economies is often seen as more of a threat than an opportunity in the US. World economic development was essentially driven by the Western world for most of the past five centuries, whereas now the baton has been partly passed to the newly rapidly industrialising economies in the East. These Eastern economies are growing in real terms at 4-8% per annum while even the most buoyant Western economies are growing no faster than 3%.

And much of what happens in the West is a reaction to economic changes originating in the East. The one area where the West still seems to be leading is in the information- and software-driven technologies promoted by the likes of Apple, Microsoft, Alphabet (the holding company for Google and related ventures), Amazon and Facebook. But even there ten of the top 25 tech companies in the world in the Forbes list are now Asian, led by Ali Baba, Tencent and Samsung.[5]

For me, besides learning at firsthand what drove economic development, the other major advantage of being brought up in Malaysia was seeing intimately the anomaly that some of us, simply through the accident of being of Western ethnic background, had so much higher living standards than people of local extraction. This got me interested in inequality.

Some people with an essentially racist approach thought that it was natural that westerners should be wealthier because in some way we were 'superior'. Fortunately I was not brought up to think that, and the economic evidence seemed to disprove it anyway. It really bothered me in my youth that we westerners lived so much better than the locals. As far as I could see we had few innate advantages of ability or knowledge. Ok, we may have been a bit less corrupt (at least on the surface). But on the other hand we worked only a fraction of the hours that most local people did. In few other areas did we seem to have any attributes that would cause us to deserve to live so much better than the Malays, Chinese and Indians who made up the bulk of the Malaysian population.

I have a theory that if there is no good economic reason for something to exist, eventually it will cease to exist. And much of my time as an economist has been spent trying to predict how soon the gap between the Eastern and Western living standards would narrow, which it has – Singapore and Hong Kong have now overtaken most of the West in GDP per capita measures – and trying to understand the consequences of this for both sides and for the world economy.

My good luck in having the twin and slightly unfair advantages of having worked at the centre of a leading tech company[6] and having seen economic development in the Far East at firsthand has certainly helped my ability to interpret economic developments and thus make predictions. I hope these insights have illuminated this book.

I would like to thank various people who have helped me. As ever Diane Banks, who is expanding rapidly as befits the best literary agent in London, helped me a lot with choosing the subject on which to write and negotiating with my publishers, Duckworth. Diane is a person of great literary judgement and a really useful sounding board for someone like me who doesn't understand the world of books. She also has an instinctive grasp of economics, which makes her possibly unique in the literary world. She was the person who suggested the title, 'The Inequality Paradox'. Martin Redfern who works with her and handles her non-fiction clients, has been especially helpful in dealing with some of the inevitable problems that emerge when one is trying to persuade those who think rather traditionally that there is a new and better explanation of how the world works. Martin also came up with the subtitle, which explains the book perfectly: 'Can capitalism work for everyone?'

The staff at Duckworth have consistently encouraged me, helping to correct my mistakes and showing considerable patience with my slowness in completing drafts. I am particularly grateful to the legendary Peter Mayer, who has helped me with his wisdom and experience. I doubt if we ever saw eye to eye on much but his constant challenge to the ways in which I have made my argument has certainly led to a better book than would otherwise have been the case. Sadly he passed away just after contributing to this book so I hope that wherever he is he will feel that I have benefited from his guidance. I am also grateful to Matt Casbourne who has taken on the role of editor since Peter Mayer's death and who has always tried to encourage me, and Deborah Blake who has been a kindly but firm copy editor and Adam O'Brien who has handled the publishing in New York.

The person to whom this book owes most is my wife Ianthe. She has constantly encouraged and driven me to keep going even when I've been close to despair at the size of the task I've undertaken, has refreshed me with delicious meals while writing, and persistently acted as a sounding board. As I said in the foreword to my previous book, *The Flat White Economy*, 'I owe my wife a disproportionate share of whatever minor success I have had in my own field and that this book might bring. She has done much more for me than any husband could possibly deserve.' This remains true. She has continued to encourage me and gently critique me. As a former civil servant who worked hard to help improve the standard of teaching, particularly maths and science, in the UK's schools, she also helped me a lot with Chapter 12 on education.

One can't write a book while trying to work in an office without placing undue strain on the other staff there. Graham Brough, Cebr's Chief Executive, has borne the brunt of the burden. But others in the office, particularly Oliver Hogan, Sarah Conkay, Nina Skero and Cristian Niculescu-Marcu, have also had to face an increased burden as a result of the time that I have spent on the book. I am very grateful to them.

Shivam Talukdar was an intern at Cebr recommended by my friend Giles Keating. Shivam was doing his first-year course at New York University when he came to work with Cebr. He helped me develop my thinking on the analysis of the persistence of wealth which is written up in Chapter 9. Most of the conclusions of that chapter result from his careful analysis.

I am especially grateful to Robert Watt, editor of the Sunday Times Rich List, for allowing me access to the Rich List data on the persistence of wealth. Although the data was already in the public domain, Robert managed to find old hard copies of the publication for Shivam to analyse and was extremely helpful in discussing our conclusions.

Two academics may not know it, but their work and research has influenced me and made the task of completing this book considerably easier. Max Roser, an Oxford academic, started OurWorldindata.org collecting data on a host of important factors, particularly in those areas affecting living standards. He and his work deserve to be much better known. I have used much of his data and I hope this book encourages more people to use it. Branko Milanovic is a Serbian American economist who has written by far the best academic book on inequality: *Global Inequality: A New Approach for the Age of Globalization*. Milanovic is very well known to the experts but less so to a wider world. I don't always agree with him but have no doubt that he is an important economist.

And he writes extremely readably for anyone, let alone an American academic, for whom English is not his first language – or possibly because English is not his first language.

Andrew Richardson was a City economist whom I knew before he became afflicted with multiple sclerosis and had to change career. He qualified as a Human Givens psychotherapist and is now a depression-recovery specialist and anti-addiction counsellor. Andrew has helped me refine this book. In the last months before I submitted the manuscript he and I met a dozen times to refine and improve the text. He has been particularly important in helping me understand the thinking of the Human Givens movement, which is a very useful approach to understanding how human beings work, though, like all approaches, it is important to understand when it works and when it doesn't.

For his immense help with this and with other things I am extremely grateful and therefore delighted to dedicate this book to him. He is a special person.

# PROLOGUE

THE INEQUALITY PARADOX IS THAT WHILE INEQUALITY HAS BEEN RISING within nations, especially in the West, poverty (and especially extreme poverty) has been falling.

Does this mean that the higher the level of inequality the lower the level of poverty?

Of course not. But the paradox draws attention to an uncomfortable fact – poverty and inequality are not the same thing and sometimes a third force (in this case mainly globalisation) can push world poverty down while at the same time increasing inequality in individual countries. In Chapter 6 we see that this has been associated with a reduction in the extent of inequality between countries.

The subtitle 'Can Capitalism Work for Everyone?' draws attention to the fact that at a time of increasing perceived inequality, liberal capitalism is under attack from Marxists on the Left and from those opposing migration and free trade and supporting various forms of protectionism on the so-called Right. Both blame increasing inequality in individual countries on liberal capitalism. This book considers the validity of the points made in these attacks and looks at what needs to be done to make capitalism work in ways that make it both more inclusive and more acceptable.

My experience, while growing up in Malaysia, of the difference in the standards of living between those of us with a Western background and those native to the Far East was what interested me in the related issues of poverty and inequality.

People often confuse the two.

By far the most important economic development in the past 25 years is that the number of people in extreme poverty (on the World Bank definition) has fallen from 1,958 million people to 769 million people between 1990 and 2013 (2013 is the latest year for reasonably hard data

..ject), from 37.1% to 10.7% of the world's population.[1] This ..tistical data is backed up by health indicators and life expectancy data. It has been confirmed by the late lamented statistician Hans Rosling who described what this data was starting to show in a highly acclaimed TED talk.[2] It is also backed up by statistics on nutrition and health (see Chapter 6). It may seem perverse that while there is evidence in Western economies of increased poverty, total poverty in the world is decreasing. Moreover the fall in poverty appears to be continuing, at least in some countries. Chinese Premier Li Keqiang, at the opening meeting of the first session of the 13th National People's Congress in March 2018, claimed that 'more than 68.5 million rural people had been lifted out of poverty in China over the past five years' with the 'national poverty rate falling from 10.2 percent to 3.1 percent'.[3] This is a fall from nearly 100 million people to 30 million. World Bank data on world poverty for the new base year of 2015 will be published around the time this book comes out.

Meanwhile globalisation has changed the geographical distribution of poverty. Poverty used to be a long way away and people in Western economies could ignore it if so inclined. While there is now much less poverty in absolute terms, much more of it is on our doorsteps, sometimes literally so with the number of rough sleepers in London having risen from 3,975 in 2010/11 to 8,108 in 2016/17.[4] This amounts to 90 per 100,000 residents. The problem of homelessness in the US is rather more serious. The data shows New York's problem as nearly ten times worse with 887 homeless per 100,000, with San Francisco nearly as bad with 795 homeless people per 100,000 residents.[5] Most people would consider that even if (as is the case) global poverty is diminishing, poverty in their own area is a problem that has to be addressed if possible.

What is superficially bizarre is that this reduction in global poverty happened mainly at a time when inequality in most Western countries was increasing at its fastest rate ever.

It is the contrast between the apparent falling poverty and the rising inequality within countries in the West until about ten years ago that has generated the title of this book.

Thomas Piketty in his best-selling book, *Capital in the Twenty-First Century*,[6] makes the case that the cause of the rise in inequality is essentially an increase in the extent of exploitation. In my view, this is responsible for substantially more than a negligible proportion (see Chapter 3 for a discussion about how much of the rise in inequality is due to this factor). And because it is the most blatant and offensive cause of inequality it is important to act to minimise inequality from this source.

But research from both Harvard University and the IMF supports my back-of-the-envelope calculations that this is by no means the most important cause of the recent rise in inequality in Western economies. The evidence seems to suggest that globalisation, particularly the combination of globalisation and the advance of technology, is a much more potent cause of both increased inequality and increased poverty in Western economies (again, see Chapter 3 for a discussion of the allocation of responsibility between different causes). Globalisation seems to have increased inequality within countries while at the same time reducing inequality between countries.

Looking forward, the jury is out on the extent to which inequality from exploitation will increase further. Piketty's argument that it would do so because the rate of interest and hence the rate of capital accumulation would exceed the rate of growth has not been supported in recent years as ultra-loose monetary policy has kept interest rates at rock-bottom levels. But as more of the world's economy shifts to countries with less well embedded traditions of law and anti-corruption, it is quite possible that so-called crony capitalism (unfair, really, to call it capitalism because it is really the antithesis of capitalism in that it is based on government controls and normally operates to exclude competition) will grow, leading to increased exploitation. In addition, the likelihood of super-high profits in tech and other monopolies could and probably would also lead to increased exploitation. But there are also trends going the other way. And there are also remedies that public policy could apply to reverse some of the trend towards increased exploitation.

My take on globalisation is that we are roughly halfway through the process of technological catch-up as the spread of education worldwide means that historic gaps between the East and the West disappear. It is likely (see Chapter 5 for a fuller discussion and explanation) that as the East continues to grow living standards will actually rise above those in the West, as they already have in Singapore and Hong Kong. So there is more impact from globalisation to come. But it is likely the biggest impact on low-labour-cost jobs has already been felt. Labour costs in many Eastern economies, especially China, are rising dramatically. The competition from the East is likely to affect work at much higher skill levels than hitherto and hence have a different impact on inequality in the West compared with that of the changes that took place over the past half century.

It is worth pausing at this point to consider whether any level of poverty is 'acceptable'. Jesus is reputed to have said 'the poor are always with us'.[7] In most modern Western societies strenuous attempts are made with considerable amounts spent on welfare to try to stop poverty. Yet it still exists. Why?

There is a mix of reasons. Obviously if you believe that the size of the economy is predetermined and that the only issue is how to slice up the cake, any poverty at all seems unacceptable. But this is an extreme view shared by few and runs in face of the evidence that the size of the cake is dependent on how it is baked. Most attempts to impose massive redistribution by the state – e.g. in the USSR, China under Chairman Mao or more recently Venezuela – have not only led to brutality on a massive scale but have also been fairly unsuccessful. There are some examples of success in small cohesive societies in some parts of Europe, especially in Scandinavia, but even these successes seem now to be breaking down under pressure from migration (see Chapter 7 for an interesting discussion of why Scandinavia has seemed to work well despite appearing to flout the obvious rules for achieving growth). It seems difficult to redistribute on a sufficient scale to eliminate poverty even in relatively affluent Western societies. Where it does seem to work best is when the redistribution is carried out on a local scale or in a relatively small and cohesive society.

The greatest success in reducing poverty ever on a massive scale has been the result of the industrialisation of the formerly emerging economies over the past 50 years. As I point out elsewhere in this book, this is not a wholly capitalist phenomenon (or 'supply side', or whatever term one wants to use to describe a partly market-based approach). In China, particularly, the policy was a clever mix of using governments to provide infrastructure and education and other relevant background support and using export markets and private investment to provide the combination of skills, markets and technologies to fuel economic growth. So the issue is not so much 'how much poverty if any is acceptable?' but 'how best to reduce poverty?' As pointed out in Chapter 11, the main harvest from reducing poverty by economic growth has probably been picked. Looking forward, it seems that other methods (in particular ending the wars that are creating so much hardship in many countries) will be necessary to reduce extreme poverty further, though it is reasonable to predict as well as hope that continuing economic growth will continue to improve the prosperity of people who, even if above the extreme poverty line, are certainly still poor by most reasonable measures.

In the future the continuing impact of exploitation and globalisation is likely to be deepened by two factors that have until now had much less impact – technology and 'superbabies'.

My experience from writing my last book, *The Flat White Economy*, and also from my time as Chief Economist for IBM (UK) is that we are now at a technological turning point as 12 key technologies leap forward – of which perhaps the most important are robotics, AI, autonomous vehicles, blockchain technologies, 3D printing and genomics.

Technology will bring back the problem of inequality and force us to think hard about solutions. It is important that we do not go for the wrong ones that would make our problems worse.

And technology is not the only new factor driving inequality. 'Superbabies', the progeny of highly educated people who meet at university, have the benefits not only of selective breeding but also the best parenting, good nutrition, regular exercise both physical and mental, as well as good education and sharp-elbowed parents determined to find the best for their children. Unless resources are deliberately channelled to the schools of the least advantaged, it is likely that the children of these meritocrats, and even more their future generations, will make it increasingly difficult for mobility to take place in society. On top of this will be the effects of genetic modification if it is allowed to take place (and it seems hard to prevent it). Any benefits from this are unlikely to be distributed evenly.

This book contains some detailed research on the persistence of wealth which suggests that it takes not three but five generations for most wealth to evaporate, but it also contains statistics on how mobility between classes is diminishing as a result of the entrenching of social positions, especially between the better and the less well educated.

The key thing with inequality is to look at the problem clearly and hardheadedly. It is understandable that those losing their jobs or seeing their pay fall back in real terms see the issue with minds that can be clouded with emotion, anger and frustration. But emotion, anger and frustration can be bad guides for action.

Perhaps the worst problems caused by inequality are those of exclusion and alienation. There is good psychological theory that suggests that if people's psychological needs are not met, ultimately they are likely to develop damaging behaviour traits or other psychological problems. Especially in the developed world in the West, many people at the less privileged end of society have a sense of a society where things are getting worse for people like them, and they see their own position in life declining, with little hope for the future for either themselves or their children. They feel that they have no control over the events affecting them, and their frustration about this has an impact on their mental and physical health.

These problems are not easy to deal with, and just throwing money at them often does surprisingly little to help. Good education (it is important to realise that in the modern world education is not just relevant to young people) is probably the single most important way of breaking into the cycle of deprivation. Providing high quality social services can also help. Continental Europe is currently handling this problem much better than either the US or the UK, though at possibly unaffordable cost and to some extent by creating a generation some of whom feel little obligation to work hard to pay their way. The increasing alienation of this group is likely to pose a future problem which will also have to be handled.

In Part IV of this book I set out how some of the problems arising from the pressures for increasing inequality can be dealt with. My contention is that it *is* possible to counteract the driving forces that are otherwise likely to increase inequality, but that it will require three things:

First, any solution needs to ensure that the economy can prosper. It would be possible to have complete equality of misery with negligible economic activity and poverty widespread. One hopes that no one would find that acceptable. Anyone who does is wasting their time reading this book.

Second, a careful and accurate identification of the main driving forces behind the growth in inequality is needed, so that their effects can be understood and where possible counteracted.

Third, when those factors driving the growth in inequality cannot easily be counteracted (or where the cost of counteracting them is excessive), policies need to be put in place to compensate so that the increase in poverty can be circumvented.

What this means is that we are likely to need to rethink a whole raft of policies, from education, through welfare, taxation and labour market policy so that the radical changes in technology that will affect us in the very near future can be absorbed with less pain than otherwise would be the case. These huge advances in technology will destroy or change most existing jobs, but they will almost certainly create many new ones, mainly in areas that we cannot possibly imagine. The impact on existing jobs might lead to either unemployment or a huge increase in inequality. But neither has to be the case if we can build the right kind of flexibility into both the product markets and the labour market. This might be complicated since the instinctive temptation when faced with such pressures is to reduce labour market flexibility by protecting jobs rather than to increase flexibility, even if the latter would ultimately be better for both jobs and people.

At the same time there is no substitute for good education, and not just for counteracting the effects of 'superbabies'. Moreover, it is vital that the schools for the most disadvantaged get the best teachers. Some may want private (or, as they are quaintly known in the UK, public[8]) schools shut down. I'm not keen on that because I hate banning things unless their side-effects are dangerously bad for society. The jury is still out on whether introducing such a disruption to the country's educational system would be justified in order to improve social cohesion, particularly as there are plenty of unused large buildings in many other countries waiting to be put to good use.[9] But something certainly needs to be done to channel the best resources into the education of the most disadvantaged. And education needs to be seen as a lifelong requirement – not just something that you do at the beginning of your life. Education needs to be backed by training and retraining to enable people to have the skills necessary at any point in time.

Although this book points out that exploitation is not even the major cause of inequality, it is vital that those excesses of capitalism that do exist (and there are many) should be ruthlessly extirpated. Not only are they damaging to both economic activity and inequality, they are damaging in a particularly offensive way. Moreover they stir up opposition to the economic system and to business. There are ways of making it much more difficult to exploit the rest of society through means such as crony deals between businessmen and politicians, crooked banking and overpowerful tech companies.

A new Teddy Roosevelt is needed to bust the trusts and ensure that politicians around the world work harder to resist the pressure of lobbying from such sources. I don't have much hope for politicians discovering backbone where none previously existed, but the best way of reinforcing good intentions is for public opinion to understand the problem and for the public to be seized with the need to ensure that their elected representatives deal with it effectively. This means an electorate who use their muscle when appropriate but who also are prepared to study issues sufficiently closely to reject unworkable and oversimplistic solutions.

Government itself needs to be careful that, through the law of unintended consequences, it does not itself cause or exacerbate inequality by imposing the wrong or excessive taxes or regulations that ossify the status quo, or by adding to costs and prices and so squeezing the standard of living, or by restrictions of supply through rental policies, planning policies, inefficient provision of public transport and other measures with less obvious effects, such as the impact of lax monetary policy on asset prices, or by keeping prices high by weak competition policy or lax regulation of so-called natural monopolies.

Western societies need to take advantage of opportunities to reduce inequality by permitting new technologies to bring down the cost of living. When Western societies had little competition we built quite a high cost way of life through strict regulation and high taxes. We may need to curb some of the practices that were affordable when we competed only with people as wealthy as ourselves. We are also likely to need to focus an increasing proportion of public expenditure on redistribution, so we will need to economise where possible on other areas to ensure that the maximum is available for this purpose.

It is worth noting that Singapore has a much higher GDP per capita than the UK yet its cost of living (despite high house prices) is about two-thirds of that in the UK. It would be worth learning from countries such as Singapore and its best practices in some areas, especially public administration and government. In many areas such as health, defence, infrastructure, education and housing Singapore manages the amazing trick of providing high quality services at relatively low cost.

High prices in the West are often added to by regulations (often gold plating prudential requirements for safety and health), tariffs, taxes and lack of pro-competition policy. And some high prices in the UK result from charges imposed by government itself, often taking advantage of its own monopoly power to raise revenues from those who cannot avoid the charges. The same is true but to a lesser extent in the US. Policy can be changed to bring down these excess charges though there will be an impact on public finances.

Technology is also driving some products and services into the world of 'post scarcity'. I was at a conference in Berlin last year where the head of one of the largest businesses in Europe openly speculated about the likelihood of energy being free (other than connection costs) within a quarter of a century as renewable resources are properly harnessed. Post scarcity in theory should make it possible for prices of some products to fall to negligible levels. It is important that this is allowed to happen so that the cost of living can be reduced.

Fifth, it seems likely that there should be a gradual introduction, as it becomes affordable, probably in the 2030s and 2040s, of a Universal Basic Income. This won't solve inequality but it will make some of the inevitable inequality less intolerable. It will also allow people to do the low (measured) productivity service, craft, lifestyle and caring jobs that will increasingly be the sensible choice for many but are at present ruled out by the combination of selective welfare and minimum wages. The fact that the premature pilot scheme for Universal Basic Income in Finland has been scrapped should not be seen as an indicator of whether this idea might or might not be appropriate at the right time. Currently the costs are not affordable, but as technology develops they should become so.

Finally, our whole system of taxation is likely to need to change. In most countries the current system of taxation mainly focuses on incomes and especially on labour incomes. This is likely to need to be rebalanced if production becomes more capital intensive and relatively less labour intensive. The first reason is that if increased labour market flexibility is required, high rates of labour and income taxation may need to be reformed. The second is that it is likely that, as technology becomes more dominant, capital incomes will become a growing share of GDP and the current focus on labour and employment taxes would mean a declining yield. The third reason is that an increasing role of the tax system will have to be the need for redistribution.

I am not a great believer in high taxes, which often cost more money than they raise as a result of their impact on incentives and hence the tax base. But despite this, there is scope for making tax itself much more redistributive, and in many countries (largely in emerging economies) there remains scope for higher rates of direct tax to finance redistribution without damaging growth and destroying incentives. Elsewhere, however, the focus needs to be more on reducing high marginal rates of direct taxes, which in many countries are above the revenue maximising rate, and moving the focus of taxation to taxing wealth instead, particularly through death duties. I believe that if the idea was sold carefully, it would also be possible to raise considerable sums through voluntary taxes, particularly voluntary death duties. It would be important for these voluntary payments to be visible, at least for private individuals.

What is interesting here is that many previous studies of inequality have focussed on great macroeconomic solutions for the problem. My take is different. The problem cannot be completely solved without throwing the baby out with the bathwater and in particular worsening poverty. But there is a lot that can practically be done with micro measures. I apologise if these don't appeal to those of a utopian disposition, but often the so-called best is the enemy of the good.

There is a growing industry of writing about inequality. In preparation for this book I have analysed more than 40 books or major articles on the subject (see Chapter 2) and I suspect many more have been left unread.

This book tries to look at the issue from a broader perspective than some. It makes a clear distinction between poverty and inequality. Sometimes increasing inequality goes hand in hand with increasing poverty. Sometimes it doesn't and, as in the recent past, the same process that has on occasions led to increasing inequality within countries has also reduced global poverty. When there is a trade-off between the two, I'm very much on the side of reducing poverty, which seems to me to be more important than reducing inequality. On the other hand, it is inequality rather than poverty per se that seems to lead to increased alienation.

The book distinguishes between three different types and four different causes of economic inequality, all of which have different policy implications, some of which are contradictory.

I make an important distinction between the psychological and material aspects of inequality. The people amongst whom I grew up in Malaysia were often amazingly poor by Western standards. But they had hope in the future. People in menial jobs, such as domestic servants, would often invest nearly half their take-home pay in private education to give their children a better life. That degree of self-sacrifice humbled me.

The contrast is the despair and alarming decline in life expectancy in white working-class males in the US, a trend I noticed first when the same thing happened earlier in Glasgow. These people in Western societies whose health is declining are in absolute terms much better off than those in Malaysia who were investing so heavily in the future. But they have lost hope. It will be important for a healthy society to address the psychological needs of these people and give them back hope.[10]

I doubt if many who have lost hope will read this book. But if some of its messages can be transmitted to them and understood by them, it may reduce their despair to a degree as they realise the causes of their frustrations and what might be done to minimise them. In some cases there is little that will actually work for them other than cushioning some of the worst aspects, which is very sad. But at least the ideas in this book should help limit the extent to which their problems are transmitted to the next generation.

Finally, this book incorporates new research into the transmission of wealth and inequality between generations. It does appear that there is some truth in the old saying 'Clogs to clogs in three generations', though the research indicates that the time taken for 95% of an initial increase in wealth to disappear is more like five generations. But the 'superbaby' phenomenon may already be starting to offset that in entrenching inequality across the generations. Already there is increasing evidence that educational inequality is much deeper rooted than income inequality.

Some of the biggest dangers from inequality are in the political backlash that it is likely to generate. If inequality causes voters in democracies to pull down the relatively liberal economic order that underpins their current living standards, even Western civilisation itself could be at risk. The Western economies are already losing their place in the economic pecking order to an Eastern world imbued with the single-minded focus and determination that comes with a still fresh knowledge of recent poverty. But the Western world still sets the moral and cultural norms for much of the world. I don't think Westerners are superior, but these norms have evolved over a long period and have advantages over the less legally based and more dictatorial approaches common in the East.

The chapters in this book are divided into four parts. Part I 'Setting the scene' defines the question that the book tries to answer. It asks whether we are more worried about poverty than simple differences of economic outcome. And its answer is 'Yes, but'; Part II 'Analysis and implications' looks at inequality and its economic impact; Part III 'The deserving and the undeserving rich' looks at the new rich and whether they contribute to society; and Part IV 'Fixing the problem' looks at what solutions might work in reality.

Although the chapters in this book are self-standing, their ordering is deliberate. The reasons why the solutions in Part IV are likely to work are based on the analysis in the earlier sections. It therefore makes sense to read them consecutively.

# PART I
## Setting the Scene

CHAPTER 1 'Introduction' provides a gentle introduction to what is a very complicated subject. It describes the growth of the winner-takes-all approach and how technology and globalisation have affected the pay of soccer players and others, and uses the English soccer player Wayne Rooney as an example to show the impact of this. The same factors that affect his pay have had economy-wide effects.

CHAPTER 2 'How Piketty created an industry' looks at Thomas Piketty's best-selling book on inequality, *Capital in the Twenty-First Century*, in detail. It also examines other approaches to inequality and shows that although the Piketty approach has some value, its single 'conspiracy theory' explanation is not even the main explanation of the recent rise in inequality, let alone the only one.

CHAPTER 3 'The three different types and four different causes of inequality' digs deeper into the problem of contemporary inequality. It distinguishes between different types of inequality and shows that in reality there are at least four causes of rising inequality, rather than just the exploitation theory put forward by Piketty.

CHAPTER 4 'Why inequality matters' looks into those aspects of inequality that are most damaging to society. There is sometimes a trade-off between inequality and poverty, so it is important to distinguish between problems caused by poverty and those caused by inequality.

## Chapter 1
## INTRODUCTION

THE BEST KNOWN SOCCER PLAYER IN ENGLAND IN RECENT YEARS HAS been a man called Wayne Rooney. When I started writing the book he still played for Manchester United, had just been replaced as captain of the England team and had scored 53 goals, a record number, for the national side. He has since retired from international football, been transferred back to his boyhood club, Everton, and at the time of writing seems likely to be transferred to the United States. Once when we were both in a bar in the Lowry Hotel in Manchester, he apparently wanted to swap his modern Aston Martin for my classic one and sent a minion to talk to me about it. The next person who wanted my classic Aston had no intention of offering something in return and simply stole it.

Wayne Rooney was paid £13.5 million in 2015.[1] His predecessor as England's top goal scorer was another Manchester United soccer player, Bobby (now Sir Bobby) Charlton (a genuine soccer hero and perhaps the biggest star of the 1966 England team who won soccer's World Cup, the only time that the England national team has ever won a major international competition), who scored 49 goals and held England's international goal scoring record for 45 years.[2]

Sir Bobby's annual salary in 1972[3] when he was close to the peak of his career was only £15,000. Even after allowing for inflation Wayne Rooney's salary in 2015 was four times as much as the whole Manchester United squad was paid in the late 1960s and early 70s.[4]

Sir Bobby earned twice the average pay for the top league and eight times the average pay of players in the lower leagues. Wayne Rooney earned ten times the average pay for the top league and 450 times the pay of players in the lower leagues.

So, relative to the players in the lower leagues, *Wayne Rooney earned a staggering 53 times more relatively than Sir Bobby did just over 40 years earlier* for doing essentially the same job.

This single figure illustrates the extent to which pay inequality in the football world has increased in the past half century.

The reasons why this has happened are widely known – UK football has globalised and technology means that it can now be broadcast instantaneously throughout the world. I have been at dinner parties in Hong Kong, Kuala Lumpur and Dubai, lunch parties in Mexico City and breakfasts in Sydney which have been interrupted by the English Premier League.

As a result, Manchester United's revenue in 2015 (not a particularly good season for the club – they finished only fifth in the Premier League, outside the top four places which entail automatic qualification for the next season's European Champions League) was 70 times higher *in real terms* than its revenue in 1969. The gap between Wayne Rooney's real earnings and those of Sir Bobby more or less entirely reflects the club's increased revenue.

The spectacular increase in inequality in soccer isn't just important because it illustrates a particular trend graphically. It is also useful because it shows how the rise in inequality in this particular sector has been driven mainly by underlying economic factors rather than the exploitation suggested by Piketty. The rise in pay of top soccer players matches the rise in earnings of the top soccer clubs. Television technology has been behind this, enabling soccer matches to be seen around the world, while globalisation has in effect poured fuel on the flames by massively increasing global television revenues for the major clubs.

But football is merely an extreme case of a phenomenon that has been widening the pay gap in most Western economies from around 1980 until the financial crash in 2008. The same trends – globalisation with some help from technology – have affected most sectors. For the UK as a whole the share of total incomes (pre-tax) received by the top 1% of income earners rose from an estimated 7% in 1975 to 16% in 2008 before falling back to 13% in 2014 (see Table 1). In the US the rise has been starker – from 6% to 18% over the same period. Even in Germany, with a more egalitarian tradition and a strong education system, the rise has been of a similar order of magnitude. The only major economies with little rise in income disparities have been Japan, France and Italy. It comes as no surprise to discover that these have been the slowest growing of the G7 economies.

The financial crash of 2007-09 marked the end of this process, at least temporarily. In the UK the share of the top 1% has fallen back to its lowest level for nearly 20 years. Even in the US the share is lower than it was ten years ago.

Table I. Shares of income earned by the top 1%

| | China | France | Germany | India | Italy | UK | US |
|---|---|---|---|---|---|---|---|
| 1980 | 6.4% | 8.2% | 10.6% | 7.3% | 8.4% | 10.7% | |
| 1981 | 6.7% | 8.2% | 6.7% | 8.3% | 11.1% | | |
| 1982 | 6.9% | 7.5% | | 6.1% | 8.2% | | 11.3% |
| 1983 | 7.1% | 7.3% | 9.8% | 10.3% | 8.2% | | 11.5% |
| 1984 | 7.5% | 7.5% | | 8.9% | 8.3% | | 12.5% |
| 1985 | 8.0% | 7.7% | | 10.5% | 8.4% | | 12.6% |
| 1986 | 8.0% | 8.2% | 10.2% | 10.8% | 8.9% | | 12.2% |
| 1987 | 7.9% | 9.0% | | 10.3% | 10.3% | | 13.3% |
| 1988 | 8.0% | 9.2% | | 11.1% | 10.6% | | 14.9% |
| 1989 | 8.2% | 9.5% | 11.4% | 11.0% | 11.9% | | 14.5% |
| 1990 | 8.1% | 9.3% | | 10.5% | 13.0% | 9.8% | 14.5% |
| 1991 | 8.3% | 9.1% | | 10.2% | 12.1% | 10.3% | 13.9% |
| 1992 | 8.8% | 8.6% | 9.5% | 10.0% | 8.4% | 9.9% | 15.0% |
| 1993 | 9.2% | 9.1% | | 12.5% | 8.6% | 10.4% | 14.6% |
| 1994 | 9.4% | 9.2% | | 12.4% | 8.6% | 10.6% | 14.7% |
| 1995 | 9.3% | 9.2% | 8.2% | 13.0% | 8.7% | 10.7% | 15.3% |
| 1996 | 9.6% | 10.0% | | 13.2% | 8.9% | 11.9% | 16.0% |
| 1997 | 9.6% | 10.4% | | 13.8% | 8.4% | 12.1% | 16.6% |
| 1998 | 9.8% | 10.7% | 11.8% | 14.4% | 8.5% | 12.5% | 16.9% |
| 1999 | 9.9% | 10.6% | | 14.7% | 8.7% | 13.2% | 17.7% |
| 2000 | 10.4% | 11.0% | | 15.1% | 9.1% | 13.5% | 18.3% |
| 2001 | 10.9% | 11.3% | 11.4% | 15.9% | 9.4% | 13.4% | 17.3% |
| 2002 | 12.5% | 10.9% | 11.1% | 16.7% | 9.5% | 13.0% | 17.1% |
| 2003 | 13.1% | 11.4% | 10.5% | 17.5% | 9.8% | 13.2% | 17.2% |
| 2004 | 13.8% | 11.6% | 11.1% | 18.4% | 10.5% | 13.3% | 18.3% |
| 2005 | 14.2% | 11.5% | 12.9% | 19.3% | 11.0% | 14.2% | 19.4% |
| 2006 | 14.8% | 11.2% | 13.2% | 19.7% | 11.3% | 14.8% | 20.1% |
| 2007 | 15.3% | 11.7% | 14.0% | 20.1% | 11.3% | 15.4% | 19.9% |
| 2008 | 15.2% | 11.6% | 14.5% | 20.4% | 10.9% | 15.4% | 19.5% |
| 2009 | 15.4% | 10.2% | 13.2% | 20.8% | 10.4% | 15.4% | 18.5% |
| 2010 | 15.1% | 10.8% | 13.1% | 21.2% | 10.4% | 12.5% | 19.8% |
| 2011 | 14.6% | 11.5% | 13.1% | 21.3% | | 12.9% | 19.6% |
| 2012 | 13.8% | 10.4% | 13.0% | 21.5% | | 12.7% | 20.8% |
| 2013 | 13.8% | 10.8% | 13.2% | 21.7% | | 14.5% | 19.6% |
| 2014 | 13.7% | 10.8% | | | | 13.9% | 20.2% |
| 2015 | 13.9% | | | | | | |

Source: World Inequality Database downloaded 5 June 2018

Another example of rising inequality can be seen in the number of billionaires in the world. In 2000 there were 470. In 2008, just before the impact of the financial crash, the number had more than doubled to 1,125 but fell back the next year to 793. In 2015 there were 1,826 billionaires in the world, according to the respected Forbes international database, although the number plateaued in 2016. In 2017, partly as a result of the impact of loose monetary policy on asset values, the number of billionaires rose to 2,043, the biggest jump in the 30-year history of the list.

In world cities such as London, Paris, New York, Los Angeles, Dubai, Singapore and Hong Kong they are obvious. Flash men (mainly) accompanied by women who look a few years (at least) younger. Noisy sports cars. They eat in the most expensive restaurants. They dance in the most exclusive clubs. In the northern hemisphere summer they can be seen on their yachts cruising into marinas in Capri, Portofino, St Tropez, Marbella, Sardinia's Porto Cervo and Monte Carlo.

It is not only the number of billionaires that has increased. A large number of studies show how income inequality increased in many different countries and regions before the financial crisis. And the number of super-rich, after falling back, rebounded to higher levels than ever.

The contention of this book is that economic inequality is going to be the major economic challenge not only for this generation but also for the next, and quite likely further ahead.

It matters hugely whether we apply the right solutions or the wrong ones. There are plenty of snake oil salesmen out there peddling ideas that at best would make both inequality and poverty worse. At worst some of these ideas could destroy what we think of as Western civilisation. Indeed a major new book released in the US while this book was being edited makes precisely the same warning.[5] It is important, in our worry about what is happening, to be sufficiently knowledgeable and hardheaded not to fall prey to such salesmen.

## Chapter 2
# HOW PIKETTY CREATED AN INDUSTRY

THOMAS PIKETTY DESERVES A LOT OF CREDIT FOR DRAWING ATTENTION to an important economic theme, the growth in inequality in many countries from about 1980 to 2008. With sales of over 1.5 million, his *Capital in the Twenty-First Century* pointed out the rise in inequality in most countries since the 1980s.[1] According to him this is partly a result of Marxist inevitability as capital accumulates and partly because the wealthy fiddle the rules in their favour.

There are very few ideas that are so misconstrued as to be entirely wrong, and Piketty's ideas are not completely wrong. But his popularity owes much to the suggestion that the problem of inequality is essentially the result of an old-fashioned conspiracy whereby the rich conspire to take advantage of the poor.

Would that it were largely so. If it were it would be quite an easy problem to solve. But actually it's a whole lot more complicated than that.[2] Piketty thinks that the rich always had the bargaining power to exploit the poor but before taxes came down to make it economically worthwhile and before it also gradually became socially acceptable for them to do so, they tended not to. The alternative explanations (see elsewhere in this book) are that inequality is much more rooted in economic factors such as globalisation and the impact of technological change and will increasingly be rooted in demographic factors as able parents marry each other and provide advantages for their offspring.

It is unfortunate for his case that, just as his book was being published, the growth in inequality which Piketty predicted would continue to rise inexorably largely plateaued and in many countries actually started to reverse. Chapter 5 of this book looks at the trends in more detail while Chapter 11 goes on to look at whether this is just a pause in an upward trend or whether the trend has reversed completely.

Piketty explains what I call Type 1 Inequality – growth in inequality caused by exploitation. This certainly exists and perhaps explains about a fifth of the rise in inequality in the past 30 years, less in the West and more in the wild East. The calculation that this explains about a fifth comes from one of the most detailed analyses ever of the change in labour income share published in the *American Economic Review* by some highly distinguished academics.[3]

The next chapter looks at other important explanations of the recent rise in inequality in the West in the period before the financial crash.

In the rest of this chapter I review some of the literature on inequality and try to explain the key theories as well as looking in more detail at some of the more recent writings on the subject.

## Adam Smith

One of the early and in many ways most radical writers about inequality was Adam Smith.[4]

A highlight of former US President Barack Obama's presidency was a high-profile December 2013 speech in which he claimed that great and growing economic inequality was 'the defining challenge of our time', a sentiment with which this book concurs.[5] The former president made much of the thinking of a man who might appear an unlikely supporter to those who operate on stereotypes rather than knowledge – Adam Smith, the alleged founder of market economics and supporter of capitalism and greed. Of course anyone who actually knows the works of Adam Smith is aware that this stereotype is grossly misleading. He never once used the term 'laissez-faire' or even the term 'capitalism', and his two most important books – *The Theory of Moral Sentiments*[6] and *The Wealth of Nations*[7] – lament the ills of what he calls 'commercial society'.

Both poverty and inequality were major concerns for Smith. Arguably he was the first Rawlsian,[8] arguing that the true measure of a nation's wealth was not that of its king or its rich people but instead the wages of 'the labouring poor'. In the passage that President Obama quoted, Smith declared that it is a matter of simple 'equity' that 'they who feed, clothe, and lodge the whole body of the people, should have such a share of the produce of their own labour as to be themselves tolerably well fed, clothed, and lodged.'

Most discussion of Smith's views suggests that he was more concerned about poverty than inequality. He developed the concept of 'trickle-down economics' which has been widely criticised by many on the left (a review of the relevant evidence is in Chapter 7). Although his concept of economic justice was essentially Rawlsian,[9] measuring the prosperity of a society by the position of the least well-off, he strongly believed that the wealthy contributed disproportionately through innovation and that their wealth improved the lot of ordinary people.

But he also believed that the rich behaved badly through conspicuous consumption, behaving with a gross degree of entitlement and with little attention to the implications for those worse off than themselves. He thought that they got away with this partly because their wealth fascinated observers who allowed them to get away with behaviour which was inappropriate. We have this today with some of the behaviour of so-called celebs who provide so much material for the tabloid newspapers.

Smith actually made a quite unusual critique of inequality, more on moral than economic grounds. Later in this book I make a case that those benefiting most from the fruits of a fairly liberal economic system have greater responsibilities than those benefiting least and need to ensure both that their behaviour is ethical and that they apply social and other sanctions to those among them whose behaviour is not.

Another important contribution of Adam Smith was his invention of the concept of the 'invisible hand'. The invisible hand consists of the income-generating and redistributing effects of diverse individuals' self-interested actions. As long as there is competition and trade, the invisible hand normally ensures that economic activity for self-interested purposes creates positive net economic benefits. My attempts to make myself better off generates wealth for other people provided that they trade freely with me as suppliers or customers.

## John Maynard Keynes

Keynes's approach was in many ways similar to that taken in this book. He did not assume that the capitalist system was self-balancing and he was sympathetic to government intervention. But he did not believe that private property should be abolished and considered that a degree of inequality was necessary as an incentive 'for valuable human activity'. He argued however that if an excessive proportion of income accrued to the rich, this might lead to underconsumption because of the lower propensity of the rich to consume. He distinguished carefully between entrepreneurs and the rentier class. The latter he considered essentially parasitic, but thought that society could benefit from the 'intelligence and determination and executive skill' of business people, which could be 'harnessed on reasonable terms of reward' under a system of progressive taxation.

## Friedrich Hayek

Apart from Keynes, the nearest to an economics superstar between the wars was Friedrich Hayek. Hayek was more traditionally minded. He argued strongly for equality before the law but made the case that because people are unequal, this must inevitably lead to inequality of outcome. Perhaps partly because he had emigrated from what was soon to become Nazi Europe, Hayek was concerned about the dangers of over-mighty governments and of the resultant coercion.

In other writings Hayek argued that inequality was necessary for economic progress, pointing out in *The Constitution of Liberty*, 'New knowledge and its benefits can spread only gradually, and the ambitions of the many will always be determined by what is as yet accessible only to the few .... This means that there will always be people who already benefit from new achievements that have not yet reached others.'[10]

Hayek's basic point is simple: before many social advancements become common, they first exist as luxuries. 'The new things will often become available to the greater part of the people only because for some time they have been the luxuries of the few.' This is remarkably similar to Adam Smith's argument that innovation requires rich people who can take the risk to experiment.

Hayek's final major work was the three-part *Law, Legislation and Liberty* (1973-79), a critique of efforts to redistribute incomes in the name of 'social justice'.

## Simon Kuznets

In the pre-Piketty period the high priest in economics of understanding inequality was Simon Kuznets who received the 1971 Nobel Economics Prize 'for his empirically founded interpretation of economic growth which has led to new and deepened insight into the economic and social structure and process of development'.

In his 1955 Presidential address to the American Economics Association, he developed the concept of the Kuznets curve.[11] He postulated that industrialisation might initially increase income inequality but that as industrialisation matured over time (based on his observations) inequality tended to diminish again. He gave a number of tentative reasons for the diminishing inequality that he had observed, of which the shift to the service sector and the importance of new technology were probably the most important at the time. While both of these factors in Kuznets' time probably worked in the way he suggested, in the modern world they may well have the opposite effects.

In my view Kuznets gave insufficient weight to the importance of the spread of education in the 20th century in reducing inequality in advanced economies. One of the effects of the spread of education in those pre-globalisation times was to create a shortage of those who were prepared to do manual jobs. There is a London joke about an employee in the financial services sector in the City of London who needs a plumber quickly. The plumber comes and fixes the problem in about ten minutes and says, 'That will be £500, sir.' The City employee responds, '£500 for ten minutes! I work in the City and don't get that much.' To which the plumber replies, 'Yes, I didn't get that much either when I worked in the City!'

Piketty is remarkably uncomplimentary about the Kuznets Curve: 'Nevertheless, the magical Kuznets Curve Theory was formulated in large part for the wrong reasons, and its empirical underpinnings were extremely fragile. The sharp reduction in income inequality that we observe in almost all the rich countries between 1913 and 1945 was due above all to the world wars and the violent economic and political shocks they entailed (especially for people with large fortunes). It had little to do with the tranquil process of intersectoral mobility described by Kuznets.'[12]

Sir Anthony Atkinson (see below) has a rather greater facility with language which enables him to be much more measured: 'The famous study in the mid-1950s by Simon Kuznets, the Nobel Prize–winning Harvard economist, of the evolution of income inequality over a period of time was based on a handful of data points for a small range of countries.'[13]

But the information now available (much of it compiled by Piketty and his followers) indicates falling income inequality in the Western world from some time in the late 19th century (and on some measures the early 19th century) to some point between 1970 and 1980. Moreover, the fall was on a dramatic scale. It runs contrary to the evidence (and even Piketty's own evidence) to try to imply as he does that the phenomenon only lasted from 1913 to 1945 and is simply a product of two world wars and the Great Depression. The increased data now available is more supportive of Kuznets' theory than of those of his critics.

But whether Kuznets was right or not about the period to around 1980, there is general agreement that there was an increase in inequality on most measures in most countries (though much more in Anglo-Saxon economies) from 1980 until the financial crisis of 2007/08. This would not be explained by the Kuznets curve.

## Milton Friedman

I have relied here mainly on a good description of Friedman's views by Julio Cole in the *Journal of Markets and Morality*.[14] He writes: 'There is a certain tension in Milton Friedman's views on the issue of freedom versus equality, which was much more nuanced than is commonly assumed. On the one hand, he argued that economic policy should focus on freedom as a primary value; stressing equality per se could lead to economic inefficiency as well as jeopardizing freedom itself. On the other hand, he famously advocated government-sponsored poverty alleviation by way of the negative income tax, a form of income redistribution that is inconsistent with his general theory of the free-market economy. His justification for this policy, however, was not on egalitarian grounds. Rather, his main motivation seems to have been compassion.'

Milton Friedman's best known statement on inequality is this: 'A society that puts equality – in the sense of equality of outcome – ahead of freedom will end up with neither equality nor freedom. The use of force to achieve equality will destroy freedom, and the force, introduced for good purposes, will end up in the hands of people who use it to promote their own interests.'[15] It is best to see this more as a statement about freedom than a statement about inequality. Indeed this book is about the dangers of focussing on the wrong solutions for the inequality problem which could even, if we make big enough mistakes, cause the collapse of the relatively liberal economic order with limited compulsion and lead to the growth of dictatorial tendencies.

Friedman is seen by some as a proponent of 'supply-side economics'. In fact supply-side economics long predated Friedman and any sensible economist would understand that regardless of one's views about demand management (I am unashamedly Keynesian about this) it would be foolish to neglect the supply side of the economy. Demand and supply are not alternative issues – they are complementary.

Friedman's case for a negative income tax[16] is quite difficult to square with his normal suspicion of government intervention. Julio Cole's conclusion is that his motivation is a mix of economic efficiency and compassion. This book puts forward a similar proposal, for a universal basic income, on the ground that this is needed to cushion the impact of the likely very rapid introduction of technology in the coming years.

One of Friedman's insights is explicitly debated with in this book. In 1953 he argued that monopoly didn't in fact do much damage to an economy.[17] That may well have been true when he said it, though he was writing at a time when the US economy was still receiving the benefits of Teddy Roosevelt's great antitrust activity and corporates were restraining their potentially oligopolistic tendencies for fear of renewed antitrust action (something of which I was well aware when I worked for IBM). Today the facts are different. Corporates show less self-restraint and in my view abuse monopolistic powers to a much greater extent. The intrinsic economies of scale in the information age and the existence of network effects give more power to entrenched incumbents, even if the pace of technological progress operates in the opposite direction. I suspect that had Friedman been still alive he would have reconsidered.

### *Economics and Equality*, edited by the Rt Hon Aubrey Jones[18]

The British Association for the Advancement of Science held a meeting in 1975 that focussed on economics and equality. The proceedings were edited by the chairman, the Rt Hon Aubrey Jones, who had headed the then Labour Government's Prices and Incomes Board in the 1960s. I have a copy of the proceedings in my library, given to me by my friend Sir Samuel Brittan, and it makes interesting reading as an historical document. The book contains ten articles covering a wide range of issues.

The issue in vogue at the time was incomes policy, which was then an approach used to bring down inflation while sustaining demand. It fell into disuse after 1979, though the alternatives, of persistent high unemployment and then highly deregulated labour markets leaving substantial power in the hands of employers also have their downsides.

One of the key topics in a world of incomes policies was what levels of differential pay between different groups of employees were appropriate. It is interesting that few contributors to the discussion were in favour of compressing differentials (even George Woodcock, the then recently retired General Secretary of the Trades Union Congress).

### Sir Anthony Atkinson

In the years between Kuznets and Piketty the economist who focussed most on inequality was the late Sir Anthony Atkinson.[19] Atkinson, who in his early work seems to have inspired Piketty, collaborated with him in various articles including 'Top Incomes in the Long Run of History' which brought the subject of income inequality to the attention of an academic audience.[20]

Sir Anthony's final work summarising his thinking is *Inequality: What Can be Done?*[21] A major virtue of this book is the attention it pays to the argument that labour-saving technological change is likely to become one of the key drivers of growing inequality (as discussed in Chapter 11 of this book). Atkinson combines his analysis with Piketty's theory of the concentration of wealth to argue that there will be a doubling up of the impacts of technology on inequality because not only will incomes be increasingly maldistributed but in addition wealth (which of course becomes even more maldistributed when incomes are so) will increasingly be in the form of robots which will force further growth in the maldistribution of wealth. His conclusion is one with which I have considerable sympathy.

Perhaps the greatest contribution of this book, however, lies in its detailed analysis of data sources and their varying implications. Atkinson shares some conclusions with those in this book. But his main policy proposals also betray a lack of realism, not entirely surprising for someone who has spent his life among the ivory towers.

The remoteness from real life can be seen in Atkinson's key conclusions, which I summarise below:

Proposal 1. Government should push innovation in a direction that enhances the employability of workers.

Proposal 2. Government should aim at a proper balance of power between stakeholders etc.

Proposal 3. Government should secure full employment by offering guaranteed public employment at the minimum wage.

Proposal 4. There should be a national pay policy consisting of two elements – a statutory minimum wage set at the living wage and a code of practice for all other pay.

Proposal 5. Government should offer a guaranteed positive real rate of interest for all savers.

Proposal 6. There should be a capital endowment paid to all adults.

Proposal 7. A public investment authority should be created to buy up companies and property.

What he is driving at is life being heavily controlled by the state, with pay levels, investment, all research and development, rates of interest and jobs organised by the government. This is, of course, the logical consequence if you believe that capitalism is failing completely and driving unacceptable outcomes. But there is no analysis to suggest that some babies might be thrown away with this capitalism bathwater, from incentives to drivers of innovation.

Having worked in the real world as well as having seen the public sector at firsthand, I cannot see how proposals such as Sir Anthony's could ever have a chance of working. How could governments control the nature of innovation, for example? The drive for innovation in the modern world seems to emerge from the decentralisation of creativity, something that would be hard to replicate if the government controlled all research. Indeed, my slightly heterodox view is that it was the emergence of this need for decentralisation with the technology revolution in the 1980s that really killed off the old-style communism in the Soviet Union.

### Goldin and Katz: *The Race between Education and Technology*[22]

This book is named after a phrase coined by the Dutch Nobel Prize–winner Jan Tinbergen. He argued that how inequality moves depends on how technology and education interplay. Technological changes raise the demand for the more skilled workers, and to stop inequality rising the supply of such workers has to rise equivalently. The balance between the two determines the direction of movement of technology.

Goldin and Katz argue that in the past 40 years three additional factors have become important – technology has been much more biased towards skilled workers, globalisation has come into play, and in the US at least education, which had improved sharply for more than a century (thus being the main cause of the decline in inequality observed over the period), has started to deteriorate.

### Autor, Dorn, Katz, Patterson and Van Reenen: 'Concentrating on the Fall of the Labor Share'[23]

This is a seminal paper arguing that a 'superstar firm' explanation of rising concentration in a sector will lead to a fall in its labour share through increased 'exploitation' or Type 1 Inequality. The paper argues that technology has made this possible. However, the calculations show that this accounts for only a fifth of the total fall in the labour share of total incomes.

### Dao, Das, Koczan and Lian: 'Routinisation, Globalisation, and the Fall in Labour's Share of Income'[24]

If increased exploitation accounts for only a fifth of the increase in inequality, what accounts for the rest? This paper from the IMF argues that the culprit is not automation or offshoring alone, but the interaction between the two. The authors point out that the labour share has been falling not just in rich nations, but in developing countries as well.

Dao and her co-authors argue that when poor countries are isolated from the global economy, they tend to specialise in things that rely on cheap labour – farming, low-end services and simple labour-intensive manufacturing. Local landlords and other capital owners do well, but don't invest heavily because they would be undercut by cheap labour.

But when trade opens up, the rich countries start offshoring manufacturing jobs to the poor countries. These jobs offer better opportunities for workers, but much better opportunities for capitalists. While capitalists in the US or Japan or France get rich cutting labour costs by shipping jobs to China, Chinese capitalists get rich because they can invest and build up business empires.

The IMF economists also predict that global financial integration should help alleviate the pressure on labour in poor countries. If American, European, Japanese and Taiwanese companies are able to invest in a developing country such as China, the inflow of foreign money will boost incomes for local workers and compete down the profits of local capital owners.

They argue that in rich countries automation and globalisation are working together – companies in rich countries can ship labour-intensive manufacturing jobs in electronics assembly, toys and clothing to China and Bangladesh, while buying advanced machine tools and robots to do more high-end manufacturing of things such as microprocessors and airplanes. As a result, workers in rich countries where routine jobs are most common have been hit hardest by both free trade and the advent of cheap automation. This paper seems to provide powerful empirical support for the approach to inequality that is taken by this book and seems to contradict the approach taken by Piketty.

### Acemoğlu and Robinson: *Why Nations Fail: The Origins of Power, Prosperity, and Poverty*[25]

This is an essentially political book that tries to explain economic progress in terms of equality of political power. It argues that failing societies have tensions between an included group, essentially of rich people who control decision-making, and excluded groups. It argues that societies split in this way do not generate prosperity for their people.

The model used in the analysis is a fairly simple one, dividing the world into a small rich elite and a large group who form the masses. Most people today would use a more general model with a higher degree of granularity that fitted modern life better. A more serious problem is that there is little distinction between the impact of the elite using their power for advantages that benefit the whole group and using their power in ways that only benefit individuals. In the former case, much of the negative impact can be diminished by different companies competing for markets and for labour, whereas in the latter case monopolistic profits increase inequality by both providing excessive rewards for the rich and reducing living standards for the poor.[26]

### Boldrin, Levine and Modica: Review of *Why Nations Fail*[27]
This review of the Acemoğlu and Robinson book makes a similar assessment to the analysis above but in rather more detail. It points out that the key test of the thesis in the book is whether China can keep on growing. My view is that it can, partly based on my experience of observing Singapore over many years. Martin Jacques's seminal *When China Rules the World*[28] agrees and sets out a range of reasons why. Acemoğlu and Robinson think not.

### L.M. Bartels: *Unequal Democracy*[29]
L.M. Bartels' *Unequal Democracy* is about one aspect of the inequality problem, which is the way in which powerful people and corporations abuse their influence, especially in the US. Some of its thinking is reflected in this book in its commentary on Goldman Sachs and the tech giants.

Where this book disagrees is that it does not see the promotion of the corporate sector in itself as necessarily a bad thing. One of the difficulties with democracy is that it tends to work in favour of individuals who consume and against the companies who produce who, naturally, do not have votes themselves.[30] Of course the corporate sector does fight back by lobbying and using its financial muscle to influence politics, so the competition is less one-sided than a simple observation of democratic rules might lead one to think – it is the abuse of this lobbying power which is the subject not only of the Bartels book but also this one. The important distinction that needs to be drawn is between measures that benefit the corporate sector as a whole where any excess that accrues to the corporate sector can be competed away provided that the sector is sufficiently competitive (hence the focus on competition policy in this book), and measures that benefit individual sectors or companies where there is less opportunity for the benefits of special privileges to be competed away. Chapter 13 contains a section that explains the distinction in more detail.

Of course, the ultimate purpose of production is consumption so there is no case to favour production at the expense of consumption. But often the long-term interests of consumption are against the short-term interests, so that measures that damage the corporate sector also damage the economy.

### Jeffery Sachs: *The Price of Civilization*[31]

Jeffery Sachs is quoted in this book because of his penetrating analysis of the effect of cronyism in Russia. His books on inequality more generally seem less penetrating. His analysis is very similar to Piketty's though he doesn't include the same weight of evidence as Piketty manages to amass.

Perhaps not surprisingly for someone who has spent a lot of time in the emerging Eastern Europe, he sees inequality mainly from the perspective of crony capitalism and does not pay much attention to the impacts of either globalisation or technology. He also fails to see the distinction between tax cuts that help the corporate sector as a whole, many of the redistributive effects of which can be competed away to the benefit of consumers or employees or both provided there is an adequate competition policy, and tax privileges that help individual companies and sectors. His take on the subject seems to focus mainly on the US and does not really come to grips with the international dimension, which is crucial.

Sachs' analysis is surprisingly political for an economist. He draws attention to the lobbying power of major corporations. Oddly he doesn't seem to pay the same attention to the lobbying powers of other groups.

### Joseph Stiglitz: *The Price of Inequality: How Today's Divided Society Endangers Our Future*[32]

I remember Jo Stiglitz from M.Phil seminars at Oxford. He was undoubtedly clever but seemed just a little too self-assured to be a proper academic. Since then he has gathered many honours and a Nobel Prize. So I guess I got that one wrong!

However, his book on inequality seems remarkably political and derivative for someone from whom we have been led to expect great insights.[33] He is clearly incensed (and rightly so) at the strength of lobbying of the top companies in finance and tech and how they manipulate governments to their advantage. That criticism we share. As someone who perhaps understands running a business better than Stiglitz, however, I don't think one ought to deal with the monopoly power of the big banks and tech companies by beating up the whole corporate sector. The sensible way to do it is to break or regulate the monopolies. The golden age for the US economy followed Teddy Roosevelt's doing just that.

Stiglitz's other weakness is an argument that *The Economist* suggested 'would benefit ... from a better sense of history and geography'.[34]

Stiglitz has written other books on the subject, notably *Globalisation and Its Discontents*. They all add to the subject, without fully expunging my view that a year managing a business would have helped him understand economics more than a lifetime in academia.

### Paul Krugman: *The Return of Depression Economics*[35] and *End This Depression Now!*[36]

My company Cebr has operationalised Paul Krugman's brilliant insights into locational economics into a series of models for examining the impact of transport on the relative economic development of different regions and I have a lot of sympathy for his microeconomic insights. He fully deserved his Nobel Prize.

Many of his takes on inequality – for example in his *New York Review of Books* review of Robert Reich's *Saving Capitalism*[37] draw attention to the dangers of oligopoly, a theme repeated in this book. However, his macroeconomic views are powerful attacks on the mainstream view that expansionary economic policies need not be constrained by concerns about debt. Had unemployment returned to the levels of the 1930s I would have made the same judgement. But with the US unemployment rate at 4.1% (much the same as the pre-depression rate in the 1920s) compared with as high as 25% in 1933, I believe that policy has to balance the need for full employment with the need to manage indebtedness, a balance that Krugman does not seem to appreciate.

Another of Krugman's weaknesses is his seeming inability to distinguish between greater and lesser causes of economic developments and of changing causes over time. One example is his complete refusal to accept that technology can affect inequality, a key theme in his review of Robert Reich. The theme of this book is that technology has been a minor cause affecting rising inequality in the immediate past but that this is likely to change in the future as the speed of technological change accelerates and the impact of globalisation wanes.

### Katz and Murphy: 'Changes in Relative Wages'[38]
### Katz and Autor: 'Changes in Wage Structure and Earning Inequality'[39]

These papers essentially provide the statistical background for the claim that technology is the key factor driving increased inequality.

### Robert Reich: *The Work of Nations*[40]

I was a contemporary of Robert Reich's at Oxford. His book, *The Work of Nations*, made the case for internationalism and the changing nature of the multinational company. He argued that changing technology and globalisation were leading to inequality, an analysis that has some resonance with that in this book. His work helped get him appointed Secretary of Labour when Bill Clinton (another Oxford contemporary) became President.

Over the historic period, my view is that he exaggerates the extent to which technology was responsible and underplays the impact of globalisation. But looking forward, it is hard to argue with his view that technology will become a major driving force for inequality.

### Mishel, Shierholz and Schmitt: 'Don't Blame the Robots: Assessing the Job Polarization Explanation of Growing Wage Inequality'[41]

This is a very powerful analysis of detailed US statistics that is claiming to debunk the theory of skills-biased technical progress (SBTP). Its statistical basis is very detailed and the analysis supports my theory that in fact because (1) change has been relatively slow and (2) machines have been made by people rather than by other machines until now, technology so far has not been a major driver of rising inequality. But looking forward it is likely that the role of technology will change. Probably the most important theorist of inequality, Sir Anthony Atkinson, took the view (which I share) that from now on technology is likely to be the most important driver of inequality as the importance of technological change in destroying existing jobs and creating different ones rises.

### Simon Johnson and James Kwak: *13 Bankers*[42]

This book is by Simon Johnson, the former chief economist of the IMF, and James Kwak. It shows how the banking industry used the bank bailouts during the financial crisis to buttress their own banks' positions at the expense of the public interest. This is a powerful book. Some of its conclusions are echoed in criticisms of the banking sector (and one bank in particular) in Chapter 9 of this book.

### Sir Angus Deaton: *The Great Escape, Health, Wealth and the Origins of Inequality*[43]

Deaton's book, by yet another Nobel Prize-winner, is a welcome antidote to the pessimism of some of the others. He starts by pointing out the international dimension of the equality issue in a very similar way to this book. Deaton points out that in recent years abject poverty has been falling and life expectancy growing. He rightly points out that the decline in poverty in the world has had some similar causes to those that have increased inequality in the US – again a conclusion shared with this book.

The Great Escape of the title is the escape, for most people in the world, from the evils of deprivation and early death. Deaton comes from a medical background and has spent a good deal of time investigating the growth of health inequality in the US among so-called middle-class (what Europeans would call working-class) Americans. His analysis is considered in more detail in Chapter 4 of this book.

### Branko Milanovic: *Global Inequality: A New Approach for the Age of Globalisation*[44]

Obviously I think my own book is worth reading, but if I were to recommend any one other book on inequality, it would be this one. Milanovic coined the concept of 'the elephant graph' and I use it in this book to look forward as the elephant mutates into a camel and then either a cobra or a spitting cobra.

Milanovic goes into great detail about how the impact of globalisation transforms not just the emerging economies but also the advanced economies. His analysis is at the core of this book, although I look more at other explanations of inequality, at the future and at policy issues.

### Martin Wolf: *Why Globalisation Works*[45]

Martin Wolf is a respected journalist for the London *Financial Times*. This mighty work describes the impact of globalisation in a very accessible way, and the book is certainly worth reading for its description of globalisation alone. He was probably the first to try to make the case that globalisation had reduced inequality in total on a global basis, though the data supporting his argument has been queried. He has also kept on the case with a series of articles in the *Financial Times*, most notably recently, where his conclusions have some parallels with those in this book.[46]

### Duttagupta, Fabrizio, Furceri and Saxena: 'Growth That Reaches Everyone: Facts, Factors, Tools'[47]

This blog by IMF authors is based on briefing for the July 2017 G-20 meeting by the IMF. Its claim that inequality is bad for growth is in line with the academic consensus, although my analysis in this book suggests a range of different relationships in different circumstances.

Many of the policy recommendations are fairly standard – more training, more education, redistribution – and are in line with those made here. One interesting angle is the suggestion that infrastructural spending on roads and airports would reduce inequality. This is unexpected since the poorest are clearly not those who would benefit directly from roads and airports, and bears further investigation (see Chapter 14).

### Kohler et al.: 'Greater Post-Neolithic Wealth Disparities in Eurasia than in North America and Mesoamerica'[48]

This article (and I am grateful to Tim Worstall of the Adam Smith Institute for a brief summary in CapX[49]) says that productivity improvements in agriculture in this period seem to have been spread unevenly and that the areas with the greatest productivity improvements had the greatest inequality. This runs slightly counter to the conventional wisdom that suggests a small negative correlation between inequality and growth, but it is in line with the 'stylised facts' in Chapter 7 of this book which looks at the complex relationship between inequality and growth.

### David Smith[50]

David Smith is one of the senior economics correspondents in the UK and has written eloquently on inequality both in his columns in the *Times* and *Sunday Times* and on his own blog page. His most recent article on the subject concludes that people are relaxed about rising inequality as long as their own position is improving but when (as recently) they believe that their own position is deteriorating they assume that inequality is rising (when in fact in the UK case it has actually been falling over the same period) and blame inequality for their own problems.[51] This is a perceptive insight.

### Hauner, Milanovic and Naidu, 'Inequality, Foreign Investment, and Imperialism'[52]

Written up by Branko Milanovic in the blog of the Stigler Center at the University of Chicago Booth School of Business, 3 January 2018.[53]

Did rising inequality cause the First World War? When I was taught politics at university a standard essay question related the cause of the First World War to imperialism and the set reading was a book by Hobson[54] relating imperialism to underconsumption at home caused by inequality and to the need to raise demand by developing captive markets overseas. Lenin and Rosa Luxembourg had similar theses.

The authors here use recent data to show that: (1) inequality was at historical highs in all the advanced belligerent countries at the turn of the century, (2) rich wealth holders invested more of their assets abroad, (3) risk-adjusted foreign returns were higher than risk-adjusted domestic returns, (4) establishing direct political control decreased the riskiness of foreign assets, (5) increased inequality was associated with higher share of foreign assets in GDP and (6) increased share of foreign assets was correlated with higher levels of military mobilization. Together, these facts suggest that the classic theory of imperialism may have some empirical support.[55]

They make a powerful case which is hard to ignore, although most of the direct evidence on decision-making at the time does not seem to be as supportive. And arguably if the capitalist class caused the First World War, they were clearly affected by the law of unintended consequences: as Piketty points out, their position was badly eroded by effects of the war, with revolution in Russia, falling profit shares and shares of income of the rich in most countries, and also high taxes in many other countries in the aftermath.

### Bloom, Guvenen, Smith, Song and von Wachter: 'Inequality and the Disappearing Large Firm Wage Premium'[56]

This is an interesting article because rather than explain the rise in inequality in the US it actually attempts to explain a factor that has prevented inequality from rising further. It argues that traditionally workers in larger firms have been paid more than those in smaller firms. But the US economy has restructured since the 1960s and smaller firms have become more important. At the same time the additional pay from working for larger firms has largely disappeared. The research suggests that this is not to do with changing relative skill sets. But my real-life experience suggests that employees in smaller firms tend to have to be more entrepreneurial, a skill that is hard to measure and which probably does not get taken into account in this analysis.

### Oxfam Annual Reports on Wealth Inequality[57]

The campaigning charity Oxfam produces an annual assessment of wealth inequality typically organised to coincide with the annual Davos meeting. The data is based on the Forbes data on billionaires and on the Credit Suisse Global Wealth Report.[58] The headlines for the 2017 report claimed that eight people owned as much wealth as half the world.[59] The next year this figure was revised to 61 for 2017 and 42 for 2018.[60] But the data is derivative. Not surprisingly (given that the organisation collecting the data is mainly concerned with investment banking and managing the wealth of the relatively rich) the Credit Suisse data does not include much of the relevant data for poor people – it does not include the data of the 800 million poorest people (Credit Suisse claims to have data for '4.8 billion adults across the globe' whereas the total number is 5.6 billion[61]), and one suspects that its data on non-investment assets is less comprehensive than its data on those forms of assets in which investment can take place. This is probably not the best data to use to compare the positions of the rich and poor.

Interestingly, Oxfam accepts the data on poverty that shows the massive decline in poverty that is referred to in this book. But it also claims that 200 million more people would be out of poverty if wealth were redistributed, making the assumption that total wealth would remain unchanged.

## Conclusion

From this chapter it is possible to see that there is a wide range of different views on inequality and its causes. This is one of the reasons that the next chapter draws attention to different types and causes of inequality.

In this book I also draw attention to how the causes of inequality can change over time and, following Sir Anthony Atkinson, my analysis suggests a major role in the future for technologically based inequality. Many of the suggestions for mitigating the growth in inequality in Part IV of this book are based on trying to cope with some of the implications of technologically caused inequality.

*Chapter 3*

# THREE DIFFERENT TYPES AND FOUR DIFFERENT CAUSES OF INEQUALITY

T IS IMPORTANT TO DISTINGUISH BETWEEN DIFFERENT TYPES OF INEQUALITY and different causes. This chapter looks at both.

## Different types of inequality[1]

There are many different concepts of equality and inequality, and the previous chapter showed how Hayek argued that some concepts preclude others. So it is important to distinguish between the different concepts before we start to analyse causes.

The first concept of inequality to be considered is that promoted by Hayek. This is essentially that each is equal in his or her legal and human rights. Hayek argues that the most important form of equality is equality under the law, giving equal legal protection for everyone. At the same time he argues that as people are different, equality of such rights is likely to lead to unequal outcomes for people.

Equality under the law is part of the constitution of most democratic countries. It is enshrined in Article 7 of the Universal Declaration of Human Rights and in Article 14 of the International Covenant on Civil and Political Rights and is part of the 14th Amendment to the US Constitution.

It is important to note that this type of equality is an equality of process. It does not guarantee equal outcomes or even equal access. Lawyers often argue that equal access cannot be guaranteed without freely available access to legal advice.

However, although equality under the law is important and most people would support it, this is not the concept of equality that is the focus of this book.

A second concept of equality is equality of opportunity. This concept is that people should be given equal chances of succeeding but whether they do in fact succeed or not is up to them. The economists Milton and

Rose Friedman describe this concept in their book *Free To Choose*:[2] equality of opportunity is 'not to be interpreted literally' since some children are born blind while others are born sighted; 'its real meaning is ... a career open to the talents'. This means that there should be 'no arbitrary obstacles' blocking a person from realising their ambitions, and that 'Not birth, nationality, colour, religion, sex, nor any other irrelevant characteristic should determine the opportunities that are open to a person – only his abilities.'

Many people instinctively support equality of opportunity, but it is hard to generate in practice. There are interesting questions about the extent to which differences in health and education can be incorporated into the concept. Moreover, since different people have different genetic endowments, the equality of opportunity argument does not really handle how to compensate for this. Finally, luck plays a major role in life and again this is not dealt with in the equality of opportunity theory. But this book is not concerned with equality of opportunity.

The third concept is equality of outcomes, meaning that whatever people do in the economic sphere they should accept the same levels of income or expenditure. For a long time this concept was seen as an ideal held only by a minority. But as inequality of outcomes has increased in Western economies especially, support for equalising outcomes has grown.

This book mainly concerns itself with this last concept of equality, equality of outcome for income and wealth, and how to move towards it without damaging the economy or other appropriate objectives, such as reducing poverty.

This brings us to four different potential causes of the recent rise in inequality.

### Type 1 Inequality

The first potential cause of the recent rise in inequality which we shall consider is the concept advanced by Piketty – increased inequality caused by increased exploitation.

It is unlikely that anyone will deny that this has happened, although there is plenty of scope for debate about how important it has been. Even if Piketty is wrong about it being the main cause, it certainly has had a role to play in these developments.

The formal definition of Type 1 Inequality is that it is the form of inequality that results when some people or groups abuse their power to extract wealth or income from the rest of society involuntarily. The simplest form is a protection racket. A more sophisticated form might come from the creation of an exploitative monopoly. A third form might be the abuse of political power to divert income and wealth to specific groups through the granting of state supported privileges.

Chapter 9 looks at this concept in more detail in the context of high pay for so-called crony capitalists, bankers and CEOs. It notes that some of the excessive pay might be a function of the disequilibrium phenomenon of a slowly adjusting labour market and that the problem of excessive pay for some might sort itself out naturally. Certainly bankers are now paid much less in London than was once the case (though in my view still far too much) and US CEOs earn less in cash terms than they did in the year 2000.

Type 1 Inequality is generally considered the most offensive form. Not only is income or wealth taken from poorer groups and given to richer groups effectively through force without creating any added value, leaving both the rich richer and the poor poorer, but in practice the existence of this type of inequality generally creates a negative sum game. The monopolies and rackets associated with it actually reduce economic activity, so the worse off suffer twice over.

In some cases tax cuts for wealthier groups might be expected to lead to increased Type 1 Inequality. This, in effect, is one of Piketty's arguments: that increased social acceptability of greed led the rich to push for tax cuts which in turn made greed more profitable. Although he does not describe them in detail, it seems clear that he is referring to the Thatcher and Reagan tax cuts mainly in this context.

Yet it is possible to argue that, particularly in the UK context, the pre-Thatcher rates of tax were so excessive that the reductions in top rates from 83% for directly earned income and 98% for investment income were merely allowing wealthier people to keep a fairer share of what they had earned. Certainly the yields from higher rates of tax actually increased when the rates were reduced.

But the question of what rate of tax maximises revenue has long been debated. One suspects that it may vary between different societies with different cultural norms.

## Type 2 Inequality

Type 2 Inequality is that caused by the early stages of globalisation. As emerging economies develop, typically they initially compete most with the developed economies in the more poorly paid jobs. At the same time global growth offers increased opportunities for those with scarce skills – especially from the more developed economies – to market their skills in a bigger market. Even if this process reduces poverty in the emerging economies (which it generally does) it might mean both more poverty and more inequality in the developed economies.

To understand the process it is worth looking at economic history, starting before the so-called 'Great Divergence' between the West and the East.

## The Great Divergence

It was the political scientist Samuel Huntington who named the sharp widening of the gap in technology and incomes between a few selected European nations and some later offshoots of these nations on the one hand, and the rest of the world on the other, the Great Divergence.[3]

Table 2. The Great Divergence. Growth of GDP per capita in selected European and Asian Nations, 1000-1950 (in 1990 Geary-Khamis $)[4]

| Year | France | Germany | Italy | UK | USA | China | India | Japan |
|------|--------|---------|-------|-----|-----|-------|-------|-------|
| 1000 | 425 | 410 | 450 | 400 | 400 | 466 | 450 | 425 |
| 1500 | 727 | 688 | 1,100 | 714 | 400 | 600 | 550 | 500 |
| 1600 | 841 | 791 | 1,100 | 974 | 400 | 600 | 550 | 520 |
| 1700 | 910 | 910 | 1,100 | 1,250 | 527 | 600 | 550 | 570 |
| 1820 | 1,135 | 1,077 | 1,117 | 1,706 | 1,257 | 600 | 533 | 669 |
| 1850 | 1,597 | 1,428 | 1,350 | 2,330 | 1,806 | 600 | 533 | 679 |
| 1900 | 2,876 | 2,985 | 1,785 | 4,492 | 4,091 | 545 | 599 | 1,180 |
| 1950 | 5,186 | 3,881 | 3,502 | 6,939 | 9,561 | 448 | 619 | 1,921 |

Source: Maddison Data Archive, Groningen University

In 1450 a betting person would probably have been at least as likely to bet that Mughal India, China or the Ottoman Empire would grow rich and accelerate clear of the rest of the world as that the European countries would do so. Because my parents lived in the Malaysian town of Malacca when I was a small boy, one of the historical figures who has always intrigued me is the Chinese admiral Cheng Ho (now in Pinyin normally called Zheng He) who if he didn't discover Malacca (there was already a Sultan when he first arrived) certainly did a lot to develop it. He visited Malacca at least five times on his seven great voyages (on one of which he may possibly have reached the Americas,[5] though professional historians think he got only as far as the Mozambique Channel). Malacca's best museum is the Cheng Ho Cultural Museum.[6]

In Cheng Ho's time, the late 14th/early 15th century, China seemed to many to be the most technologically advanced nation in the world (although GDP per capita is estimated to have been slightly lower than in most European countries).[7] His ships were many times larger and more advanced than those in which the great Spanish, Italian and especially Portuguese navigators discovered the world half a century later. (His biggest ships were about 400 feet long and 180 feet wide whereas Columbus's *Santa Maria* was 60 feet long and about 20 feet wide.) Chinese nutritional standards and life expectancy at that time were significantly higher than those in Europe.

If you go to the Maritime Museum in Lisbon (in many ways, for those of us interested in globalisation, one of the great museums of the world) you can see how tiny and how technologically backward were the ships in which the daring adventurers from Portugal and elsewhere visited much of the world. Where they had an advantage was that their navigational skills were more advanced than others so they could cross oceans while others did not sail far away from the coast.

One of the most readable accounts of the Great Divergence is by the former BBC Economics Correspondent Peter Jay.[8] One of the reasons that he writes so well about the voyages of discovery is that he is himself, as well as a distinguished economist, a highly competent sailor who has personally undertaken epic voyages (including returning from his stint as UK Ambassador in the US by sailing the Atlantic himself in a race).[9]

During the 15th century the Ottoman Empire conquered Constantinople, besieged Vienna, fought the battle of Lepanto, captured Hungary and raided Moscow as well as conquering many parts of Central and Eastern Europe. Technologically it too looked well ahead of the European nations who were hard pressed to hold it off militarily.

So how did Europe get ahead?

The main theories explain the Great Divergence as to do with the competition for ideas spurred by the Reformation in Europe (a slight problem for me having been brought up as a Catholic in various Jesuit monasteries) compared with the generally anti-business attitudes of the Chinese and the Muslim empires[10] as well as of those parts of Europe that remained most heavily Catholic. Indeed the arrival of French Huguenots in Holland and England were major spurs to growth. Ironically, immigrants to London today working in Spitalfields and the area nearby, the same area colonised by the Huguenots, have created the new 'Flat White Economy' which has done so much to push the UK economy forward in the past ten years.[11]

Trade was considered by the Confucians to be 'unproductive, uncultured and preoccupied with profit rather than the good of society'[12] – they obviously hadn't yet made the discovery of Adam Smith's 'invisible hand'.

Exploitation of the New World and, sadly, of slaves from Africa, were also probable contributory factors to the Great Divergence. If we ever think of ourselves in the West as somehow intrinsically superior to other peoples, it is sobering to think of the deception and violence that accompanied these processes. Although many others might have behaved just as badly had they had the resources to do so, it remains a fact that the West did have the resources and initiated the violence and deception.

It is arguable that persistent warfare in Europe during most of the next 300 years from 1500 also stimulated technological development. It certainly helped develop the weapons technology which enabled European nations to conquer and colonise much of the world.

Eventually the growth in per capita incomes created a world with a sufficient surplus over subsistence to finance an industrial takeoff. The combination of technology and capital generated the industrial revolution which took over the UK in the 18th and 19th centuries and which was rapidly copied by the other European nations.

As an interesting aside, much of the technology for the industrial revolution was contributed by my fellow Scots.[13] The Scottish Education Act of 1496 made it compulsory for sons of barons and substantial freeholders to be educated in grammar schools. From 1560 education was encouraged as a result of the Scottish Reformation. For people to be enlightened they needed to be able to read so that they could read the Bible. In 1696 the Scottish Parliament passed the 'Act for Setting Schools', making it compulsory for each kirk (parish) to have a school. Thus education in Scotland was widespread throughout society at an early stage, creating a sufficient breadth of ideas and knowledge among people doing manual jobs. The mix of education and practical manual jobs provided the engineering knowledge that made the Scots of the era such great inventors.

In most other countries those who were educated did not actually do practical work and so were generally unable to apply their education to the artisan processes involved in the work of the educated but still artisan Scots. Thomas Telford, the great engineer, was a stone-mason originally but his mix of practical building knowledge and his education, which was not much more than most Scots of his era received, turned him into someone who could change the face of a nation.[14] The experience of Scotland and indeed of émigré Scots in the US, Canada, Australia and New Zealand is powerful support for the theory that the most important means of securing equality is education.

One of the consequences of the Great Divergence was a massive increase in inequality, especially between countries. Even poor people in rich countries became typically much better off than the bulk of the population of poorer countries.

The industrial revolution – despite fears to the contrary which led to the Luddite rebellion of 1811-15 and the breaking of machines – in fact created more jobs than it destroyed (though real wages of manual workers fell in the UK in the early part of 19th century, both the two series commonly available show drops of around 25%).[15] These declines in wages were however reversed during the second half of the 19th century.

## Globalisation

I had got excited about globalisation while I was being brought up in Malaysia. It is hard for someone who was not in South East Asia through the third quarter of the 20th century to comprehend the scale of the change in living standards that took place in the country during that period. Between 1953 and 1976 when my family lived in Malaysia, per capita GDP in the country more than doubled from $1,440 to $2,910 despite rapid population growth.[16]

What this meant was that conditions in the country changed from the majority of people living below the breadline (or in their case the rice equivalent) to living with some minor creature comforts. Bicycles had become widespread during the 1950s and early 1960s. In the late 1960s and early 1970s small motorcycles started to flood the roads. By the 1980s the motorcycles had been replaced by cars, creating the epic traffic jams that are now so characteristic of the Far East.

In the early 1970s economic growth really started to take off with offshore manufacturing of electronic components.

Asia in the 1950s and 1960s was mainly thought of economically as a producer of commodities and very cheap basic goods. In 1968 that changed. The electronics company Fairchild made the first offshore electronics investment in Hong Kong. I have a personal view which has been rarely mentioned in the literature (the main study on this is in Korean, though it has now been translated) that the Vietnam War was catalytic in causing the first investments in East Asia.[17] Young American soldiers were drafted into the war and sent to Asia. I'm sure that their unusual experience abroad in Asia (remember that at that time very few Americans of their generation ever left the US) may have influenced their attitude to investment in East Asia when they returned to civilian life and made business decisions.

The peak level of annual expenditure by the US on Vietnam was (coincidentally) also in 1968 when, according to the Congressional Research Service, $111 billion was spent on the war, which they have helpfully translated into $738 billion in 2011 (financial year) dollars and about $800 billion in today's money.[18] As Senator Everett Dirksen pointed out, 'a billion here, a billion there, pretty soon you're talking about real money'. $800 billion is real money and had already started to leach into the domestic Asian economies in the provision of basic supplies before Fairchild came in and started to make electronics products in Hong Kong.

We talk these days of wars creating 'collateral damage', which I feel is a nastily sanitised phase to describe the killing of innocent people which often occurs during a war. But there are occasionally also 'collateral benefits', such as the stimulus given to economic development in East Asia.

When I was studying for my Master's at Oxford in 1972-74, the phenomenon of offshore electronics manufacturing in Asia already seemed developed enough for me to choose to perform a social cost–benefit analysis of the first two electronics plants in the Kuala Lumpur area for my thesis, which showed how massively these projects benefited all parties.[19] The first plant took no more than a year to pay back its entire capital investment. The second took only ten months. Employees working in the plants typically tripled their living standards from their previous levels while, even though the plants were in tax-free zones (meaning no import or export duties and no profits taxes), government revenue was boosted strongly by income taxes, employment taxes and indirect taxes on the employees' expenditure.

Incidentally, this is one reason why I am careful not to confuse companies who pay little or no corporate taxes with companies paying no tax at all. While I think companies should pay a reasonable amount of corporate tax on their profits, their main contribution to overall tax revenues is through sales and value-added taxes on their products, the various payroll taxes they pay and of course the taxes that their employees pay on their incomes and on their expenditure. Direct corporate tax payments on profits tend to be relatively unimportant in comparison, and if low rates of corporate taxes promote increased inward investment and hence economic growth, the government tax take is likely to gain much more than it loses from a reduction in corporate tax rates. This may change in the future though, if new technologies make businesses more capital intensive and reduce employee income shares.

This offshore manufacturing was clearly going to transform those medium-income developing countries that took it up, such as Hong Kong, Singapore, Taiwan, Thailand and Korea as well as Malaysia. It would transform the world economy as well as the economies of those countries in which manufacturing previously took place when countries such as China and India (who between them make up nearly two-fifths of the world's population) emulated them.

What we saw starting to happen in Malaysia and Hong Kong, and also in Taiwan, Korea, Thailand and especially Singapore, was an important economic theme of the 1970s and 1980s, though because these economies were still relatively small as a share of the world economy, the impact on the global economy was muted.

These Asian countries plus Taiwan accounted for 3.2% of the world economy in 1870 and were about the same percentage, 3.3%, in 1970. Their share rose to a peak of 8.0% in 1997 before the Asian currency crisis.[20] The rise was very rapid, but despite this the net impact on the scale of the world economy was limited.

Let me digress for a short time just to deal with Japan. Japan was the first East Asian economy to industrialise. This started after the Meiji restoration in 1868 and led to a process that finally saw Japan catch up with the Western economies. Japan's standard of living doubled between 1870 and the First World War, doubled again by 1939, and after a major slump during the war – much more than in most of the other belligerent countries – had recovered its pre-war level by 1956 and caught up with Western Europe by 1973.

Japan is an outlier. It was the only Asian economy to industrialise so early. Although it had scale, with a population which reached 100 million in 1967, and its industrialisation was distinctly faster than in Western Europe, nevertheless its total impact on the world economy was still relatively minor because it represented just one country. Japan's share of world GDP rose from 2.3% in 1870 to 8.7% at its peak in 1991, which is non-trivial but still not enough to mark a qualitative shift in things such as world demand for resources.

There are two other reasons (that is, other than the Second World War war) why Japan has been less disruptive: first, the speed of industrialisation – though rapid – has been about half that of East Asia and China. The second is that after the Second World War the US had the power to influence Japanese economic policy and the Japanese have been forced to allow the yen to appreciate to reflect its competitiveness. Thus the super-competitive conditions that we have seen elsewhere existed for only a short period before the appreciation of the yen changed the position.

But Japan has been important in the story. It proved conclusively to any racist who believed that only white people could industrialise that this was emphatically not the case. And of course, Japan's actions in the Second World War, though ultimately self-defeating, spelt the end of the Western, especially British, empires in the East. My once fellow Gresham Professor, Sir Richard Evans,[21] has written eloquently about this.[22]

The examples of the emerging economies in East Asia as well as that of Japan were bound to affect other Eastern economies. With Taiwan and Hong Kong on their doorstep, the Chinese in China would have had to be immensely obtuse or blinded by ideology not to realise that Chinese people everywhere other than mainland China seemed to be doing remarkably well while those in China were not. And once Chairman Mao had died, the new Chinese leadership was not obtuse or blinded by ideology. From the mid-1970s onwards they decided to copy what was being done in the economies on their doorstep.

In the 1960s President Johnson used to defend the actions of the US in Vietnam by talking about what he called the Domino Theory – that if one country fell to communism it would knock over its neighbour country. In the end, what happened was the Domino Theory in reverse. The economic success of East Asia changed China, which was one of the factors leading to President Gorbachev wanting to reform Russia and which over time was one of the factors that led to the fall of the Iron Curtain. I remember once explaining to Lee Kuan Yew, the eminent Singaporean leader, that he had caused the fall of the Iron Curtain – he was amused by the idea, though he seemed less amused when I explained that the previous time I had visited Singapore as a rebellious teenager in transit to Kuala Lumpur I had been kept in preventative detention at the airport because my hair was too long.

And of course we are not just talking about these economies alone. Latin America saw which way the wind was blowing and changed course. More importantly, other emerging economies, of which the most important was India, also began to change.

A coincidental factor that was hugely important in all this was the emergence of information and communications technology. The new electronic technologies created a mass demand for cheap mass-produced electronic components and products which have been the main driving technology for East Asian economic development. They have also reduced the tyranny of location and allowed businesses throughout the world to enter into the software industry. This has been especially important for India, since it allowed Indian software exports to escape the so-called Permit Raj that had – very much with the help of the professors of economic development – done so much to slow down India's emergence from the economic doldrums.

The effects of globalisation have been to remove the Western world's dominance of the production of economically sophisticated goods. This in turn has meant that ordinary workers in the Western world have lost their jobs or been forced to accept a squeeze in their living standards. Note that this does not mean that had the West put up protectionist barriers to this trade they could have avoided this squeeze. The squeeze has also resulted from changed terms of trade. Protection would not have helped the West improve its terms of trade by much and would have come at a cost in lost economic growth which would also have weakened the position of the worst off in the Western world.

It is argued elsewhere in this book that we may now be moving to a point where globalisation no longer increases inequality even in the Western economies. If this is so it will be because the Eastern economies compete with the more skilled jobs in the West just as aggressively as they previously competed with the less skilled jobs.

## Type 3 Inequality

Type 3 Inequality is the growth in inequality that comes from changes in technology. Technically this results from what the experts call 'skills-biased technical progress', suggesting that technical progress is resulting in the substitution of machines and software for unskilled labour, while creating increased opportunities for skilled labour.

There is no a priori reason why technology should be labour substituting – it could easily go the other way, as Anthony Atkinson points out. But in recent years, since the 1960s, information technology has been the most pervasive source of economic advance and has been largely substituting for labour. One possible reason why technology has tended to be labour substituting is that in much of the world the main taxation base is labour incomes through payroll taxes, social contributions and income taxes.

The historic evidence on the extent of skills-biased technical progress is mixed[23] but seems to suggest that technology on its own has not yet been the major driving force behind growth in inequality. However, Sir Anthony Atkinson, who specialised in the subject, believed that this was about to become much more important. From my background as chief economist for IBM UK, from being on the board of Marconi plc and from writing *The Flat White Economy*, I suspect he may be right.

The IMF economists Mai Dao, Mitali Das, Zsoka Koczan and Weicheng Lian, who have tried to explain what is happening, have suggested that it is not so much technology on its own but the interaction between technology and globalisation that has been particularly important.[24] This seems plausible to me.

There are some examples of information technology reducing inequality. To give an example from my own field, it used to be possible for only major banks and other large institutions with access to huge and expensive mainframe computers to produce economic forecasts. Now a competent economist with access to a £300 desktop computer can do so. In the late 1980s the top economists in the City earned close to £1 million a year. Today there are many more economists employed but few earn as much as £250,000 (although of course other factors have been at work as well as technology).

In general, however, the technological divide has boosted inequality. First, communications technology has permitted the best to sell their services many times over rather than be limited to those whom they could easily reach physically. Second, the powerful tools permitted by technology can do much more to boost the incomes of those with the greatest skill in using them. For example, at some point the most sophisticated piece of capital equipment was a spade. No matter how good you were with a spade there was a physical limit to what you could do compared with an average wielder of a similar spade. But think of a modern IT system. A sophisticated user can find highly profitable arbitrage opportunities for derivatives trading yielding returns many million times more than those available to someone who can only use the system for word processing.

The impact of technology is about to face a further leap forward with advances in robotics and autonomous vehicles and a wide range of other technologies. A major study across 29 countries by the consultants Price Waterhouse Cooper has suggested that by the mid-2030s about 30% of current jobs are likely to be automated and 44% of unskilled jobs.[25] Because of the pace at which this is likely to happen, it is probable that the labour markets in many countries will not adjust and that many may lose their jobs before others emerge. Obviously new jobs will emerge eventually unless prevented by social security benefit levels and minimum wage laws. But there may be an extremely painful period in between while the current jobs are being automated.

### Type 4 Inequality

The rise in Type 4 Inequality emerges from an increasing influence from parenting and genetic inheritance, creating so-called 'superbabies' and their corollary in the lower socioeconomic classes. It is not patronising to point out that many mothers (often single) from lower socioeconomic groups achieve results that are close to miraculous in supporting their families and bringing up children at the same time. Yet these children are unlikely to have the advantages of those from more privileged backgrounds.

One cause of the increase in these so-called 'superbabies' is homogamy – the tendency for people to mate with similar people. It is not just that people like people who are like them, though there is evidence going back to 1943 that this seems to be the case.[26] Rather it is the fact that this is combined with the tendency for people to mate with those whom they meet when they first leave home – in many cases when they go to the same university. This is discussed in much more detail in Chapter 8. But an unfortunate consequence is that the inequality that it perpetuates can become a real threat to social cohesion and can be difficult to counter. The data suggests not just that people tend to partner with others at the same university but even from the same course.

On top of this, and even more frightening in some ways, are the potential effects of genetic manipulation and modification on inequality. There is quite a good review article in *Forbes* magazine on this.[27] Fortunately both taboos on human genetic manipulation and the difficulties of experimentation mean that this is still some way into the future.

But even without genetic manipulation the tendency for homogamy combined with the experience of co-education at university seems likely to be a disruptive social force that unless countered will entrench the position of the privileged.

## Conclusions

What this chapter shows is that there are some quite different driving forces behind high and rising inequality and that different periods in history are likely to be associated with different factors pushing changes in the level of equality. The key is not to be blinded by ideology and to understand what is actually happening at any time. This is necessary to achieve the best mix of responses that can reduce inequality most without jeopardising the levels of economic activity necessary to provide prosperity.

## Chapter 4
# WHY INEQUALITY REALLY MATTERS

THIS CHAPTER EXPLAINS WHY INEQUALITY MATTERS. FIRST IT DISTIN-guishes between the problems of inequality and those of poverty. Because there is sometimes a trade-off between inequality and poverty, it is important to understand which problems reflect the former and which the latter.

The analysis here suggests that there are two particular problems associated with inequality as opposed to poverty. The first of these is the sense of despair from which those who fear that they and their descendants face an increasing exclusion from society may suffer. The second is the loss of cohesion that emerges as society becomes increasingly divided. The loss of cohesion can lead to various problems, one of which might be a scale of political partisanship that can make a country ungovernable.

The end of the chapter looks at the development of a new dynamic in London and other parts of the world (especially Sweden) – a sort of grunge chic – where excessive conspicuous consumption is frowned upon and the rich self-consciously try to live a similar lifestyle to poorer people using public transport and the public health services. It argues that in egalitarian societies people react against those who try to behave as if they are different and that there are centrifugal forces making for cohesion. Such a greater degree of homogeneity of behaviour can make for better policymaking (if the articulate middle classes use public services, they tend to be less tolerant of bad service) and can reduce partisan behaviour.

### Inequality and poverty
The difference between problems caused by poverty and those caused by inequality depends on whether making poorer people better off will solve them. If making poorer people better off will solve the problems, then they are essentially problems of poverty. If the problems come as a result of the breadth of the gap between different people in the pecking order, then they are problems of inequality.

## Health inequality

It is often claimed that differences in health outcomes reflect health inequality. In most cases they do not, reflecting instead simple lack of access to healthcare and medicines that would cure diseases. Making people better off would largely solve these problems, even if inequality remained the same.

There is, however, a different category of health problems of poorer people in wealthier economies that seems to reflect psychological factors rather than the simple cost of medicine.

Some indication of the ability to confuse health problems caused by inequality with those caused by poverty can be seen from the widely respected State of Child Health report in the UK which provides a comprehensive list of 25 measures of the health of UK children, ranging from specific conditions such as asthma, diabetes and epilepsy, to risk factors for poor health such as obesity and a low rate of breastfeeding, to child deaths.[1] The data provide an 'across the board' snapshot of child health and well-being in the UK.

The report concludes 'Nearly one in five children in the UK is living in poverty and inequality is blighting their lives, with those from the most deprived backgrounds experiencing much worse health compared with the most affluent. Despite some improvements in the health of UK children over the last decades, there is clear disparity with Europe, and major cause for concern.'

The quick jump from poverty to inequality in the statement makes it likely that the reporting of the study confuses the two. It is possible that making poor people richer might solve some of these problems. But one also suspects that lifestyle issues, which are discussed below in the context of status and loss of it, are more important. While not all lifestyle issues are to do with relative position and hence inequality, one's position in the pecking order in a society can be a factor affecting health.

## Positional goods

The economist Fred Hirsch coined the phrase 'positional goods' to describe goods which are in limited supply and which command a premium because of their special quality.[1] They are only available to those who want them so much that they will outbid anyone else. Housing in the most desirable locations in the world is probably the best example.

The London housing market shows this. The best houses are quite quickly being taken over by rich foreign buyers. One often suspects that complaints about inequality by London-based government employees and by journalists reflect the loss of access to the best houses that at one point were affordable for the likes of them but now are priced way beyond their reach.

I have always used Fred Hirsch's thinking as good investment advice and bought assets such as houses and classic cars on the basis that the supply was limited. When I moved into a terraced house in Regent's Park in 1991, 15 of the 18 houses in the terrace were owned by other people of British origin and (as I discovered subsequently) the other person bidding for the house which I bought turned out to be the then Prime Minister, Mrs Thatcher. Previous owners of the house included the Chairman of the Scottish Banks and the North British Railway company that built the Forth Bridge (he was also an MP) and the former Chief Economist of the Colonial Office.

In my 26 years in the house there has been only one journalist living in the terrace (admittedly he was editor of *The Times*) and no civil servants other than my wife. But now 14 of the owners are of foreign descent, and only four British, though the foreign owners do generally work and have increasingly strong roots in the UK as bankers or entrepreneurs of some other kind and indeed are active socially in the local community.

Globalisation has meant that many buyers of such property are now from abroad. Those that are domestic tend to be entrepreneurs, bankers or lawyers. Not long ago they might have been members of the chattering classes like academics, journalists and civil servants. There is no god-given law that says that such people should live in fancy houses. But if their expectations are unsatisfied, it would be understandable if they felt the system wasn't working for them. And these are people who are skilled at making themselves heard. So the result of their unsatisfied expectations is likely to be quite loud complaints against the system.

It is realistic to blame these effects on inequality, though many of them particularly relate to the combination of inequality and globalisation.

Other positional goods which are likely to be affected in a similar way are unique items such as works of art and classic cars. It is not widely known that the most comprehensive index for art prices, from Artprice.com, shows art prices in most currencies sharply down from their peak in January 2008 (the dollar index is down 30%). But at the same time the top prices paid have risen. At the time of writing the highest price ever paid for a work of art is $450,312,500 paid in November 2017 for Leonardo da Vinci's 'Salvator Mundi'. In 2008 the record price ever paid was \$164.5 million for Jackson Pollock's 'No.5, 1948'. So while the prices of ordinary art are falling, the top prices are rising by not far short of a factor of three, yet another indicator of rising inequality.

The fact that only the very richest have access to those goods in limited supply might not appear to be a major social problem. Arguably no one has a right to smart London houses or Leonardo paintings. And if different rich people can access them today from those who could a few years ago, does it really matter? Even if the group hit most is made up of the vocal chattering classes such as people working in the public sector and journalists.

But the problem with inequality and positional goods becomes more serious if the London housing market is looked at in total. In *The Flat White Economy* I drew attention to housing in London having become so expensive that people were being forced to share bedrooms with those other than partners. And the Parliamentary report on the state of housing in the UK[3] makes the following points:

(1) There has been a reduction in the number of 25- to 34-year-olds owning homes in England. In 1991, 67 percent of this age group owned homes, but this had fallen to 36 percent by the year ending 2014. Over the same period, home ownership among 16- to 24-year-olds fell from 36 percent in 1991 to 9 percent in 2014.[4]

(2) In 2015, the Cambridge Centre for Housing Planning Research published research on the number of young people, aged 16 to 24, experiencing homelessness. The study found that during 2013-14 83,000 homeless young people had been accommodated by local authorities or homelessness services. It also estimated that there were 'around 35,000 young people in homeless accommodation at any one time across the UK'.[5]

(3) Our new research into housing affordability for generation renters shows that buyers may now have to save for 19 years in order to buy their first home (assuming the deposit has to be raised entirely from their own savings without family assistance). In 2000, the same group would have been able to buy after saving for just 6 years; and in 1990 it took only around 2 years.[6]

It is because housing is in scarce supply with its supply affected by planning controls and rent controls that it becomes a positional good where your ability to buy or rent is not a function of your absolute ability to pay but of your ability to pay relative to other people. Hence if housing is made scarce, income inequality leads to housing inequality. There is a fuller discussion of the impact of planning and rent controls in Chapter 14.

## Alienation

The concept of social cohesion emerged with industrialisation. To quote from a highly referenced study by Larsen:[7]

> In Durkheim's (1858-1917) terms, the question was what could replace the so-called mechanical solidarity found in pre-modern societies – the solidarity that is established among people who are similar. This similarity could be both material: similar work, housing and food; and non-material: similar beliefs, morality and feelings. Durkheim labelled the non-material part of the community the conscience collective, which is the academic origin of the term 'social cohesion'. Pre-modern societies were according to Durkheim characterized by a sizeable and strong 'collective consciousness', which typically had a strong religious fundament, so that any deviation from the moral codex was typically interpreted as a religious violation. Thus, strong norms of right and wrong and intense monitoring in small communities upheld non-material similarities. Or using the provided definition of social cohesion, the strong religious fundament and close monitoring made the member of society believe that they shared a moral community that enable them to trust each other.

Durkheim developed the concept of 'anomie' where individuals lose their relationship with society in his major book, *The Division of Labour in Society*.[8] Alienation, which is much the same concept, was at the core of Marx's work and again associated with the rootlessness resulting from industrialisation.

A more literary and less intellectual description comes from the former Conservative Prime Minister Stanley Baldwin in his speech to the annual dinner of the Royal Society of St George at the Hotel Cecil on 6 May 1924:[9]

> And there comes into my mind a wonder as to what England may stand for in the minds of generations to come if our country goes on during the next generation as she has done in the last two in seeing her fields converted into towns.

> To me, England is the country and the country is England ... The
> sounds of England, the tinkle of the hammer on the anvil in the coun-
> try smithy, the corncrake on a dewy morning, the sound of the scythe
> against the whetstone, and the sight of a plough team coming over
> the brow of a hill, the sight that has been seen in England since Eng-
> land was a land and may be seen in England long after the Empire has
> perished and every works in England has ceased to function, for cen-
> turies the one eternal sight of England.

Earlier he argues 'The Englishman is all right as long as he is content to
be what God made him, an Englishman, but gets into trouble when he
tries to be something else.'

There is a sense of social breakdown associated with change, particularly with the move to the city from the countryside. Marx sees this
as an opportunity; conservatives as a threat. But both make the same analysis of change and alienation and can be contrasted with old-fashioned
Liberals who are much more enthusiastic about change.

Unfortunately for those who dislike it, globalisation and technology
have given the West change in a dramatic fashion. This is unsettling even
for those benefiting from the process – how much more so must it be for
those who lose out?

### Despair and falling life expectancy

The first evidence of falling life expectancy in a developed economy came
from Glasgow. A survey of the Calton area of Glasgow between 1998
and 2002 showed male life expectancy of only 54.[10] Recent data casts
some doubt on this figure, however – in the latest data for the period
2008-2012, male life expectancy at birth was estimated by the Glasgow
Centre for Public Health to be 67.8 years, while female life expectancy
was estimated at 76.6 years.[11] It seems unlikely that life expectancy in
Glasgow has improved that much that quickly.[12]

Recent deaths of pop musicians in their fifties and early sixties draw
attention to the dangers posed by drug abuse which does shorten lives
through a variety of routes. And many in the more poverty-affected parts
of Western economies suffer from a toxic cocktail of exclusion, lack of
direction and substance abuse that means that their quality of life, even
if objectively they have access to resources, is low. These people need to
be helped directly if possible. Giving them money alone with no assistance does little to solve their problems and can make them worse.

Meanwhile, Case and Deaton have shown a very serious and sharp rise in the death rate of white non-Hispanics in the US and their data has recently been updated.[13] To quote the summary of the updated paper (I apologise for quoting at such length but the study is so important and so relevant that to fail to quote it would impoverish this analysis):

We build on and extend the findings in Case and Deaton (2015)[14] on increases in mortality and morbidity among white non-Hispanic Americans in midlife since the turn of the century. Increases in all-cause mortality continued unabated to 2015, with additional increases in drug overdoses, suicides, and alcohol-related liver mortality, particularly among those with a high-school degree or less.

The decline in mortality from heart disease has slowed and, most recently, stopped, and this combined with the three other causes is responsible for the increase in all-cause mortality. Not only are educational differences in mortality among whites increasing, but from 1998 to 2015 mortality rose for those without, and fell for those with, a college degree. This is true for non-Hispanic white men and women in all five year age groups from 35-39 through 55-59. Mortality rates among blacks and Hispanics continued to fall; in 1999, the mortality rate of white non-Hispanics aged 50-54 with only a high-school degree was 30 percent lower than the mortality rate of blacks in the same age group but irrespective of education; by 2015, it was 30 percent higher.

There are similar crossovers in all age groups from 25-29 to 60-64. Mortality rates in comparable rich countries have continued their pre-millennial fall at the rates that used to characterize the US. In contrast to the US, mortality rates in Europe are falling for those with low levels of educational attainment, and have fallen further over this period than mortality rates for those with higher levels of education. Many commentators have suggested that poor mortality outcomes can be attributed to contemporaneous levels of resources, particularly to slowly growing, stagnant, and even declining incomes; we evaluate this possibility, but find that it cannot provide a comprehensive explanation. In particular, the income profiles for blacks and Hispanics, whose mortality rates have fallen, are no better than those for whites. Nor is there any evidence in the European data that mortality trends match income trends, in spite of sharply different patterns of median income across countries after the Great Recession.

We propose a preliminary but plausible story in which cumulative disadvantage from one birth cohort to the next, in the labour market, in marriage and child outcomes, and in health, is triggered by progressively worsening labour market opportunities at the time of entry for whites with low levels of education. This account, which fits much of the data, has the profoundly negative implication that policies, even ones that successfully improve earnings and jobs, or redistribute income, will take many years to reverse the mortality and morbidity increase, and that those in midlife now are likely to do much worse in old age than those currently older than 65. This is in contrast to an account in which resources affect health contemporaneously, so that those in midlife now can expect to do better in old age as they receive Social Security and Medicare. None of this implies that there are no policy levers to be pulled; preventing the over-prescription of opioids is an obvious target that might be helpful.

What this is saying is that the long-term diminution of status, generation by generation, is creating a serious form of alienation that turns into depression.

Obviously it is difficult to see exactly how to reverse this trend. But my experience from the Far East may be helpful. That experience suggested that even people whose own economic circumstances were unfavourable could still be fairly content with life as long as they could see an improving trend for themselves and their offspring. The experience in the US in the 1930s seems consistent with this. Also the experience in Europe, where fewer people seem to feel excluded, seems to lend support.

This suggests that finding ways of helping people appreciate that they have a stake in society is a mixture of carrot and stick. Some relief from the pressure of current conditions is necessary. Some realisation of what expectations are appropriate and realignment of them is also necessary. But the most important ingredient is hope, and this has to be partly for the people themselves and partly for their children. Encouraging people to believe that their children can have a better life than themselves can be a huge incentive for people who are getting a bad deal from any given set of economic circumstances.

The conclusion of this book revisits some of these issues to understand their policy implications.

## Social cohesion

There is another sense in which inequality creates problems which are different from those of poverty itself. Although the rose-tinted memory of everyone living in much the same way is misleading, there is a sense that, particularly in the US and to a lesser extent in Europe, for a long period the bulk of people had remarkably similar lifestyles. Obviously the poor living in the projects or in council houses lived differently from the rich in their gated communities or in flats in Eaton Square. But a large number of people had lives that differed only in degree from each other and not in essence.

They shopped in roughly the same shops, watched the same TV programmes, drank the same drinks and ate the same food. And one of the consequences of this was a shared experience of life that led to a remarkable degree of consensus about how to handle problems.

Both in the US and in Europe there was a consensus about economics, with a view that problems should be approached broadly from a market perspective and that there should be some welfare, that governments had a significant role to play and politicians of different parties worked together to make life better for everyone.

The breakdown of this consensus is not just a function of growing inequality and the resultant differences in lifestyles. It goes much further than that. Technology, the breakdown of the nuclear family model and other social factors have caused a fragmentation of consumption patterns. But the growth in income inequality has made an important contribution.

On top of this, technology has increased the remoteness of power from most people. At work in the past, your foreman might have been a bully and might have given you a hard time. But at least he had a face and if you were feeling brave (or stupid) you could argue with him. Today the person who makes the decisions that affect your working life is probably a faceless person many miles away. If you don't hit your targets, your job goes. There is no one with whom you can argue the toss. You get sacked by email or text.

A policeman might once have given you a kicking if you were a petty offender. But, particularly if he caught you near the end of his shift and didn't fancy the paperwork, and if you hadn't actually hurt anyone, you had a good chance of being let free at least the first couple of times. Now he has targets set by faceless officials that he has to satisfy. You get nicked if he has half a chance and generally for breaking the letter of the law rather than being a real nuisance to society. The serious criminals often get off scot-free because they are too hard to pursue, while minor infractions of the law that can be easily proved are pursued with vigour.

There is a lot of research that connects both physical health and mental health with feelings of powerlessness. Although the study of health inequalities often confuses the impacts of poverty with those of inequality, the detailed analysis of mental health and the physical symptoms associated with mental health problems seem to indicate that feelings of powerlessness are often causes of such problems that lead to bad health. And as the anecdotes above indicate, modern society and automation increase the perception of powerlessness.

Meanwhile inequality has a habit of entrenching itself. Particularly at the bottom end of society, the toxic mix of undisciplined lifestyles, family breakdown and the low quality of publicly provided services makes it difficult though not impossible for people to break out of the situation in which they are trapped. To escape needs a mix of character and intelligence, some bravery and a lot of luck.

Two generations ago your chances of getting on were much higher. My father, who is still with us aged 92, became Lord Mayor of London, ending up with the prestigious award of a GBE (Knight Grand Cross of the Order of the British Empire), despite having had a father who was unemployed for most of his childhood and whose only work was occasional evening jobs clearing up in a pub (and probably paid in cash).

My father has great charm, intelligence and iron self-discipline and the great good fortune to have found a soulmate in my mother that has made their marriage a love affair that has lasted for nearly 70 years. But even he would have admitted that for him and others like him, getting on required a great deal of luck as well as talent and persistence. This extract from his eulogy at his sister Helen's funeral describes the situation:

> Our parents were not what you would call well off. Our father was unemployed for most of the thirties, though he got some pin money from helping in a bar in the evening. Our mother was formidable and a good manager. She found all sorts of ways of extending what little she had, cooking with marrow bones which the butchers were happy to be rid of and sending the children to our relations in Fauldhouse in the summer so that she could take in paying guests from Glasgow to stay in our flat in Portobello just a stone's throw from the beach. My brother John and I loved Fauldhouse but my sisters hated it.

Helen and I were talking a few years ago about an incident which I subsequently wrote about. Let me quote from what I wrote in my memoirs:[15]

'I was talking to my sister Helen recently about the occasion when my mother sold a beautiful oval shaped rosewood table. I think she had inherited it from the Robbs, her former employers. I was in the house when the second hand furniture dealer came. He looked at the table, sucked his teeth, and said it was awfu' heavy and that nobody would want it. He would however as a friendly gesture take it off her hands and give her 10 shillings (that is 50p in modern money). Lord knows what such a table would be worth today.

'Helen remembered the sale of the table and the reason for it. It was a typical example of my mother juggling with her resources. My eldest sister Isobel and Helen had joined the Girl Guides. The table was sold but the proceeds would only buy one new and one second hand uniform. Because she was the eldest Isobel got the new uniform. Helen to her chagrin had to be content with the other with the hat several sizes too large resting on her ears.'

We had to stuff the hat with newspaper to make it fit better.

Helen should have gone to university as she had the capacity to do so. Unfortunately she had to leave secondary school early because my mother was ill at that time. Also at that point not many women went on to higher education unless to become teachers.

Obviously I am hugely proud of my family history. But I wonder to what extent the ladder my parents climbed would still be available today. At the more privileged end of society, the rich and clever marry each other and bring up their children with fanatic attention to such matters as nutrition and health and of course to education, creating 'superbabies' with the skills and strength of character to take over the world. It seems unfair and it is.

But isn't it also unfair to punish people for trying to be good parents?

There are no very simple solutions. This book looks in much more detail at how to get education right in Chapter 12.

## Political partisanship

The loss of social cohesion has had an effect on political partisanship. One has an image of a world where there was substantial consensus on how to take society forward; where the bulk of society accepted conventions and the differences between political parties were in their tribal roots.

Political partisanship is a long-term phenomenon. But particularly because one of the defining events of British history, the Second World War, was fought under a coalition government, in much of the post-war period there were limits to the extent to which politicians were partisan. Clement Attlee, who had led the Opposition against Churchill, nevertheless was a pall bearer at his funeral in 1965. The 1950s introduced a period of what was called Butskellism when the Chancellor of the Exchequer, Rab Butler, and the previous Chancellor and then Shadow Chancellor, Hugh Gaitskell, seemed essentially to agree with each other.

In Britain that consensus shattered in the 1970s and 1980s as the left tried to bring the country to its knees through trade union power and then the right responded with what some have called sado-monetarism, leading to the collapse of companies, the disappearance of jobs and unemployment close to three million for five years.

In the 1990s, even when the left under Tony Blair adopted more moderate policies, they still exacerbated political partisanship with a dangerous ideology of spin that fairly successfully tried to stigmatise the Tories as figures of hate. This was taken to extreme levels under the wildly partisan Gordon Brown. When back in government it is not surprising that the Conservatives responded in kind. But while retaliation may give some satisfaction, what it means is that both major parties have contributed to the demeaning of British politics. The British used to be famous for their moderation and common sense. One can understand how people from other countries may no longer think that. Since then this problem has been exacerbated by the after-effects of the Brexit referendum. This has polarised the media. While inequality has had some impact on both the holding of the referendum and the result, the extent of partisanship on both sides has exacerbated the sense of a decline in the traditions of British moderation and common sense. Possibly it also reflected the reduced standing of the press and the growth of social media. Increasingly many people appear only to take in information that reinforces their prejudices.

As someone who has made a career out of forecasting I have always been anxious to take in information that might disprove my predictions and therefore search out information that might contradict me. It is for this reason that I find the extent of the partisanship on both sides, particularly in the UK's debate on Brexit, extremely disappointing.

In the US political partisanship has also grown. Pew Research Center[16] has been tracking political partisanship since 1994. In 1994 74% of Republicans and 59% of Democrats saw the other party unfavourably. In 2016 these numbers had increased to 86% and 91%. That isn't entirely surprising – you obviously don't like the other side a certain amount otherwise you would support them. Much more alarming is the jump in extreme partisanship. In 1994 21% of Republicans and 17% of Democrats saw the other party 'very unfavourably'. By 2016 these proportions had more than doubled on each side to 58% of Republicans and 55% of Democrats.

According to the *New York Times*:[17]

> The Republican Party strikes fear in the hearts of 55 percent of Democrats surveyed, Pew found. Among Republicans, 49 percent felt the same way about the Democratic Party.
>
> At the same time, 47 percent of Democrats said Republicans made them angry, while 46 percent of Republicans said the Democratic Party made them feel angry.

Jane Mansbridge, the Charles F. Adams Professor at the Harvard Kennedy School and president of the American Political Science Association from 2012 to 2013, created the Task Force on Negotiating Agreement in Politics to respond to the crisis of polarisation in the federal legislature. Coming from academia at Harvard and writing in the *Washington Post*, her views are by no means neutral but this does not mean they are wrong.[18] Her take on polarisation is 'Get used to it. It's not going away anytime soon.'

> Americans have not, by and large, grown grumpier over the years. But members of the two major parties have stopped speaking to one another across the aisle. They don't vote together, either.

She argues that:

> Three major structural changes – gradual party realignment, closer elections and inequality – largely explain the huge decline in the numbers of party members willing to vote for legislation that the other party has sponsored, and in particular the number of Republicans willing to vote for measures the Democratic Party has sponsored. None of these causes is likely to change.

She explains how the 1964 Civil Rights Act changed the party composi-tion in the US:

> A massive transition began after President Lyndon B. Johnson signed the Civil Rights Act in 1964. As he told then-White House Press Secretary Bill Moyers the night of the signing, 'I think we just delivered the South to the Republican Party for a long time to come.' He had set in motion a train of events that, over time, would slowly lead conservative white southerners to leave the Democratic Party and join the Republicans. As the Southern conservatives left the Democratic Party, they left behind a relatively liberal remnant (in significant part, African Americans).
>
> Democrats outside the South did not become much more liberal in the ensuing years, but the change in the composition of the party in the South made the national party more liberal and receptive to people of color. As the conservative Southerners joined the Republican Party, they also changed its center of gravity. Their perspectives and demands empowered the right wing of the party that had long chafed under the moderate Republican establishment. Evangelicals rose in strength; businesspeople fell. The Republican Party began to look for support less in Maine and more in Georgia. Its members became more extremely conservative, while the members of the Democratic Party became only a little more liberal.
>
> With this shift, the parties in Congress became more electorally competitive. Southern conservatives leaving the Democratic Party gradually added their numbers to the Republican Party, which in 1980 won a majority of seats in the Senate (and in 1994 a majority in the House) for almost the first time since the New Deal.
>
> The period of bipartisanship in Washington, from 1940 to 1980, was actually a period of Democratic dominance. With the Democrats in more or less permanent power, it behoved individual Republicans to play nice in order to get their bridges and roads. But by 1980, the parties began a period of intense competition.
>
> As Frances Lee at the University of Maryland points out, when the minority party thinks it might win in the next election, it has a great incentive not to let the majority party have any 'wins' that it might run on in that next election. She quotes then-House Chief Deputy Minority Whip Kevin McCarthy (R-Calif.) from 2009: 'If you act like you're the minority, you're going to stay in the minority. We've gotta challenge them on every single bill.'

But what is most relevant to this book is her third cause:

> The now-famous U-curve of income inequality in the United States shows that after a period of relative equality from about 1940 to 1980, we have today become as unequal as we were in the last Gilded Age. That U-curve of income inequality tracks uncannily the U-curve of polarization, which in 1910 was almost as high as it is now, then fell precipitously – along with income inequality – until it bottomed out in the bipartisan era from 1940 to 1980. It rose again, in exact parallel with inequality, to its present heights. Why? Inequality seems to cause polarization and polarization to some extent causes inequality.
>
> Nolan McCarty and his colleagues at Princeton are beginning to tease out the mechanisms. In state politics, they find that states with increasing income inequality experience two polarizing effects. First, state Republican parties shift to the right overall. Second, state Democratic parties shift to the left because their moderates lose. Rich Republican donors could well be responsible for both outcomes if, as seems likely, they fund more extreme candidates in Republican districts and target the Democrats they have the best chance to dislodge, namely those in politically moderate districts.
>
> The big picture is that the extraordinary growth in incomes at the top of the income distribution makes possible the discretionary money that can then be poured into politics, and those who contribute to politics are, on average, a good deal more extreme in their views than the average voter.
>
> The gradual party realignment after 1964, the closeness of elections since 1980, and the growth in income at the top of the distribution are the three deep causes of polarization. Gerrymandering is not the cause; the Senate is as polarized as the House. Primaries are not the cause; primary reforms have had relatively little effect. Changes in the rules of the House and Senate have had some effect, as have the increasing number of hours that legislators now have to spend fundraising and the increasing number of hours they now spend in their home districts with their constituents. But of the three deepest causes, at least party realignment and income inequality are likely to continue. Close elections may well continue, too. So polarization is here to stay – for the indefinite future.

I think Ms Mansbridge misses one of the key contributory factors – the growth in social media and the increasingly partisan press – which has led to polarisation in both the UK and the US. We have just as much political partisanship in the UK as in the US even though the main factors quoted by Ms Mansbridge have not affected the UK.

### Some hope for the future

Fortunately I can see inequality itself generating a backlash.

One thing I have noticed is that there is a reaction to inequality in tastes and fashions. When I was writing *The Flat White Economy* I noticed that London seemed to be leading the way. A sort of grunge chic is emerging. Mean streets are fashionable not just with the alienated. Ideals are changing. Rich people are changing their lifestyles and behaving more like poorer people. Sports cars are unfashionable – people associate them with the types that have more money than sense (mainly the highly entitled kids of rich foreigners).

For six months in 2017 a gold-plated Maserati was parked in various locations around Marylebone to universal derision on social media, a derision enhanced when it was discovered that the owner had forgotten to tax it and it got impounded by the police.

Even though the UK economy has partly recovered from the banking crisis, champagne consumption has not recovered. In 2014 UK champagne consumption was a quarter lower than at its peak in 2007. Though it rose again by 4.5% in 2015, it fell back by 10% in 2016, to reach a level nearly 30% down on its peak. Meanwhile sales of coffee – a much more democratic drink than champagne – have been increasing by 10% per annum in London.

One indicator in London that a place is unfashionable is the nature of its clientele. If it is patronised mainly by rich foreigners it loses its appeal to the locals. The locals prize the places that offer best value. One restaurant that is good but very expensive and largely boycotted by the locals because of its pricing is Sketch in Conduit Street in the heart of Mayfair. Unusually I was invited to its opening, not because they wanted me but because they wanted my car (the classic Aston Martin mentioned earlier in the book, which has since been stolen) to be parked outside. The last time I was taken there was as a guest of an Embassy official, and I was one of only two Brits in the restaurant, the other being a former Labour Cabinet Minister and quangocrat whom one suspected of dining at public expense. I very much dislike the place. Although the food is good, it is overpriced. As a Scot I hate waste. And I hate conspicuous waste even more (and waste at taxpayers' expense even more still!).

At the other extreme is the London restaurant Pidgin in Hackney, which provides by far the cheapest food of Michelin rosette quality available in London. Set in Hackney in a former café with a minimal kitchen, the young chef (until recently Dan Graham) manages to cope with limited space by setting a single menu for the week and only making alternations for dietary reasons. Its prices are low and it is by far my favourite London restaurant and not too far from my office – we took over the whole restaurant for our office Christmas lunch in 2017. It is permanently full and a great source of joy for those in the know.

One suspects that the reaction to inequality in tastes and fashions will spread to politics. Most rich people prize a society where people are treated relatively equally and they are prepared to pay quite a lot in taxes and charitable contributions to ensure that that is the case, which is why I think that the idea of voluntary taxes described in Chapter 17 is an idea whose time has come. It is not just that, in order to keep their property and to stem off a revolution, they want to ensure that the masses are not too restless. It goes much further than that.

Some rich people may prefer the sort of country where judges are bribed because they are the ones who can afford to bribe them. But in the kleptocracies another person normally comes along with a bigger bribe and outbids you. It is notable that many Russians of whatever background come to London to try to sort out their legal disputes. The judges may get it wrong, for law and evidence are difficult things. But no one expects them to be bribable. If they make a mistake at least it will be an honest one.

One of the reasons that London is so popular as a destination is its liveliness. This reflects the diversity of views and backgrounds that it contains. The most fashionable part of London in recent years has been Shoreditch.

Shoreditch started as the centre of London's art scene, buoyed by easy availability of cheap property. It was claimed in the early 1990s (when I moved my office there) that the density of artists' studios per square kilometre in the area was the highest in the world. Since then and particularly since about 2005 it has become London's tech centre, a rise I chronicled in *The Flat White Economy*.

The tone of the area is chic but very deliberately not expensive. The predominantly young people who work in the Flat White Economy are not especially highly paid, particularly when London's huge cost of accommodation is taken into account. So compared with the previous fashions set by the burgeoning City in the 1980s, it is much less based on 'loadsamoney' spending. Porsches have been replaced by bikes; champagne by coffee; houses in Kensington by flatshares in Hackney. Increasingly Londoners of all levels of wealth are using public transport, state schools and the NHS and all working to make these services work.

At the same time fashions change quickly, as if deliberately to confuse the uninitiated. New cafés, bars and restaurants come and go.

London has swung right and left in local elections in recent years but the surprise has been how little policies have changed. Both major parties have adopted centrist economic policies with the focus on infrastructure and on keeping the businesses that have made London so successful. Both have supported migration and integration.

Sweden is another example. I was visiting Stockholm in late 2017 to discuss an early draft of this book with some of Sweden's most successful businessmen, kindly arranged by my friend Mikael Pawlo. We couldn't find a taxi and I encouraged him to take the underground which we did (he pretended to be unaware of how to use it). Meanwhile I joked that I had expected him to pick me up in a chauffeur-driven Rolls. He looked shocked – 'If I tried that sort of thing people would throw stones at me!' My sense is that a long history of an egalitarian approach to life has left Swedes with a much greater sense of and desire for equality of outcomes than many other countries. But (as I used to joke before they reduced top tax rates in Sweden) one thing that successful Swedes used to have in common was that they didn't generally live in Sweden.

The new generation of Swedish entrepreneurs is different. The top marginal rate of tax peaked at 90% in 1980 and since has fallen to 57%.[19] Although this is still high by international standards, many Swedes are happy with the situation and Stockholm is second only to London as a hotbed of entrepreneurialism in Europe.

Perhaps Sweden and London can be a template for reducing political partisanship in other areas. But if this does not happen, extreme politics of both right and left could be seriously destabilising.

## Conclusion

Many of the problems allegedly caused by inequality are really caused by poverty. It is important to distinguish between the two because quite often the policies that would reduce inequality would increase poverty by reducing economic growth.

There are, however, some problems that directly result from inequality per se. Health inequalities from mental stress seem to result more from a person's position in the pecking order and a sense of lack of control over their lives than from poverty as such. And although neither health nor education is largely allocated by the market in most countries, it does look as though the middle classes get access to better services through using their knowledge and in some cases their financial power.

Meanwhile access to positional goods is allocated by relative not absolute income and so inequality does matter there. But often people complaining about inequality want to have their cake and eat it – they have chosen professions on a basis other than expected career earnings and in effect made a lifestyle choice. When they complain, they do not seem to realise that making a lifestyle choice means being prepared to give up income.

The worst problems of inequality leading to negative social outcomes seem to be associated with despair. This is why it is important not only to examine the current static position of inequality but also to understand the dynamics – whether those in the worst-off positions have much chance of improving their own and their children's positions.

In Part II I examine the extent to which inequality and wealth and people's positions in the pecking order are entrenched and the extent to which they change over time.

# PART II
## Analysis and Implications

PART II LOOKS AT the data on inequality and its effects.

Chapter 5 'Has the world become more unequal' looks at the data on inequality using different measures. It looks at both wealth and income and at Gini coefficients when available. It points out that there have been essentially three periods in recent history with different trends in inequality.

First there was a long period from about 1890 to about 1970 when in most Western countries inequality on most measures diminished. This is dismissed by Piketty and by more serious commentators such as Atkinson as an historic anomaly caused by wars and the great depression. It seems hard to dismiss a period of 80 years as an historical anomaly and I am not so sure they are right.

The second period is between about 1970 and roughly ten years ago when the financial crisis struck. In this period inequality generally rose within Western economies though inequality between countries, especially between rich and poor countries, generally fell.

The third period is the past ten years when inequality has largely fallen in advanced economies. There is less data in emerging economies but one should not be surprised if inequality there has risen. Again, inequality between rich and poor countries has almost certainly fallen.

Chapter 6 'The paradox of rising inequality and falling poverty' looks at the link between inequality and poverty. Unfortunately many confuse the two and hence put forward policy proposals on the grounds that they will reduce inequality even though the side-effects might increase poverty. This chapter shows that in the Piketty period from 1970 to around 2008, while inequality was rising in most Western economies, global poverty fell dramatically. Rising inequality in individual countries can be combined with falling poverty and it is critically important to distinguish between the two. They are different phenomena.

Chapter 7 'Inequality and growth' looks at the links between them. It shows that the links are mixed and often due to third factors ignored in some analyses.

It finds that naturally cohesive societies even with quite high public spending and taxes can have low inequality and high standards of living and often relatively rapid growth. It shows that countries which are very diverse and have large-scale inward migration can have quite high inequality and also have rapid growth but tend to need to have relaxed labour laws, low taxation and public spending to achieve rapid growth. It also finds that some highly equal societies can be stagnant with little growth, but this can also be the case for unequal societies.

By far the greatest driver of growth is good education throughout the population, which both reduces inequality and boosts growth. But it is also the case that low taxes tend to be associated with faster growth and sometimes with reduced inequality in the West. So different mixes of inequality and growth are possible. Raising taxes to reduce inequality, for example, might not only reduce growth but increase poverty. But improving education to reduce inequality is much more likely to increase growth and reduce poverty at the same time.

## Chapter 5

# HAS THE WORLD BECOME MORE UNEQUAL?

THIS CHAPTER DESCRIBES HOW INEQUALITY OF INCOME AND WEALTH have changed in the major Western and Eastern economies. It updates the data in the Piketty book (most of which ends in 2011 or 2012) to 2015 or the most recent years for which data is available. It draws an important distinction between the rise in inequality within countries and the decrease in inequality between countries.

The chapter also considers the critique of the concept of income inequality: that it fails to measure incomes accurately because of the informal economy and that consumption inequality is not only a better measurement but also a better representation of reality.

## Measurement issues

I apologise, especially to non-technical readers, for having to start with this. But without understanding the relevant measurement issues, it is hard to interpret the data.

The seminal article on the measurement of inequality is by the late Sir Anthony Atkinson in the *Journal of Economic Theory* in 1970. He deals with conceptual issues. He argues that two conventional measures (the coefficient of variation and the Gini coefficient) are inappropriate since one needs to have an understanding of the social welfare function before attempting to measure inequality.[1] One senses that this is the work of a young man looking for perfection rather than trying to deal with the real world of measurement problems. He completely fails to deal with data issues!

In their important work on measuring income inequality in the US, Auten and Splinter show that using US tax data carefully gives a very much smaller rise in income inequality than Piketty and Saez's earlier work.[1] The key conceptual problems with income inequality data are these:

(1) Many at the lower end of the income spectrum and a proportion at the upper end operate in parts of the economy where their income is not measured – data shows consumption (which itself is also probably underestimated) consistently exceeding income even after adjusting for transfers for low-income groups.[3]

(2) Many at the upper end of the income spectrum have international aspects to their income that are not fully reflected in the national tax data.

(3) A large number of people at both the top end and the bottom end of the income spectrums are there as a result of temporary changes in their income levels (loss of job; large lump sum payments, etc.) so that their income is not representative of their normal position. It appears that the temporary component has got larger in recent years.[4]

(4) Should post-tax or pre-tax data be used?

(5) How to account for transfers?

Looking at wealth inequality, the difficulties are even greater.

In theory, wealth is assets minus liabilities. But measuring assets without constant revaluation is hard, and revaluation is costly. Liabilities are often easier to measure, but contingent liabilities are less easy to evaluate. Entitlement programmes such as pensions are again difficult to evaluate and are often excluded. Small amounts of wealth are often excluded. The Credit Suisse Global Wealth Report data quoted by Oxfam tends to be weaker for those unlikely to be using the services of an investment bank (obviously predomininantly the poorest groups) than for the richer groups who do use such services, and weaker for assets that tend not to be marketable, such as the property of people in poor countries. By contrast they measure marketable assets relatively well. In addition, as wealth tends to accumulate with age on most saving hypotheses, even if everyone had the same average wealth over their lifetime, the statistics would show very large variations in wealth as it accumulates with age before being run down when people stop working and then start to spend and redistribute their wealth. And societies that are ageing will tend to have more apparent maldistribution of wealth than those that are getting younger, even if the average wealth of everyone is the same over their lifetimes.

It is beyond the scope of this book to construct data series corrected for all the weaknesses outlined above. They are pointed out to encourage a degree of scepticism that might help a shrewd observer not to be blindsided by the data. In general the weaknesses will tend to mean that data sets exaggerate inequality. But issues such as tax avoidance (let alone evasion) probably work in the opposite direction.

Although some of the weaknesses affect the changes in the data over time, my view is that the problems with this are fewer. It is for this reason that most of the analysis in this chapter looks at changes in inequality over time.

### Inequality within countries

It is wrong to think of inequality as a single variable. Different measures in different countries show different things. I have looked at six different measures (shares of income for top 1% and top 10%, shares of wealth for the same groups, and Gini coefficients for both income and wealth) for seven countries (India, China, Japan, France, Germany, UK and US when the data is available).

It is also important to be aware of the deficiencies of the data. Income and (even more) wealth data are hard to calculate.

What do the data indicate?

First, the income shares of the top 1%.[5] These typically trended down from the first quarter of the 20th century till around 1980. Since then they have trended up in all seven countries (see Table 1 in Chapter 1), in some cases quite sharply. In India the share rose from 7.3% in 1980 to 20.4% in 2008; in China the share rose from 6.4% to 15.2% over the same period. For the European countries the increases between 1980 and 2008 were relatively modest: in France from 8.2% to 11.6% and in Germany from 10.6% to 14.5%. In the Anglo-Saxon world with strong financial services sectors the increases were stronger over the same period: from 6.7%[6] to 15.4% in the UK[7] and from 10.7% to 19.5% in the US.

These data are from the World Inequality Database (WID) originally set up by Piketty and Saez. They do not take into account the analysis from Auten and Splinter which suggests a very much smaller increase in inequality in the US – about a quarter of the increase suggested by the Piketty and Saez data. Although the Auten and Splinter analysis looks amazingly thorough and detailed, it does not entirely chime with one's gut reactions after nearly 50 years of observing economic data. One's suspicion is that there is some international tax leakage that would allow wealthy people to earn rather more than is indicated from their tax returns. I admit that I might be completely wrong on this – no doubt time will tell. A less strong reason for not using the adjusted data is that it is not internationally comparable.

On the WID data, since the financial crisis in 2007/08 this measure of inequality has fallen back in all countries except India. This is consistent with Cebr's analysis of financial sector bonuses in London, which fell from £12 billion in 2007 to £4 billion in 2015.

Looking at the top 10% share of income, the information presents a broadly similar picture. But there is no upward trend from 1980 for France. The scale of the rises from 1980 is smaller than for the top 1% in general. And (presumably reflecting the lesser representation of bankers in the top 10% than in the top 1%) there is a less marked falling back after 2007/08. Indeed (though as there is a series change it is difficult to compare), it looks as though the share of the US top 10% reached a new peak in 2015. Meanwhile, on this measure the rise in inequality in the UK is one of the least in the advanced countries and by 2015 income inequality in the UK even pre-tax was less than in Germany.

*Shares of wealth*
The WID has less data on wealth than on income and quite a lot of wealth data that was once available on the Piketty-Saez database is no longer posted, possibly reflecting the Giles critique mentioned below. There is now data only for China, France, the UK and the US (and Russia where I assume that the wealth data is not totally reliable). One would normally assume that the richer groups had higher shares of wealth than of income since they combine higher income with typically higher savings ratios and in addition wealth accumulates with age. The earlier data (which is no longer posted on the web) indicated that while the shares of income of the top 1% vary from around 10% to 25%, the shares of wealth vary from around 30% to around 50%.

There is now only long-term data for the wealth share of the top 1% from the 19th century for France and the UK. For France the peak share was 56.9% in 1906, although the rapid decline only started just after the First World War, bottoming out at 15.9% in 1984. Since then it has recovered to 28.1% in 2000 before settling at between 22% and 23% since 2004. For the UK the peak was earlier and higher, with the share of wealth of the top 1% ranging from 70-75% from 1895 to 1906 but falling thereafter and bottoming out at 15.2% in 1984. There has been a small recovery since to 19.8% in 2012. It is worth noting that the share of wealth of the top 1% in the UK is less than in any other country for which the WID has data!

The data for the US share of the top 1% starts in 1960 and falls more or less in parallel with the data for the UK until 1975 where it plateaus at around 22-24% for ten years. The share then recovered to 40.1% in 2012 although it edged back a little in the two subsequent years.

The data for China is interesting. The share remained (suspiciously) flat (even when measured to three decimal places) at 15.797% from 1978-95 but has since nearly doubled to 29.6% in 2015.

The WID data for the wealth of the top 10% mirrors that for the top 1%, though the movements are moderated and with a slight lag. Again there is data for only five countries, one of which (Russia) is probably fairly inexact.

In France the share fell from 86.0% in 1905 to 50.0% in 1984 and in the UK from 92-93% in 1895-1914 to 45.6% in 1991, and in the US from 72.4% in 1964 to 61.8% in 1985. Since then the shares have edged up in each of these countries, to 55.3% in 2014 for France and 51.9% in 2012 for the UK, and to 73.0% in 2014 in the US. The only place where the rise has been really dramatic has been in China where the share of wealth of the top 10% has risen from 40.8% in 1995 to 67.4% in 2015, but this is not surprising given the transition from a regime where private property was largely not allowed to a more capitalist system.

### The Giles critique[8]

The *Financial Times* Economics Editor Chris Giles has analysed the Piketty data carefully. He has not identified any particular difficulties with the income data, but he argues that much of the wealth data has been constructed with little or no admission about the sources of the data. To quote *The Economist* magazine:

> Several oddities surfaced, such as discrepancies between numbers in the source material Mr Piketty cites and those that appear in his spreadsheets; a large number of unexplained adjustments to the raw data (often in the form of a constant written into the Excel spreadsheet cell); inconsistency in how underlying source data were combined; and the frequent interpolation of data, without explanation, when underlying sources were missing. For instance, none of the sources Mr Piketty used had data for the top 10% wealth share in America between 1910 and 1950. So he assumed their wealth share was consistently that of the top 1% plus 36 percentage points. All told, Mr Giles found 'problems' in 114 of 142 data points in Mr Piketty's wealth inequality tables.[9]

It is clear from the discussion in the preceding paragraph in this chapter, which refers to the updated data (from Piketty's colleagues) for the wealth of the wealthiest 10%, that they have now adjusted their data from that criticised by Giles, presumably to meet the criticism.

What emerges after the data has been adjusted is that the new data for the upward trend in the shares of wealth of the richer groups in the years after 1980 is much less prominent than had been asserted in Piketty's book and has done very little to reverse the huge fall in the share in wealth of the top 10% from the early to the late part of the 20th century.

We should all be grateful to Giles for his persistence and attention to detail. It is to his credit that Giles, whom many might consider left-wing and therefore from a political position not too diametrically opposed to Piketty's, has done the job that Piketty's opponents on the right have failed to do.

It is important to note, though, that Giles, who clearly checked the numbers closely, gave a clean bill of health to the data compiled by Piketty and his colleagues for shares of income.

*Other criticisms*

The other main criticisms of the data, which apply more to the income data than the wealth data, are as follows:

(1) The income data ignores the informal economy which is (allegedly) particularly important at the bottom end of the income scale.

(2) The income data does not take account of the extent to which the tax system redistributes income.

These criticisms suggest that it might be better to look at consumption data or disposable income data. The recent UK data confirms that inequality has fallen since 2007/08 measured by the comparison of the disposable incomes of the top quartile versus the bottom quartile. Increased employment and protected job benefits have relatively helped the poorest groups, while declining real salaries and rising taxes have hit the highest groups.

Although it seems clear that in many countries the incomes of the very rich have risen relatively sharply, at least until 2007/08, some of this progress has since been checked and it remains an open question how much inequality in individual countries is rising at the moment.

For this reason economists have looked at another measure, the Gini coefficient. This is the official definition of the Gini coefficient from the Office for National Statistics website:[10]

The Gini coefficient is a measure of the overall extent to which these groupings of households, from the bottom of the income distribution upwards, receive less than an equal share of income.

The concept is expressed more formally by the Lorenz curve of household income distribution, from which the Gini coefficient can be calculated.

Based on a ranking of households in order of ascending income, the Lorenz curve is a plot of the cumulative share of household income against the cumulative share of households.

Complete equality, where income is shared equally among all households, results in a Lorenz curve represented by a straight line.

The opposite extreme, complete inequality, where only 1 household has all the income and the rest have none, is represented by a Lorenz curve which comprises the horizontal axis and the right-hand vertical axis.

The Lorenz curve in most cases will lie somewhere between these two extremes.

The Gini coefficient is the area between the Lorenz curve of the income distribution and the diagonal line of complete equality, expressed as a proportion of the triangular area between the curves of complete equality and inequality.

Complete equality would result in a Gini coefficient of zero, and complete inequality, a Gini coefficient of 100.

All the Gini coefficients shown in the effects of taxes and benefits on household income are based on distributions of equivalised household income.

Equivalisation is a standard methodology that takes into account the size and composition of households and adjusts their incomes to recognise differing demands on resources.

The Gini coefficient is used to show the degree of income inequality between different groups of households in the population.

It can also be used to show how inequality of incomes has been changing over a period of time.

Table 3. Gini coefficients of income inequality, mid-1980s and late 2000s

|  | Mid 80s | 2008 |
|---|---|---|
| *Rising inequality* | | |
| Mexico | 0.45 | 0.48 |
| US | 0.34 | 0.38 |
| Israel | 0.33 | 0.37 |
| UK | 0.32 | 0.35 |
| Italy | 0.3 | 0.34 |
| Australia | 0.3 | 0.34 |
| NZ | 0.27 | 0.33 |
| Japan | 0.31 | 0.33 |
| Canada | 0.29 | 0.32 |
| Germany | 0.25 | 0.3 |
| Netherlands | 0.27 | 0.3 |
| Luxembourg | 0.25 | 0.29 |
| Finland | 0.21 | 0.26 |
| Sweden | 0.2 | 0.26 |
| Czech | 0.23 | 0.25 |
| Norway | 0.22 | 0.25 |
| Denmark | 0.22 | 0.25 |
| *Little change in inequality* | | |
| France | 0.3 | 0.3 |
| Hungary | 0.27 | 0.27 |
| Belgium | 0.25 | 0.25 |
| *Decreasing inequality* | | |
| Turkey | 0.43 | 0.41 |
| Greece | 0.33 | 0.31 |

Table 3 shows how Gini coefficients had increased in most but not all Organization for Economic Cooperation and Development (OECD) countries. The original source is the OECD inequality database, but the chart comes from my Gresham Professorial lecture 'How does globalisation affect equality'[11] from the OECD report 'An overview of growing income inequalities in OECD countries: Main findings'.[12]

The chart shows that the recent rise in income inequality observed in the US is part of a more general though not completely ubiquitous trend.

The OECD concluded:

> Over the two decades prior to the onset of the global economic crisis, real disposable household incomes increased by an average 1.7% a year in OECD countries. In a large majority of them, however, the household incomes of the richest 10% grew faster than those of the poorest 10%, so widening income inequality. Differences in the pace of income growth across household groups were particularly pronounced in some of the English-speaking countries, some Nordic countries, and Israel. In Japan, the real incomes of those at the bottom of the income ladder actually fell compared with the mid-1980s.

In OECD countries today, the average income of the richest 10% of the population is about nine times that of the poorest 10% – a ratio of 9 to 1. However, the ratio varies widely from one country to another. It is much lower than the OECD average in the Nordic and many continental European countries, but reaches 10 to 1 in Italy, Japan, Korea, and the United Kingdom; around 4 to 1 in Israel, Turkey, and the United States; and 27 to 1 in Mexico and Chile. Although what is happening to the very rich is interesting, I believe that it is much more important to see what is happening to the poorer income groups.

The OECD conclusion (which is limited to a much shorter period than the US income distribution data and so has a very limited historical basis) is as follows:

> Increases in household income inequality have been largely driven by changes in the distribution of wages and salaries, which account for 75% of household incomes among working-age adults. With very few exceptions (France, Japan, and Spain), the wages of the 10% best-paid workers have risen relative to those of the 10% lowest paid. This was due to both growing earnings' shares at the top and declining shares at the bottom, although top earners saw their incomes rise particularly rapidly (Atkinson, 2009). Earners in the top 10% have been leaving the middle earners behind more rapidly than the lowest earners have been drifting away from the middle.

A separate study on a wide range of countries is by Toth, who discusses the evolution of inequality in a set of 30 countries according to six groupings:[13]

(1) Five Continental European welfare states
(2) Four Nordic countries and the Netherlands
(3) Five English-speaking liberal countries
(4) Four Mediterranean countries
(5) Two Asian countries
(6) Ten Central and Eastern European countries

To get more insight into the magnitude in the trend in inequality, he models the trend in Gini coefficients using fixed effects for country, allowing country-specific intercepts. The linear trend is definitely upward, with 0.25 points increase each year, or 0.43 points if controlled for GDP per capita. He concludes that for the window of the data the increase thus equals 7.35 points, more than half of the within-year range of Gini coefficients between countries.

Interestingly, the English-speaking countries do not stand out in terms of inequality trends; the average growth in inequality is 0.15 Gini points, not much higher than in Continental Europe (0.12 Gini points per year). The trend in the Nordic countries is much larger, with 0.26 Gini points per year on average, and also in Central and European countries (0.30 Gini points) and the Baltic States (0.54 Gini points per year).

In all groups of countries, except in the Mediterranean countries, inequality has been on the rise. However, as will become clear below, there are large discrepancies in inequality trends between countries within these groups. In certain countries (such as Austria, Belgium, France, Italy, Ireland, Slovenia) the level of inequality remained largely unchanged.

The most dramatic increase in inequality was experienced by some transition countries and, to a lesser but still significant extent, by the Nordic countries, most notably Sweden and Finland. In some of these countries the increase was sudden and large (as in the Baltic states, Bulgaria and Romania); in others it accumulated gradually over time (the Nordic group, Netherlands).

Figure 1 shows very recent data for the Gini coefficient for disposable income for the UK. Earlier data indicates a sharp rise in the Gini coefficient from the late 70s (and I believe that there was a rise immediately before that) to the early 1990s, but shows a slight falling back since then and the latest data shows a further decline in inequality on all three measures.[14]

Figure 1. ONS data for the UK. Movement of Gini coefficients over time

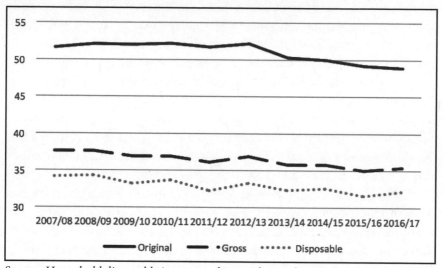

Source: *Household disposable income and inequality in the UK: financial year ending 2017, Office for National Statistics, 10 January 2018.*

It would appear that in the UK there have been a number of different trends that explain the fall since the early 1990s in contrast with the evidence for the top 1% and top 10%. Essentially the protection and indexation of benefits and the fall in unemployment helped the worst off over the period from the early 1990s to the late 2000s. Then the fall in bankers' bonuses was the key explanation of the further fall in the past decade.

It is important to understand the basis of regional variations also. In the UK the regional data from the Office for National Statistics suggests that in fact inequality measured on any sensible basis is much lower than is generally assumed because the income data fails to take account of the lower costs of living in the parts of the country where incomes are lower.

The latest report that supports this is the relatively new data published by the ONS looking at country and regional public-sector finances. It considers how much money gets taken in tax from the wallets of the people in an area, and how much of the government's spending they are then able to benefit from.

What it shows is that London and the South East of England pay much more into the common pot than they get, the East of England gets as much as it gives, and everyone else is a net beneficiary. This is not very different from what everyone thought was happening, partly because my colleagues and I have carried out this analysis on a similar basis on eight occasions since we first did so in 1993, nearly a quarter of a century ago, in a series of reports on London's contribution to the UK economy.[15]

To understand why Gini coefficients overstate inequality for a country like the UK which has large regional differences it is a convenient simplification to see the British economy as two different parts. One part is London and the area around it – which are hugely productive and an important part of the global economy and the network of global cities. Then there's everything else – which has been described as 'really just a rather boring middle-ranking Northern European economy'.[16]

That huge difference in productivity, in tandem with a national taxation system, explains why the government gets nearly £16,000 a year in tax revenue from each Londoner and under £8,000 from each Welsh person on average. Even though a person earning £30,000 a year in London pays the same tax as someone earning the same amount in Bridgend, the hugely different costs of living in each place mean that one is much better off than the other. It is the differences in the cost of living in different parts of the country that mean that real income inequality is much less than measured income inequality.

In reality the high cost part of the economy has much lower living standards than is allowed for by the Gini coefficient, which does not take account of either the higher real rate of tax or the higher real cost of living in London and the South East of England. Equally the low cost and low income part of the economy has a much higher living standard than is allowed for by the Gini coefficient because it does not take account of the lower real rate of tax and the lower cost of living.

The same is true for the United States where again regional differences in the cost of living are not reflected in the national Gini coefficient which exaggerates income differentials.

## Global Gini coefficients

Milanovic has made estimates of global income inequality. These are shown in Figure 2.[17] What he shows is that at the time when income inequality in individual countries in the West was falling, income inequality for the world was rising. And when income inequality in the individual countries in the West was rising, worldwide income inequality was falling. The fact that there seems to be an inverse correlation over this particular period between income inequality in most Western countries and income inequality worldwide should not be taken to show causation but should at least hint that some economic factors connecting the two are at work.

**Figure 2. Estimated global income inequality over the past two centuries, 1820-2013 (using 2011 PPPs)**

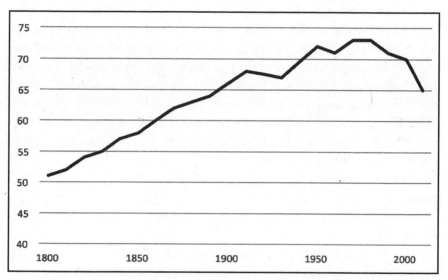

*Source: 'Inequality in the Age of globalisation', presentation by Branko Milanovic to EU Annual Research Conference, Brussels, 20 November 2017, Lecture in Honour of Anthony A. Atkinson.*

## Gini coefficients for wealth

There is little data available for the trends in Gini coefficients for wealth, but I include data for the UK (Table 3), for Canada (Figure 4) and for the US (Figure 5).

**Table 4. Great Britain, July 2006 to June 2014 Gini coefficient**

|  | July 2006 to June 2008 | July 2008 to June 2010 | July 2010 to June 2012 | July 2012 to June 2014 | July 2014 to June 2016 |
|---|---|---|---|---|---|
| Property Wealth (net) | 0.62 | 0.63 | 0.64 | 0.66 | 0.67 |
| Financial Wealth (net) | 0.81 | 0.81 | 0.92 | 0.91 | 0.91 |
| Physical Wealth 2 | 0.46 | 0.45 | 0.44 | 0.45 | 0.46 |
| Private Pension Wealth | 0.77 | 0.76 | 0.73 | 0.73 | 0.72 |
| Total Wealth 1 | 0.61 | 0.61 | 0.61 | 0.63 | 0.62 |

*Source: Wealth and Assets Survey, Office for National Statistics.*

The UK data[18] show little trend since 2007, but with a slight increase in the more recent years and a falling back in the latest period. The trends in pensions wealth seem to be in the opposite directions to the trends in property and financial wealth.

There is some Canadian data available which suggests a fall in wealth inequality in Canada: 'there has been a 17% decline in the Gini Coefficient (the most popular indicator of inequality) on Canadian net worth between 1970 and 2012. As well, both top decile share and top quintile share have declined over the same period, although by a smaller percentage.'[19]

Figure 3 shows estimates for the US Gini coefficient for wealth since 1962. It shows a jump in the concentration in recent years and is consistent with the picture produced by the analysis of the shares of wealth of the top 1% and the top 10%.

### Inequality between countries

So far we have looked only at inequality of income and wealth within countries.

Milanovic has examined measures of inequality of wealth that don't simply look within countries but also cover the world as a whole. He demonstrated in his so-called 'elephant graph' that while inequality within countries has risen, with globalisation and the rise of the Asian and other economies, inequality between countries has fallen.

As a result, looking at the whole world, the groups of income earners whose incomes have been most squeezed in recent years have been those who are relatively well-off by international standards.

Figure 4 from Milanovic shows how the different parts of the global distribution of income have been affected by the globalisation of recent years. It shows clearly that those whose incomes have been most badly affected have been poor people in rich countries who in terms of the global distribution of income are in fact among the relatively rich. These are concentrated between the 75th and 90th percentiles in the global income distribution.

Figure 3. Gini wealth coefficients for the US

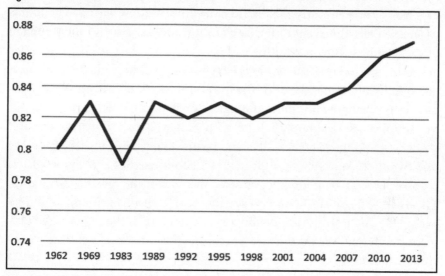

Source: Edward N. Wolff, 'Household Wealth Trends in the United States, 1962 to 2013: What Happened Over the Great Recession?', Russell Sage Foundation Journal of the Social Sciences 2(6), 2016. pp. 24-43.

Figure 4. The 'elephant graph' — the change in real income between 1988 and 2008 at various percentiles of global income distribution (calculated in 2005 international dollars)

Source: Branko Milanovic, Global Inequality: A New Approach to the Age of Globalisation, Harvard University Press, 2016, fig. 1.3, p. 31. The vertical axis shows the percentage change in real income, measured in constant international dollars. The horizontal axis shows the percentile position in the global income distribution. This runs from 5-95 in increments of five (technically called vigintiles as they represent one-twentieth each) while the top 5% are divided into two groups, those between the 95th and 99th percent and the remaining top 1%.

*The Resolution Foundation critique*[20]

The Resolution Foundation, in its pamphlet 'Examining an Elephant', has made three criticisms of the elephant graph. The first is that the shape of the graph is distorted by the inclusion of some important economies in the end period that are not in the beginning period. This does not fundamentally affect the shape of the graph but does shift it up slightly for the higher income vigintiles (apologies for using this obscure word but the sample is divided into 20 parts – 5 percentage points each, so the first point is 0-5%, the second 5-10% and so on. The technical name for these one-twentieth parts is vigintiles). The second is that the shape of the graph is affected by population growth in some of the specific economies. This is true, but it does not necessarily mean that this growth should be excluded. The third is that if China is excluded then the results are completely different. Again this is true, but it does not seem sensible to exclude China.

Another way of testing the Resolution Foundation conclusions is to look at my conclusion, in my Gresham lecture, that inequality between countries has diminished.[21]

At an OECD Policy Forum on inequality, Richard Freeman, professor of economics at Harvard University, noted that 'the triumph of globalization and market capitalism has improved living standards for billions while concentrating billions among the few. It has lowered inequality worldwide but raised inequality within most countries.'[22]

The reason for this paradox is that although inequality has risen within countries, it declined significantly between countries.

The first decade of the 21st century has seen both the middle income grouped countries and the poor countries catching up with the rich. The upper-middle-income countries have done best, mainly because of China, and the lower middle income countries have done nearly as well, mainly because of India. The poorer countries have done much better than the richer countries but not as well as the middle income countries. Figure 5 shows the definitions of these country groupings by income and shows how all the groups have grown faster than the rich countries.

Because this period includes the financial crash of 2007/08 it clearly may exaggerate the pace at which the economies are converging, but this was in fact happening before the crash and has actually accelerated, with the poorer economies doing even better since the crash. Cebr's latest global forecasts, released on Boxing Day 2017,[23] show continued convergence, with incomes in the poorest countries growing especially rapidly.

Figure 5. Annual GDP Growth by different country income groupings (per capita income annual percentage real PPP growth 2000-10)

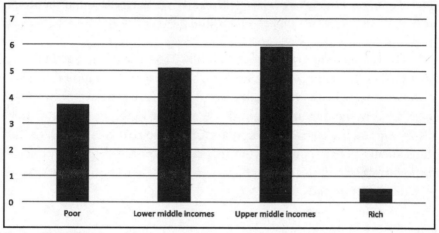

*Source: World Bank.*

The conclusions of the Canadian Conference Board report support those of Professor Freeman that there has been convergence in incomes between rich and poor countries since 2000 using data that is unweighted by population (because of the very large weights of India and China when weighting by population). The same trend appears to be have been in existence since 1960, though the evidence here uses data that is weighted by population and so is dominated by the experience of India and China.

Figure 5 shows that the rich countries have grown very much more slowly than the middle income countries especially but also more slowly than the poor countries. And this is one of the reasons for the basic shape of the elephant graph.

There seems to be an inbuilt resistance to accepting that globalisation can have an effect on the distribution of income. But this is surprising, since it would seem pretty obvious that the least skilled jobs are most likely to be competed against by the newly upskilling emerging economies. My M.Phil thesis in 1973 on the first two electronics plants in Malaysia showed how these were likely to suck jobs out of the developed economies and into the emerging economies with the corresponding effect on income distributions. As I predicted it before it happened and then it happened as I predicted, I guess I have some basis for saying that I am probably right in my explanation!

To be fair it is not only the least skilled jobs that are affected. Classical musicians are amongst the world's most skilled workers. Yet their pay in the UK appears to have stagnated in nominal terms in recent years as the numbers wanting to work in the UK has risen dramatically.[24] Interestingly this has not been the case in the US where the musicians are heavily financed by private patronage and pay is kept up by an aggressive trade union.

The last piece of evidence is from the 2016 issue of the Credit Suisse Global Wealth Report. This is an enormous resource on global wealth. It shows how wealth was distributed in 2016 and that the bulk of the most wealthy people are still in the West. But looking at past history shows a dramatic change in the share of the world's wealth held in the traditionally poorer countries. As this continues, the degree of concentration of wealth in the richer countries is unlikely to remain the case as globalisation proceeds further.

### Longer-term inequality analysis

An interesting longer-term analysis of inequality in England and Wales and subsequently the United Kingdom going back to the 13th century has been produced by the economists Max Roser and Esteban Ortiz-Ospina.[25] They make the important but often ignored point that the scope for inequality grows as economies grow. A wholly subsistence economy has very little opportunity for inequality since there is a lower limit (the subsistence level) below which people cannot survive for any length of time. As economies get more prosperous, the opportunities for inequality increase.

They point out that 'The United Kingdom is the country for which we have the best information on the distribution of income over the very long run.'

The message from the long-term analysis is that inequality on all measures drifted upwards slightly between 1200 and 1800, probably because of the rise in incomes and hence the increased scope for inequality. But from 1800, on the Gini coefficient measure, and from around 1870, on the 'share of top 5%' measure, there was a dramatic drop in income inequality. From 1980 till 2008 there was a rise in inequality which appears to have plateaued out since. Indeed on the Gini index inequality has fallen in recent years. There appears to have been a divergence between the behaviour of the Gini measure and the share of incomes of the top groups in the 21st century. The Gini measure fell; the share of incomes for the top groups rose until the financial crisis but then fell. It is highly likely that this phenomenon is largely a result of the overpayment of bankers discussed in Chapter 6.

## The impact of tax

If you ask most people in the UK whether the tax system reduces inequality they would conclude that it does.

The official data also suggests that it does, though mainly through financing benefits and not so much through the tax system.[26] Although the official analysis says that income tax is redistributive, it suggests that this is offset by the negative redistribution of indirect taxes. Many academics accept this, some to the point of being quite outspoken.[27]

It is important to distinguish between two entirely different concepts. The first is whether tax is regressive. This is analysing what happens to the same person as they get richer – do they pay proportionately more in tax? This is of course affected by spending patterns and there is a theoretical problem, namely how much to allow for the changes in actual spending patterns that take place as one gets richer. There is also a problem with what to do with the fact that the rich save more – do you treat their savings as money eventually to be consumed and therefore to be taxed at some point, or do you just ignore the taxes paid on this money when it is eventually consumed? There is also the problem of the allocation of taxes on property. The ONS data ignore these taxes, which means that they considerably understate the taxes on expenditure paid by the better-off groups.

The second point is whether a tax system redistributes. The conventional measure of tax progressivity is the Kakwani Index, based on an article in the *Economic Journal*.[28] But this is actually a measure of redistribution, not progressivity. In my investigations of this I was delighted to discover that my distinction between progressivity and redistribution had already been written about more than 40 years ago by no less than one of my predecessors as Chief Economist of the Confederation of British Industry, the distinguished economist Dr Barry Bracewell Milnes. In an article in the *Economic Journal* replying to the Kakwani article he wrote: 'The distinction between progressivity and redistribution is the essence of the proposed measure of progressivity.'[29] He pointed out that on the (then) new measure if all taxes were doubled the alleged progressivity of the tax system would increase, whereas, since progressivity relates to proportions, this should not be the case.

The ONS states that 'In the financial year ending in 2016, the richest fifth of households paid 14.4% of their disposable income in indirect taxes, while the bottom fifth of households paid the equivalent of 27.0% of their disposable income.'[30] This result appears to emerge from different savings patterns, different spending patterns and the failure to take property taxes into account. It also inflates the proportion of indirect tax paid by the poorest groups by including the tax paid on spending financed by benefits even though the benefits are not included in the income level – this is why the figures give a high ratio for indirect tax to incomes.

There is a further problem with the ONS data which purport to show that that the poor pay much more in indirect tax than the rich. This is that surveys of the kind that generate the ONS figures are heavily affected by income variability. People in the survey whose incomes are low are often only suffering from temporary low income. Their spending is likely to be based on their average income over a longer period and so will be high relative to their temporary income. Equally people with high incomes often are only benefiting from temporarily high incomes and again would be basing their spending on what they believed to be their longer-term average income. As a result their spending in relation to their temporarily high income is low and gives a misleading impression of what people with consistently high incomes might spend. This in turn means that the indirect contribution of well-off people is understated while that of less well-off people is overstated.

The top 1% of income earners in the UK pay just under 30% of all income-based taxation. This compares with the equivalent figure in the US where they pay roughly 50% of all federal income tax.

## Conclusions

What all this shows is that the position is mixed.

The most important phenomenon is the huge fall in inequality on all measures between the late 19th or early 20th century and the late 20th century. On only one measure in one country (share of top 1% in the US) has the more recent rise in inequality fully reversed this fall. On all other measures in all other countries the recent rise is small in comparison with the scale of the fall in inequality.

The second phenomenon is that since around 1970 or 1980 the very rich (the top 1%) seem to have got relatively richer except over the recent period when bankers' bonuses have been squeezed from their disequilibrium high levels achieved in 2007/08 (see Chapter 6 for more on the future of bankers' pay).

Inequality has increased as a problem especially in the Anglo-Saxon world, though the increase has been very much less in Japan and in Continental European countries. This hints that the scale of financial markets, much larger in the Anglo-Saxon economies, has had a role to play in the increase in inequality. Since 2007/08 bankers' salaries have fallen sharply and inequality in the Anglo-Saxon world has diminished. In the UK on all measures of inequality, the extent of inequality is now at its lowest for 20 years. In the US it is at its lowest for ten years.

The latest data seem to suggest that inequality is at least temporarily plateauing. This would not be surprising because the persistence of low interest rates seems to be driving out some of the excesses of financial capitalism and reducing some of the excessive salaries paid in financial services, so reducing inequality, even while other forces such as technology and globalisation are working in the opposite direction. Also some of the poorest in countries such as the UK have had the real value of their benefits protected while better-off groups in work have faced falls in dis-posable income (partly through tax rises to pay the benefits for the poorer groups). This has meant that on the Gini Index inequality has fallen by much more than on measures that simply look at the shares of the top 1 or 10%.

There are some issues of inequality that I have not attempted to address in this book. One is the growth in intergenerational inequality, especially in the UK. One reason that I do not do this is because the problem is much more serious in the UK than elsewhere and is essentially largely a result of excessive housing costs caused by planning rules that heavily restrict the building of new houses. I deal with this in some detail in Chapter 14 'Attacking the law of unintended consequences' where I show how better balance between economic and environmental requirements are needed to prevent inequality from emerging or to reverse the inequality that has emerged. Another reason is that the problem has been well described by David Willetts in his book *The Pinch: How the Baby Boomers Took Their Children's Future – And Why They Should Give it Back*, and there is very little that I can usefully add.[31]

## Chapter 6

# THE PARADOX OF RISING INEQUALITY AND FALLING POVERTY

## Introduction

THE INEQUALITY PARADOX THAT PROVIDES THIS BOOK WITH ITS TITLE IS that while inequality in rich countries has been growing – at least until recently – at the same time as the fastest rise in inequality, there took place a quite extraordinary reduction in poverty. We have seen that until the 1980s poverty was pervasive worldwide. Interpolation from the data in Figure 9 suggests that in 1950, 65% of the world's population lived in extreme poverty. The latest estimate for 2013 suggests that this has fallen to 10.7%[1] (since updated to 10.9%).

The other side of reduced poverty in the East is that – although the nature of the poverty is not comparable – the extent of poverty in the West is growing. I observed in a Cebr report on the US economy in 2013 that San Francisco, near Silicon Valley and one of the most prosperous regions in the world, now has more than 6,000 people homeless and that this type of poverty is a problem that is increasingly affecting the United States.[2] To a visitor their difficulties are very obvious. The total homeless has since risen further, according to the data mentioned in the prologue to this book.

Oddly, surprisingly few people in the West know about the fall in poverty. A recent survey in the UK showed that only 12% agreed with the proposition that 'In the last 30 years the proportion of the world population living in extreme poverty has decreased.'[3] In other words, 88% of the population don't believe something that every person who has made an objective study knows to be true about one of the most important issues in world economics and politics. If you ever wanted an explanation of why democracy often doesn't produce the right answer, this perhaps gives a clue.

A different survey showed that only 8% of the adult populations in the US and in Germany agreed with the proposition that global extreme poverty had fallen in the past 20 years. But interestingly, in a country where the fall in poverty would be much more obvious than in the West, fully half the population of China covered in the same survey knew this.[4]

The Marxist assumption of false consciousness is used to explain why the poor don't rise up against their exploitation. But you could use the same phrase to describe the situation where people believe in things that are completely untrue, to the detriment of their political understanding.

One doesn't need to go down the whole Donald Trump 'fake news' route to suggest that in the area of poverty the mainstream media in the West need to raise their game in keeping the public informed.[5] Some might suggest a conspiracy to mislead among left-wingers, of whom there are many in the media. But in my experience of life, serious academics and commentators do not get together to try to work out how to mislead people. If they do mislead it is generally unintentional, and results from a combination of ignorance, 'group think' and arrogance.

This chapter looks at six issues – how much has poverty fallen and on what measure; why poverty has fallen; a discussion of the measurement issues affecting poverty; the links between poverty, education and health; a geographical analysis of where extreme poverty is now concentrated; and a brief examination of the prospects for further poverty reduction.

## How much has poverty fallen?

This section relies heavily on an excellent note available on the web prepared by two outstanding economists, Max Roser and Esteban Ortiz-Ospina.[6]

The main statistics on world poverty that are widely used relating to recent years since 1981 are those provided by the World Bank. The best source of earlier data is in a seminal paper written by Bourguignon and Morrisson in 2002.[7] In this paper, the two authors measured poverty as far back as 1820 using a measure of 'one dollar a day'. The current poverty line of $1.90 a day was only introduced in 2015. There has been some discussion of the changing official definitions of extreme poverty amid worries that these definitions have been changed to choose the data that gives the best presentation of the results, so it is sensible to look at this in some detail.

### How is poverty defined and measured?

One of my advantages as an economist is that having lived and worked in an emerging economy, worked in a major corporate and run my own company I have some sense about which statistics are likely to be reliable and which might not be.

When I worked for IBM in the UK we discovered that the official data suggested that the prices of computers were going up. Since we produced a third of the computers produced in the UK at that time and we were pretty certain that the opposite was true, I thought it was worth investigating in our own organisation what statistical data we were contributing to the government on this.

Eventually we discovered how IBM's contribution to these statistics was emerging. A relatively junior employee whose day job was stacking shelves had been tasked with filling in the government forms. It turned out that the government sent IBM three forms, one of which related to a machine that had gone out of production roughly 20 years earlier. I asked the person who filled in the form how he dealt with that problem 'Oh, I just put in the price of the successor machine,' he responded. 'But,' I asked, 'what about the fact that the successor machine is 10,000 times more powerful?' 'Don't worry,' he said. 'It's only a government form.'

I also asked how he took account of discounting, which is meant to be taken into account when the official forms are filled in. His expurgated reply was on the lines of: 'Do you think I have the time to waste on finding out who got what discount for each machine – of course I only put down the list price!' This taught me a lot, and ever since I have been extremely careful to understand the basis of any figures before I assume that they are correct. My impression is that qualitative data from senior figures in a position to know is often superior to quantitative data from people who are not in a position to have the relevant information at their fingertips.

The potential unreliability of statistics has to be considered when looking at the data here.

The World Bank is the main source for global information on extreme poverty today and sets the International Poverty Line. This poverty line was revised in 2015 – since then a person is considered to live in extreme poverty if he or she is living on less than $1.90 per day. The poverty measurement is based on the monetary value of a person's *consumption*, but since consumption measures are unfortunately not available for all countries, the World Bank has to rely on income measures for some countries.

A key difficulty for measuring global poverty is that price levels are very different in different countries. For that reason it is not sufficient to convert the consumption levels of people in different countries simply by the market exchange rate; it is additionally necessary to adjust for differences in price levels between different countries. This is done through Purchasing Power Parity (PPP) adjustments (explained below), which allow consumption and incomes to be expressed in so-called 'international dollars'.

It is important to notice that the International Poverty Line is extremely low. Indeed, 'extreme poverty' is the right name for those living under this low threshold. Focusing on extreme poverty is important precisely because it captures those most in need. However, it is also important to point out that living conditions well above the International Poverty Line can still be characterised by poverty and hardship.

The data mainly comes from surveys and has been criticised for various defects such as non-response and urban bias. That is why I have cross-checked the data (see below) with other indicators which might confirm this or otherwise.

I have looked particularly to see if the extreme poverty data is consistent with data on health, on malnutrition and on life expectancy. I have also checked to see if it is consistent with conventional views on the returns to education and the data on the spread of education.

In October 2015 the World Bank's new definition of poverty became $1.90 a day in 2011 US Purchasing Power Parity dollars. The International Poverty Line (IPL) is the generally accepted measure below which people are considered to be living in extreme poverty and is meant to represent a level of income that would buy $1.90 worth of goods in the US in 2011. The previous IPL was $1.25 in 2005 US Purchasing Power Parity dollars set in 2008. Previous to that the IPL (set in 1990) was $1.00 in 1985 dollars, which was raised in line with inflation to $1.01 also in 1990, to $1.08 in 2001 before the rise to $1.25. The poverty line is set in line with the median poverty line in a sample of countries which are carefully chosen to be representative and investigated in detail. In 1990 these countries were Kenya, Nepal, Tanzania, Bangladesh, Indonesia, Morocco, the Philippines and Pakistan. The data on poverty is then extended to cover the whole world using the International Price Comparison project which compares the cost of living around the world.

## Weaknesses in the data

Measuring poverty is hard to make scientific. Different people have different ideas of poverty. Many anti-poverty campaigners now use relative poverty rather than absolute poverty, although it would be hard to measure progress against issues such as malnutrition on such a basis. And the countries where poverty is rife are unlikely to have the skills to make measurement, particularly on an internationally comparable basis, easy. And frankly, if poverty is that severe, the first policy priority is more likely to be food than statistics.

The first problem is that there is a group of 30 countries ranging from Zimbabwe to Argentina which do not normally provide poverty data at all. Their total population was 225 million in 2008 out of a world population (then) of 6.7 billion. Because they account for only 3.6% of the world's population, this is a relatively minor problem since even if everyone in each of these countries was in extreme poverty they would not change the statistics dramatically.

There is an additional group of countries of which the most extreme example is Syria where the data has not been collected recently because of conflicts. Here it is likely that the bulk of the population *is* in extreme poverty and the numbers in these countries should be added in. Syria's population was 24.5 million pre-war and is currently estimated to be slightly over 16 million of whom 13.5 million are estimated by the UN to be in need of humanitarian assistance.[8] This boosts the official numbers in extreme poverty by at least 20 million and probably by something more like 50 million (300 million people lived in countries with war happening somewhere in their country in 2014).[9]

The third problem is that many have criticised the definition of extreme poverty because it is too tight and excludes many malnourished people (it is estimated that about 60% of those living on the IPL are malnourished). For this reason the World Bank has published separate data using a much wider definition of extreme poverty, with the IPL set at $3.20 a day instead of $1.90 (the equivalent of the $3.20 measure consistent with the $1 a day 1990 measure was $2 a day in 1985 dollars). The reduction in extreme poverty is slightly less (see below in this chapter for data on the $3.20 a day basis of measurement) but the figures still show an essentially similar picture.

Thomas Pogge, the German philosopher based at Harvard, claims, based on a 2010 UN report, that malnourishment is still increasing worldwide, which would be unlikely if poverty was falling.[10] But this UN data is contradicted by more up-to-date data from the same source. The latest data from this source (actually the Food and Agriculture Organisation, which is a sub-branch of the UN) contradicts this view.[11] What it shows is that the number malnourished rose from 900 million to 925 million from 2000 to 2005, fell dramatically to 777 million in 2015 on the latest data, and was projected to rise to 815 million in 2016. The falls in percentages are much more impressive because of the growth in the world population. The fall is from 14.7% in 2000 to 10.6% in 2015. I find the projected rise in the number malnourished in 2016 to be improbable because 2016 was a year when food prices fell dramatically – by about a third.[12] If it indeed turns out to be an accurate estimate, one suspects that the fall in food prices in 2016 will bring down the 2017 figure for malnourishment sharply.

The World Health Organisation collects different data which show, in the latest World Health Report, that malnourishment among children has declined from 198 million people worldwide in 2000 to 156 million in 2015.[13] The decline in percentage terms is much more impressive – a decline from 32.7% to 23.2% over the same period, roughly in line with the World Bank estimates of the declining proportions in extreme poverty, although it is important to note that with a quarter of the world's children undernourished, we have a long way to go before we have declared victory in this battle.

Another criticism is that the bulk of the reduction in poverty has been in India and China. Since nearly 40% of the world's population lives in these two countries and they have both grown especially quickly, this is exactly what one might expect. But it does make the data especially dependent on the methodology of collecting data in these two countries. This is why I have deliberately cross-checked the data on poverty with independently sourced data on life expectancy, health and malnutrition. They all point to the same thing – that world poverty has fallen sharply, though of course the extent of the fall depends on the measure used.

The importance of the dependence on results from only two countries is enhanced because there appear to be many people, especially in India, living on a subsistence level that is quite close to the International Poverty Line, and the results are therefore sensitive to precisely where the line is drawn. The fall in the proportions on the $3.10 (and $2) measure is therefore slower than that on the $1.90 (and $1) measure (see Figure 9). One suspects that the fall in poverty on the $3.10 measure is about to increase in speed while that on the narrower measure will slow and may even go into reverse. It would be improbable that different ways of measuring the same thing could derive completely different conclusions over a long period.

There is one final criticism which seems to me less easy to accept. To quote Pogge again: 'Between 1990 and 2008, the number of people living in extreme poverty shrank only incrementally, from 1.2 billion to 1.1 billion, when you exclude China. And you should exclude China, because its radical poverty reduction has been achieved via methods that are completely at odds with World Bank and World Trade Organization policies'.[clx] In other words, poverty hasn't fallen because it didn't fall in the right way. My response to this would be to ask the poor themselves whether they feel that their poverty hasn't diminished because it didn't diminish 'in the right way'. I am extremely uncomfortable with this suggestion that poverty hasn't reduced because it didn't reduce in the right way.

### History of poverty

For most of the world's history, poverty has been the general state of mankind. The Reverend Thomas Malthus, writing at the end of the 18th century in his classic 'An Essay on the Principle of Population', argued that as agricultural production essentially grew arithmetically while populations grew exponentially, unless people abstained from having children, famine to limit populations would be inevitable. For example, world GDP (1990 Geary-Khamis dollars) is estimated at $121 billion dollars in the year 1000 AD and twice that at $248 billion dollars in 1500 AD. Yet GDP per capita grew only slightly, rising from $453 per person per year in 1000 to $566 in 1500. Indeed, from 1500 to 1820 GDP more than doubled yet again, to $693 billion, but GDP per capita again rose only slightly to $666 per person. Malthus' concept that populations would rise to consume the resources available would not have seemed entirely fanciful to someone observing that data.[15]

Only a very small proportion of the world's population did not live in extreme poverty in 1820. But economic growth and trickle-down economics (where economic growth does enough to mean that the number of poor diminishes) means that the world since then has not only managed to reduce extreme poverty by more than three quarters but also to accommodate a sevenfold increase in the world's population from one billion to seven billion.

From 1820 to 1950 the fall in world extreme poverty was gradual – from 94% to 72% on the $2 a day measure and from 84% to 55% on the $1 a day measure. But since then the amount of poverty in the world has fallen dramatically. There is no consistent series, but interpolation suggests that about 65-70% were in extreme poverty in 1950; this had fallen to 44% in 1981 and to the conventionally accepted figure of 10.7% for 2013 (just revised to 10.9%).

Until the 1960s, because of population growth, the gradual fall in the share of the world's population in extreme poverty was not enough to prevent the total number of people in extreme poverty rising – from around one billion in 1820 to around two billion in the 1960s. But since the 1960-90 period the share has fallen so fast that the number in extreme poverty has itself fallen to around a third of its peak level. The World Bank estimate for 2013 was originally 705 million people in extreme poverty, though this number has been increased in the latest estimates to 783 million.

The first countries in which people improved their living conditions were the first to industrialise. Martin Ravallion from the World Bank (measured against the older poverty line of $1.25 in 2005 prices) writes:[16] 'Today there is virtually no extreme poverty left in today's rich world, when judged by the standards of poor countries today.' An exception to this is the US – a country with exceptionally high inequality among rich countries – where a small but sizeable fraction of the population is still living in extreme poverty (see my comment about San Francisco above and those about New York and Los Angeles in the prologue).

Although poverty in rich countries had largely ended a generation ago, there are increasing signs that it may be returning. For example, the number measured as sleeping rough in England (and one can imagine that this number is almost certainly an underestimate) doubled from 1,768 in 2010 to 3,569 in 2015[17] (more recent data mentioned in the prologue of this book suggests a further increase to over 8,000 people). Most poverty measures in Southern Europe have shown rising poverty since the Euro crisis started and the latest measure (for 2014) shows 36% of all Greeks at risk of income poverty.[18] By contrast, the levels of homelessness in the US, admittedly starting at a high level, have fallen in recent years. The official estimate of the number of chronically homeless individuals has fallen from 119,813 in 2007 to 83,170 in 2015.[19] But from casual observation it seems likely that with a long-lasting period of economic underperformance since the financial crisis and time-limited welfare that this may now be rising.

Many would argue that people are in extreme poverty even on incomes higher than $1.90 a day. Figure 6 shows the trends on both the $1.90 definition and the $3.20 definition. What it makes clear is that the number in poverty on the $3.20 measure – by no means a high measure – was relatively recently nearly three times that on the $1.90 measure. This shows that even if the world can claim substantial success in reducing the worst of poverty, there are still very many people living in desperately tough conditions.

Figure 6. Comparison of those in poverty on $3.20 per day with those in poverty on $1.90 per day

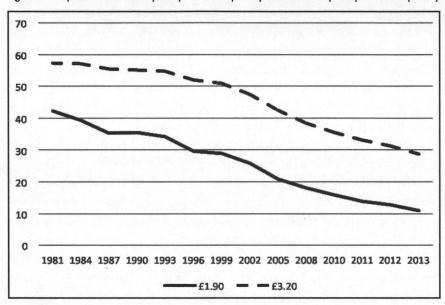

*Source: World Bank databank http://databank.worldbank.org/data/reports.aspx ?source=poverty -and-equity-database.*

## Why has poverty fallen?

The answer that most analysts will give to this question is the rate of economic growth in the poorer economies. Growth particularly in India and China has been behind the fall in poverty. But what has caused the growth?

*The Economist* has looked at this issue in some detail and come to similar conclusions to those in this book. First, *The Economist* confirms the scale of the reduction in poverty that is a key point in this book:

> To people who believe that the world used to be a better place, and especially to those who argue that globalisation has done more economic harm than good, there is a simple, powerful riposte ... In 1981 some 42% of the world's population were extremely poor, according to the World Bank. They were not just poorer than a large majority of their compatriots, as many rich countries define poverty among their own citizens today, but absolutely destitute. At best, they had barely enough money to eat and pay for necessities like clothes. At worst, they starved.
>
> Since then the number of people in absolute poverty has fallen

by about 1bn and the number of non-poor people has gone up by roughly 4bn. By 2013, the most recent year for which reliable data exist, just 10.7% of the world's population was poor (the modern yardstick for destitution is that a person consumes less than $1.90 a day at 2011 purchasing-power parity). Poverty has almost certainly retreated further since 2013: the World Bank's finger-in-the-wind estimate for 2016 is 9.1%.[20]

The assessment that poverty is still falling is backed up by Homi Kharas of the Brookings Institution, who calculates that someone escapes extreme poverty every 1.2 seconds.[21] Kharas also supports the 'trickle down' explanation of the reduction in poverty: 'Middle-class growth in most countries is a function of growth in incomes and in population, and not due to changes in inequality.'

Then *The Economist* goes on to explain why poverty has fallen – so-called 'better economic policies' or a move from highly socialist policies that had been followed hitherto to a more successful mix of government intervention and free market policies:

> Until recently the world's poorest people could be divided into three big groups: Chinese, Indian and everybody else. In 1987 China is thought to have had 660m poor people, and India 374m. The concentration of destitution in those two countries was in one sense a boon, because in both places better economic policies allowed legions to scramble out of poverty. At the last count (2011 in India; 2013 in China) India had 268m paupers and China just 25m. Both countries are much more populous than they were 30 years ago.
>
> Some of the decline in poverty in China and India is artificial, caused by more accurate household surveys and new estimates of purchasing power. But most of it is real. In both countries, economic growth has benefited the poor as well as the rich, peasants as well as city-dwellers: the magic ingredient in China's poverty-reduction formula since the 1980s has been not its factories but its highly productive small farms. Much the same is true of other Asian countries. Carolina Sanchez, a manager at the World Bank, is particularly impressed by Bangladesh, where many sparsely educated women have been able to find good jobs in textile factories.

Looking forward, *The Economist* comes to the same conclusion as this book does – that the low-hanging fruit of poverty reduction has already been picked:

> Unfortunately, this happy chapter in world history is drawing to a close. The share of people living in absolute poverty will almost certainly not decline as quickly in the future—and not because it will hit zero and therefore have nowhere to fall. Even as the global proportion of poor people continues to drift slowly downwards, large pockets of poverty will persist, and some of them are likely to swell. The war on want is about to settle into a period of grinding battles in the trenches.

Then the magazine goes on to explain why it will be increasingly difficult to reduce poverty as rapidly in the future and that doing so will require a mix of economic growth and welfare reform – the same conclusion as this book reaches in Chapter 11 (although *The Economist* misses what I believe to be a crucial point, the establishment of stable governments in states that are at war):

> ... these days about four-fifths of all extremely poor people live in the countryside, and just over half of them live in sub-Saharan Africa. Africa is as studded with examples of failure as Asia is filled with success stories.

Allegedly the most controversial cause of the fall in poverty is the role of increased international trade, or globalisation.[22] Capital and goods, and to a lesser extent people have moved around the world increasingly freely over the period when poverty fell most. Not only has there been very rapid growth in trade between developed and developing nations, but trade between developing nations has grown even more quickly.

Underpinning this growth in trade have been various 'infrastructural' developments.

First, education has moved from being an exception to being the norm in emerging economies. Second, health has improved dramatically, as is evidenced by substantial increases in longevity. Third, the rule of law and the protection of property (it is necessary for property to be protected for investment to be made by private individuals and corporations) has increased. And there has been investment in the physical infrastructure in emerging economies as well.

Meanwhile, technology has also played a role, enabling globalisation.[23]

But what is startling is that charity and overseas aid have played a minor role, if any. Indeed, given the extent of anti-globalisation campaigning by charities over this period (though recently some have started to change their views) one could argue that the reduction in poverty has taken place despite these charities.

Although some campaigners have genuinely tried to help the poor, more have campaigned against globalisation, even as this process has worked its magic to reduce poverty. Christian Aid, for example, provides a globalisation 'trading game' for students, filled with such propaganda claims as trade is 'unfair'.

Oxfam appears to have changed tack dramatically, and has broken with many in the anti-globalisation movement. But it had previously made some tough claims, such as 'the rules that govern [international trade] are rigged in favour of the rich'. CAFOD, the Catholic charity, has worked with Christian Aid to assert that globalisation could not succeed in reducing poverty on anything like the scale implied by the Millennium Development Goals. This turns out to have been not just wrong, but the precise opposite of the truth.

Why do so many think that globalisation has had such disastrous consequences? One answer is that part of the process of making the poor in poor countries richer has been associated with falling real wages for poorer people in rich countries. And rich countries have built a high cost base into their systems, with heavy regulation, expensive housing and costly energy all combining to raise the cost of living. Charities based in rich countries have paid more attention to the increase in poverty in the rich countries than to the decrease in poverty in the poor countries.

Another possible answer is that globalisation has been a partially capitalist process, though supported by government activity, particularly for education, sanitation, health and infrastructure. And many campaigners may be more ideologically anti-capitalist than genuinely interested in the fate of the poor. Because of their ideological predisposition some feel that anything capitalist cannot yield good results. I try (though it is dangerous to think one is open-minded and others are not, even in those circumstances where it is true!) to have an open mind on capitalism, a system which works quite well but has its weaknesses and of course doesn't work perfectly (what system does?). And having seen with my own eyes the poor getting richer in Malaysia in my youth and having had the economic tools to understand the process, perhaps my take on the subject has some extra validity compared with the views of those whose understanding is purely statistical.

Of course the fact that the less well-off in the developed world have clearly suffered a worsening in at least their relative position and in many cases their absolute position as a result of globalisation is a genuine problem resulting from globalisation. But one would need to be extremely callous to argue that the number in extreme poverty, in effect facing starvation, should rise four times to prevent a 10-30% at most worsening in the levels of disposable incomes of people in the rich world who, though by no means rich themselves, do at least have enough to live on.

What this book aims to do is to propose policies that would lead to the worse excesses of inequality in the West being prevented without forcing the poor elsewhere in the world back into poverty. The solution to this problem is not to go back to an autarchic pre-capitalist world where the poorest people slide back into poverty again. It is to find ways of bringing down the cost of living in countries such as the US and Britain and improving the skills of poorer people so that they can get decent jobs.

### The links between poverty, education and health

Yet again the wonderful Max Roser has provided an invaluable data source to show how living conditions around the world have changed.[23]

The first major item of data is the fall in child mortality.[24] We are often unaware of how bad conditions were in previous eras and so have no basis for comparison with the present. In 1800 43% of those born died before their fifth birthday. Even as recently as 1960 child mortality was still 18.5%. Almost every fifth child born in that year died in childhood. But by 2015 child mortality was down to 4.3%.

Not only has infant mortality fallen but life expectancy has increased. Over the last 200 years people in all countries in the world achieved the type of progress in health that has led to increases in life expectancy. As an aside, improvements in hygiene and sanitation have probably had as much to do with this as improvements in medicine. In the UK, life expectancy doubled over the 200-year period and is now 79.2 for men and 82.9 for women. In Japan health started to improve later, but the country caught up quickly with the UK and overtook it during the 1960s. In South Korea health started to improve later still and the country achieved even faster progress. Now life expectancy in South Korea is higher than life expectancy in the UK.

A century ago life expectancy in India and South Korea was as low as 23 years. A century later, life expectancy in India has almost tripled and in South Korea it has almost quadrupled.

But there are still huge differences between countries: people in Sub-Saharan countries have a life expectancy of less than 50 years, while in Japan, Hong Kong and Singapore it exceeds 85.

The average life expectancy worldwide today is 75. Interestingly, although as a region Sub-Saharan life expectancy is the lowest, increasingly low life expectancy is also being found in pockets of more advanced economies, such as Russia and parts of Glasgow in Scotland and among white working-class people in the US.

Meanwhile education has spread, which has increased the likelihood of escaping from poverty.[25]

In 1870 only one in four people in the world attended school, and only one in five was able to read. Today, in contrast, the global estimates of literacy and school attendance are above 80%, and the inequality between world regions – while still existing – is much lower.

It is the contention of this book that the role of education in reducing poverty and promoting globalisation has been understated compared with economic causes. Clearly it is difficult to prove the case because so many things have been happening at the same time. But my personal experience growing up in the Far East makes me believe that the spread of education has been crucial. Other factors of course contributed, but had education not become widespread, it seems very unlikely that globalisation as we know it would have happened. Certainly none of those employed in the two offshore manufacturing plants that I studied right at the beginning of globalisation would have been employed had they not been literate.

### Where is poverty now concentrated?

In 1990 the world region with the largest number of poor people was Asia (505 million in South Asia, plus 966 million in East Asia and the Pacific). With the rapid economic growth in Asia over the following two decades, the number of people in extreme poverty fell rapidly to 327 million in 2013 – by that time Africa was the continent with the largest number of people living in extreme poverty.

The breakdown of extreme poverty by continent in 2013 was as follows:

- 383 million in Africa
- 327 million in Asia
- 19 million in South America
- 13 million in North America
- 2.5 million in Oceania
- 0.7 million in Europe

India is the country with the largest number of people living in extreme poverty (218 million people). Nigeria and the Congo (DRC) follow with 86 and 55 million people.

Since then it has become clear that further low-hanging fruit have been gathered. The Chinese premier Li Keqiang recently claimed that more than 68.5 million rural people had been lifted out of poverty in China over the past five years, meaning that 37,000 people escaped poverty every single day, and that the national poverty rate had fallen 10.2% to 3.1%.[26]

### How can we reduce poverty further?

The aim of the World Bank is to end extreme poverty by 2030. How realistic is this?

A continuation of present growth trends would roughly halve the rate of extreme poverty between 2015 and 2030 to 4.8%.[27] While a fall is likely, I would be amazed if we do as well as this.

Microsoft founder Bill Gates (who has a pretty good record in forecasting, but gets it wrong occasionally) predicts that:

> By 2035, there will be almost no poor countries left in the world. (I mean by our current definition of poor – specifically, I mean that by 2035, almost no country will be as poor as any of the 35 countries that the World Bank classifies as low-income today, even after adjusting for inflation.) Almost all countries will be what we now call lower-middle income or richer. Countries will learn from their most productive neighbours and benefit from innovations like new vaccines, better seeds, and the digital revolution. Their labour forces, buoyed by expanded education, will attract new investments.

I would love to be as optimistic as Bill Gates. But I fear (as does *The Economist* – see above) we have picked the low-hanging fruit of poverty reduction – that part that is most amenable to economic growth through the trickle-down effect. Much of what is left is due to less easily eradicable causes.

First, while poverty is reducing in the emerging economies, especially in India and Sub-Saharan Africa, there are also signs that poverty is increasing in the developed world. The persistence of welfare and a culture of joblessness has been combining with problems like addiction to leave people in poverty with growing problems of lack of physical health leading to low and in some cases falling life expectancy.

And the fact that in some Western economies a bad economic policy response to globalisation mean that some groups are almost completely excluded from society means that increasing numbers are mired in poverty. One of the most unfortunate examples is Greece. In 2010 I pointed out that Greece had no option but to devalue and default[28] and was accused for my sins of being 'irresponsible' – by the leader of the Greek Communist Party, a fine example of pot and kettle![29] Successive Greek governments took a different line and refused to leave the euro, prompting a fall in GDP of over a quarter. As a result a Greek friend has described the situation in Greece as 'much like after the war' when many cannot find enough food and are suffering from malnutrition. My prediction that Greece would leave the euro has been proved wrong, though the underlying economic prediction that if they did not do so there would be an economic disaster was not.

The result of what I believe to be bad economic policy decisions, combined with the fact that the later economic developers in the Western world are on the front line of globalisation, have hit Greece badly. Even had my economic policy recommendations been accepted the country would still have faced a tough time but would be recovering by now after nearly a decade. The Greek economy does now seem to be starting to edge upwards again as the stabilisation policy stops intensifying and as the benefits of the 'internal devaluation' cutting costs in the tourist sector bear fruit.

The impact of the past decade on Greek poverty is tragic and dramatic. Since 2008 the proportion of Greeks assessed by Eurostat (the European Statistical Agency) as 'severely materially deprived' has doubled, reaching 22.2% in 2015.[30]

Greece is not the only example in the 'developed' world of sharply rising poverty, but it is the most dramatic.

Second, much of the poverty that remains has specific causes – failed states such as Venezuela or Zimbabwe, or states where there are civil or other wars. Without restoring the rule of law and creating peace in these countries, reducing poverty seems unlikely.

There is some interesting evidence about this from Iraq, where the Coalition forces after the Gulf War produced some good statistical measurements to try to show the effects of their efforts at nation-building. There the position at one point started to improve but has since gone into reverse. Abdul Zahra al-Hindawi, the spokesperson of the Iraqi Ministry of Planning, told a journalist that the data suggests that 'the poverty rates dropped from 23 percent in 2010 to 19 percent in 2013 [as a result of] the application of a strategic plan to decrease poverty, which aimed to reduce it to 10 percent by the end of 2014. But because of the current circumstances and the high numbers of displaced people, the plan is no longer effective. The shock of Daesh [the local name of the IS] which raised the numbers of displaced people and the fall in oil prices have raised the poverty rates in 2014 to 22.5 percent.'[31]

Meanwhile, poverty rates in provinces seized by the Islamic State are higher at 41% than they were during Saddam's era, according to the Ministry of Planning, though it may not be a totally unbiased source.

This short discussion with statistics indicates the impact of civil war on poverty. Clearly the situation is much worse in Syria, where there are no measurements but where between two-thirds and three-quarters of the population have become refugees.

Where the rule of law has failed for whatever reason it is likely that no matter how beneficial the external environment, poverty will not fall. So, although official aid and charity have played a minor role in reducing extreme poverty worldwide in recent years, their roles and that of peacekeeping agencies are likely to be greater in the future.

My three priorities for reducing poverty in the coming years are:

(1) It is important that the economic growth worldwide continues so that the forces that have been reducing poverty in the past 25 years can continue to operate.

(2) The world will need to deal with problems in specific states where governments have failed or where law and order has broken down or where there are wars taking place.

(3) As the scale of extreme poverty diminishes, the next problem to be dealt with is to reduce slightly less extreme poverty – with still near to a quarter of the world's population subsisting on less than $3.20 a day.

This means keeping growth going and not holding it back as a result of mistaken policies that are an emotive response to inequality. It means reforming countries where failed policies have been entrenched – Zimbabwe and Venezuela are most obvious. It means finding ways of bringing peace to countries at war – more easily said than done. And it means working with those families where problems of poverty and addiction have become intertwined in order to give them hope and help them out of their problems.

As we shall see in Chapter 17, in many emerging economies there is plenty of scope for increased redistribution from higher rates of taxation without doing too much damage to the incentives that drive growth. But welfare systems need to be carefully planned to minimise their impact on perpetuating poverty. My impression is that such systems often work well initially but as they become entrenched frequently lead to a 'cycle of deprivation' of welfare dependence.

Ironically, although aid and charities have played a surprisingly small role in the massive reduction in global poverty so far (and arguably some, through their anti-globalisation campaigning, have actually hindered the process), over the next 25 years poverty reduction is likely to need the kind of targeted help that can be provided from these sources. Their time is likely to come.

*Chapter 7*

# INEQUALITY AND GROWTH

THIS CHAPTER LOOKS AT THE COMPLEX RELATIONSHIPS BETWEEN IN-equality and economic growth. Rather than accept the simple proposition that inequality is good (or bad) for growth, the chapter looks at how different types of inequality have different effects on growth and how some solutions to the inequality problems reduce growth while others increase it.

There have been many attempts to formalise a relationship between inequality and growth.

One theory is that income differences drive incentives. If that is so, the most highly incentivised should be those who are generating most growth, in which case one might expect high inequality to be combined with rapid growth. In 1975 Arthur Okun, an American economist, wrote *Equality and Efficiency: The Big Tradeoff*.[1] He argued that societies cannot have both perfect equality and perfect efficiency, but must choose how much of one to sacrifice for the other. Many economists today continue to believe this. Okun wrote:

> Contrast among American families in living standards and in material wealth reflects a system of rewards and penalties that is intended to encourage effort and channel it into socially productive activity. To the extent the system succeeds, it generates an efficient economy. But that pursuit of efficiency necessarily creates inequalities. Hence, society faces a trade-off between equality and efficiency. Tradeoffs are the central study of the economists. You can't have your cake and eat it, too, is a good candidate for the fundamental theorem of economic analysis. We can't have our cake of market efficiency and share it equally.

The theory has an intuitive plausibility but suffers from one major defect – the facts do not seem to fit it. Most cross-sectional examinations of the relationship between inequality and growth over a range of economies show either that there is no significant relationship or that the relationship is that the less the inequality, the faster the rate of growth.[2]

Indeed an IMF study concludes that a one-percentage-point increase in the income share of the top 20% will drag down growth by 0.08 percentage points over five years, while a rise in the income share of the bottom 20% actually boosts growth.

Given that the evidence seems to hint that inequality harms growth, research in recent years has concentrated on trying to explain the transmission mechanism. One theory is that inequality could impair growth if those with low incomes suffer poor health and low productivity as a result or if the poor struggle to finance investments in education.

An alternative theory is that inequality boosts pressure for bad economic policies (i.e. protectionism and limits on immigration or anti-capitalist policies) which were mentioned at the beginning of this book as likely to inhibit growth.

There is also some evidence to show that inequality can cause a savings glut. Well known economists such as Ben Bernanke and Larry Summers have argued that inequality contributes to the world's 'savings glut' since the rich tend to spend a lower proportion of their incomes than the poor. And they argue that there are consequential results – higher savings cause interest rates to fall, boosting asset prices, encouraging borrowing and making it more difficult for central banks to manage the economy.

On the other hand, those advanced economies that have not had significant growth in inequality in the 1980-2008 period were those who also had the least GDP growth, such as Japan, Italy and France. Those with a larger rise in inequality, such as the UK and the US, showed stronger economic performance.

It seems probable that a range of mechanisms are at work, not all pointing in the same direction.

The Kuznets theory would imply that the early phases of economic development, when growth is often especially fast, are often phases where inequality is large and is increasing. At later phases when an economy is maturing and growth as a result is slowing, inequality would likely be diminishing.

It is important therefore to compare countries that are at the same phase of economic development. Yet even there, countries have widely differing social approaches. One typical contrast in advanced economies is between countries with a fairly homogeneous structure and ones which may be very open to migration but where the different groups are segregated. It is possible that the homogeneous structure, particularly if associated with a small underclass and a strong educational performance at the bottom end of the ability range, would generate both higher average productivity and faster GDP growth. It is possible that some of the Scandinavian countries have benefited from this in the past, though there are hints of evidence that increased migration is causing their social structures to become less homogeneous.

There is a fascinating analysis, so far available only in Dutch, that tries to unpick some of the social influences behind the different levels of equality and inequality in different but otherwise relatively comparable countries in Europe. Bert Bakker, a Dutch financial journalist, has written about how the economic history of different European economies has led to different social backgrounds that have resulted in different levels of equality.[3]

In a letter published in the *Financial Times* on 28 April 2018 Mr Bakker wrote:

> The hypothesis I worked out in Onbegrepen Europa (loosely translatable as 'Europe under the surface') is that some regions of Europe have always been part of an empire (Roman, Frankish, Habsburg) governed along feudal, centralistic lines. Large landownership for a few and serfdom for the majority was the economics and societal model.
>
> However, in some other – often remote – regions, such as Scandinavia, the Low Countries and Switzerland, the conditions (lack of vast estates of arable land) prompted a large proportion of the people to make a living on their own, as small-scale farmers, tradespeople, traders, transporters, shipbuilders (Viking's Frisians and later Hanseatic shippers).
>
> The proportionately large middle class in these countries ruled themselves, knew material autonomy and thus laid the basis for the egalitarian, trust-based, individualistic attitudes we know now in the Nordic countries, the Netherlands and Switzerland. But also, for the same reasons, in the north of Italy and in Catalonia, Spain. This accounts for two very different European value systems.[4]

I suspect that a rigorous examination of different sets of circumstances would discover the following 'stylised facts' about the relationship between the level of inequality and GDP growth:

(1) Homogeneous societies with strong social networks and good education tend to have lower inequality and high GDP and fairly high rates of GDP growth.

(2) Highly capitalistic and free market societies with less strong social networks tend to have high levels of inequality and high rates of GDP growth.

(3) Economies with high levels of immigration and weak social networks tend to have high levels of inequality and high rates of GDP growth.

(4) Economies with high levels of inertia and historic inequality tend to combine high levels of inequality and low rates of GDP growth.

(5) Dictatorial and autocratic societies tend to have high levels of inequality. Their rates of growth can sometimes be high but over time tend to become lower and sometimes even negative.

(6) Communist societies can have low levels of inequality (though not all do) but typically have low rates of GDP growth and quite often have falling GDP (though measuring GDP and GDP growth in countries where there are no proper markets can be difficult).

(7) Emerging economies tend to have high rates of inequality and high rates of growth.

(8) Mature economies tend to have lower rates of inequality and lower rates of growth.

The key point about this is that even though on balance the data seem to show a correlation between less inequality and higher growth, it is not clear that reducing inequality, for example by redistributive taxation, will lead to higher economic growth. It is the underlying factors affecting the inequality, such as social structures, incentive systems, educational inequality and the quality of parenting that affect economic performance as well as the pervasiveness of social and economic incentives that are more important.

### Inequality and economic development[5]
The relationship between aggregate output and the distribution of income is an important topic in macroeconomics.[6] The World Bank Group has included among its key global objectives for development the eradication of extreme poverty and boosting the incomes of the bottom 40% of developing countries. The IMF has also involved itself in the discussion about the role of income distribution as a cause and consequence of economic growth.[7]

In a recent paper Brueckner and Lederman provided estimates of the within-country effect that income inequality has on aggregate output.[8] Their empirical analysis started from the premise that the effect of changes in income inequality on GDP per capita may differ between rich and poor countries. This premise is grounded in economic theory.

In a seminal contribution, Galor and Zeira proposed a model with credit market imperfections and indivisibilities in investment to show that inequality affects GDP per capita in the short run as well as in the long term.[9] Galor and Zeira's model predicted that the effect of rising inequality on GDP per capita was negative in relatively rich countries but positive in poor countries. Brueckner and Lederman tested this prediction by introducing in the panel model an interaction term between income inequality and countries' initial GDP per capita. Their empirical analysis showed that for the average country in the sample during 1970-2010, increases in income inequality reduced GDP per capita.

Specifically, they found that a one-percentage-point increase in the Gini coefficient reduced GDP per capita by around 1.1% over a five-year period and that the long-run (cumulative) effect was larger and amounted to about –4.5%.

The estimates from the interaction model thus suggest that in poor countries, increases in income inequality raise GDP per capita while the opposite is the case in high- and middle-income countries.

## Redistribution and growth

Because the evidence seems to show that high inequality is correlated with lower growth, one might think that redistributing income and wealth from the rich to the poor would boost growth. But real life is messy and the studies seem to show that policies involving high rates of tax and redistribution in various ways if anything reduce growth.

The seminal work suggesting that high levels of government (current) spending hinder economic growth was by Robert Barro in 1991.[10]

His study showed that 'for 98 countries in the period 1960-1985, the growth rate of real per capita GDP is positively related to initial human capital (proxied by 1960 school-enrolment rates) and negatively related to the initial (1960) level of real per capita GDP'. Barro concluded:

> Countries with higher human capital also have lower fertility rates and higher ratios of physical investment to GDP. Growth is inversely related to the share of government consumption in GDP, but insignif-

icantly related to the share of public investment. Growth rates are positively related to measures of political stability and inversely related to a proxy for market distortions.

There is also an interesting concept called the Scully Curve.[11] This is like the Laffer Curve but has a stronger scientific basis.

What it says is that there is a quadratic relationship between economic growth and public spending as a share of the economy. Economic growth varies positively with the share of public spending and negatively with the square of public spending. This gives a curve where initially growth rises with higher public spending but as the quadratic term starts to dominate, the relationship between growth and public spending first levels out and then shows lower growth for higher public spending.

When public spending is too low, the economy lacks the public infrastructural support to grow strongly. When it is too high, public spending crowds out the entrepreneurial sector and causes taxes to be so high that they destroy incentives. The latest estimates of the Scully Curve from the Fraser Institute in Canada show that the difference between public spending at 25% of GDP as in much of Asia and 45% as in the UK can be the difference between GDP growth at 1.5% per capita per annum and growth at 3%.[12] If this really is the case, it points out that in this area there is likely to be a trade-off between inequality and growth since one of the purposes of public spending is in many circumstances to reduce public spending.

The analysis of public spending and growth has developed more dimensions since the initial work. In general, the latest research suggests that educational spending can boost growth and that infrastructural spending at least does not hinder growth, but that other areas of public spending remain generally negative for growth. Spending on welfare in particular can have a dramatic effect on inequality but appears to reduce growth both through the public spending mechanism and more directly through impacting on the labour supply.

And research confirms that the damage to growth from public spending rising as a share of GDP grows substantially as the share rises from 40%. The Institute of Economic Affairs in the UK has produced a useful table of studies on this and their conclusions (Table 5).

## Table 5. Studies of public spending and growth[13]

| Author | Data coverage | Main explanatory variables | Comment |
|---|---|---|---|
| Barro (1991)[14] | 98 countries in the period 1960-85 | Human capital, government consumption, political instability indicator, price distortion | 1% point increase in tax-to-GDP ratio lowers output per worker by 0.12% |
| Koester and Kormendi (1989)[15] | 63 countries for which at least five years of continuous rate, data exists for the 1970s | Marginal tax rates, average tax mean growth in labour force and population | 10% decrease in marginal tax rates would increase per capita income in an average industrial country by more than 7% |
| Hansson and Henrekson (1994)[16] | Industry level data for 14 OECD countries | Government transfers, consumption, total outlays, education expenditure government investment | Government transfers, consumption and total outlays have a negative impact on growth whilst government investment is not significant |
| Cashin (1995)[17] | 23 OECD countries over the 1971-88 period | Ratio of public investment to GDP, ratio of current taxation revenue to GDP, ratio of expenditure on transfers to GDP | 1% increase in tax to GDP ratio reduces output per worker by 2% |
| Engen and Skinner (1996)[18] | US modelling Together with a sample of OECD countries | Marginal tax rates, human capital, investment | 2.5% rise in tax to GDP ratio reduces GDP *growth* by 0.2-0.3% |
| OECD (Leibfritz et al.) 1997[19] | OECD countries over the 1965-95 period | Tax to GDP ratio, physical and human capital formation, labour supply | 10 point increase in tax to GDP ratio reduces GDP *growth* by 0.5-1% |
| Alesina et al. (2002)[20] | 18 OECD countries over the 1960-94 period | Primary spending, labour taxes, transfers, government wage consumption, indirect taxes (all as shares of GDP) | 1% increase in government spending relative to GDP lowers the investment to GDP ratio by 0.15% and a cumulative fall of 0.74% after 5 years |

**Table 5.** *(Continued)*

| Author | Data coverage | Main explanatory variables | Comment |
|--------|---------------|---------------------------|---------|
| Bleaney et al. (2000)[21] | 17 OECD countries over the 1970-94 period | Distortionary tax, productive expenditure, net lending labour force growth, investment ratio | 1% increase in distortionary tax revenue reduces GDP growth by 0.4% points |
| Folster and Henrekson (2000)[22] | Sample of rich OECD/non OECD countries over 1970-95 period | Tax to GDP, government expenditure to GDP, investment to GDP, labour force growth, investment ratio | 10 point increase in tax to GDP ratio reduces GDP growth by 1% |
| Bassanini and Scarpetta (2001)[23] | 21 OECD countries over the 1971-98 period | Indicators of government size and financing, physical capital, human capital, population growth | 1% point increase in tax to GDP ratio reduces per capita output levels by 0.3-0.6% |

In this section I draw heavily on Patrick Minford, 'Tax and Growth'.[24]

An important set of work that became known as the 'Barro growth regressions' has been widely used to investigate policy impacts since Barro's 1991 work).[25] These take the form of a regression of either GDP growth or productivity growth on initial income (to control for convergence or 'catch-up'), some factors to account for other influences, and a variable measuring the policy factor under investigation. Models of this type are often estimated in a panel of cross-country and time-series data with observations averaged over five-year periods to smooth out the impact of the business cycle. Barro used data for 98 countries between 1960 and 1985.

Leach[26] and OECD document the empirical literature on the effects of taxation on growth and output levels. Table 5 sets out a selection of the major studies, noting their data set, the explanatory variables used and the main effects of tax on growth that are found. All control for various factors other than taxation (usually different variables across different studies). Some of these studies use tax as the explanatory variable and others use government spending.

In theory, the latter is preferable because government spending measures the total claim on the economic resources of government. Barro did, in fact, consider that some government spending, in theory at least, might have a positive impact on growth.

He believed that there may be a positive effect of education spending on human capital formation and therefore on growth and takes that into account. As such, he examined the impact of real government consumption net of spending on both education and defence as a percentage of real GDP over the period 1970-85 on both real economic growth (averaged over the period 1960-85) and on private investment. He found a negative correlation between net government spending (so defined) and growth.

Koester and Kormendi examined the effect of measures of the marginal and average tax rates, as well as population and labour-force growth on economic growth. In a cross-country analysis for the 1970s, they found a significant negative effect of marginal tax rates on the level of real GDP per capita, but not on the rate of growth when this was controlled for the initial level of income. They suggested that, holding average tax rates constant, a 10 percentage point decrease in marginal tax rates would increase per capita income in an average industrial country by more than 7% (and in an average developing country by more than 15%). Thus, a revenue-neutral tax reform which reduced tax progressivity would raise incomes.

Alesina et al. focussed on the extent of government spending of various sorts on the investment-to-GDP ratio (and hence by implication on growth). They concluded that, via the effect of raising private sector labour costs, a 1 percentage point increase in government spending relative to GDP resulted in a decrease in the investment-to-GDP ratio of 0.15 percentage points and a cumulative fall of 0.74 percentage points after five years. In general these studies, with their varying methodologies, find that there are measurable negative effects of higher tax rates on growth.

The order of magnitude of this effect was estimated to be around 0.5-1.0% for a 10% rise in the ratio of taxation (or government spending) to GDP. The OECD's own conclusion from its survey was as follows:

A number of studies, influenced by the new growth theories, have taken a top-down approach to assess the impact of taxes on per capita income and growth at the macro level. Several of them purport to demonstrate a significant negative relationship between the level of the tax/GDP ratio (or the government expenditure ratio) and the growth rate of GDP per capita, implying that high tax rates reduce economic growth ... our estimates [using a top-down cross-country regression] suggest that the increase in the average (weighted) tax rate of about 10 percentage points over the past 35 years, may have reduced OECD annual growth rates by about 0.5 percentage points.

The OECD study suggested that a 10 percentage point cut in the tax-to-GDP ratio could increase economic growth by 0.5-1.0 percentage points. Thus they also argued that 'up to one third of the growth deceleration in the OECD [over the 1965-95 period] would be explained by higher taxes. In some European countries, tax burdens increased much more dramatically than the OECD average, which would imply correspondingly larger effects on their growth rates'.

Taken together, all these studies seem to show that subsidies and government current expenditure other than on education have the worst negative effects on growth on the spending side. Overall, the tax (or government spending) and growth studies indicate a strong association between the two variables.

As a rule of thumb, the conclusion of the studies is that it would appear that a 10 percentage point fall in the share of national income taken in tax would lead to around a 1 percentage point increase in the growth rate – results of this order of magnitude occur over and over again. This does not mean that the US or the UK can automatically expect to increase their growth rate by 1 percentage point if the government reduced the proportion of national income it spends from (say) 45% to (say) 35%. First, there is the issue of causality. For example, does high government spending lead to low growth or the other way round? Second, the results are averages using data taken from a wide variety of situations. Third, the effects are likely to be non-linear. The impact of a 1 percentage point change in government spending relative to national income cannot simply be multiplied by ten to find the impact for a 10 percentage point change. Intuitively, it is likely that the gains in terms of extra growth at the margin will reduce as the tax burden falls and rise as the tax burden increases.

The analysis of the Scully curve suggests that the growth-maximising average spending ratio is 17.5-22.5% of national income and the welfare-maximising point is 27.5-32.5% of national income. Broadly, the model suggests that a cut in government spending to the welfare-maximising point from current levels might imply a rise in the economic growth rate by around 1 percentage point; and a cut to the growth-maximising point would imply a rise in the economic growth rate by a further 0.8 percentage points. These are clearly orders of magnitude and the effects of cutting government spending are unlikely to be a simple linear function of the extent of the cut. However, there is a lot of evidence from different sources that points towards figures of this order.

## Profits and investment

The relationship between profits and investment is a complicated one. And extremists on all sides make seemingly plausible assertions which do not stand up to the test of empirical economic analysis.

One extreme view is that there is no relationship between profits and investment. The opposite view is that all profits get ploughed back into investment. Neither is correct, though those that argue with the view that profits lead to investment often forget that redistributed profits are often reinvested and that high income earners have a high investment ratio.

The most highly cited paper on profits and investment argues that there is a very strong relationship between profits and investment.[27] The argument is not a cashflow argument (although this probably provides an element of the correlation) but more that profits act as a signal to investors and hence encourages them. This seems intuitively plausible, especially if one has some experience of investment decisions in the financial sector or at board level.

## Redistributing to the poor

Obviously if a sum of money is taken from a rich person and given to a poor person it initially reduces both inequality and poverty. But whether redistribution to the poor helps reduce poverty in the long term is more controversial.

In the United States, members of both the Republican and Democratic Party (as well as third parties such as the Libertarians) have favoured reducing or eliminating welfare. The landmark piece of legislation which reduced welfare was the Personal Responsibility and Work Opportunity Act passed under the Clinton administration though on the basis of strong pressure from the Republicans who controlled both Houses of Congress at that time.

Conservative and libertarian groups such as the Heritage Foundation[28] and the Cato Institute[29] assert that welfare creates dependence and a disincentive to work, and reduces the opportunity of individuals to manage their own lives. This dependence is called a 'culture of poverty' which is said to undermine people and prevent them from finding meaningful work. Many of these groups also point to the large budget used to maintain these programmes and assert that it is wasteful.

In the book *Losing Ground*, Charles Murray argues that welfare not only increases poverty but also increases other problems such as single-parent households and crime.[30]

All this is not to say that any kind of redistribution is bound to fail. What it says instead is that when redistributing two things are critical: first, any redistribution has to be in a form that minimises the disincentives to work; and second, any redistribution needs to ensure that it has as little impact as possible on the tax burden, particularly the tax burden on the rich who are both mobile and typically have enough income and wealth to make choices about how many hours they work.

## Conclusions

All this shows that the relationship between inequality and growth is a mixed one. The trick is not to make crude assumptions based on correlations. For example, it seems to be generally the case that higher inequality is associated with less growth. So one might be tempted to recommend raising taxes to redistribute from rich to poor to boost growth. But then one discovers that higher taxes are (generally, although it does depend on the starting point) also associated with lower growth. What to do?

The answer is to redistribute in the right way. First, concentrate on universal benefits. These do not create the negative work incentives that other forms of redistribution can. Second (because affordability is critical here) get the cost of living down, especially for those elements which affect the cost of living of the poorest groups. Third, redistribute while keeping taxes down to the extent possible. There probably has to be a trade-off here. What this also means is that government has to be rigorous about avoiding spending on non-mission-critical items and on eliminating waste. It is possible that one escape from the impact of high compulsory taxes on growth is to look at voluntary taxes, and I devote a section of Chapter 17 to this.

# PART III
## The Deserving and the Underserving Rich

PART III LOOKS AT the rich and whether they are good for society or not. Few will be surprised to discover that the answer is that sometimes they are and sometimes they aren't.

Chapter 8 'Who are the super-rich?' looks at how the rich live and how and where they spend their money. It is clear that there are a number of global cities in which the world's rich, who mainly operate on a global scale, congregate. The chapter looks at their knock-on spending, which is considerable. Although sometimes the spending, especially on property, has negative knock-on effects on others, there are ways in which this damage could be mitigated or eliminated.

Chapter 9 'The undeserving rich' looks at crony capitalism, overpaid bankers and CEOs and tries to determine when they move over from being good for the economy to being bad. The worst excesses of cronyism tend to be outside the West, and it should be possible to use administrative measures such as travel bans and freezing of assets to affect their activities. Because the rule of law remains prevalent in much of the Western world, many of the beneficiaries of crony capitalism need the West to enable them to store their stashes of loot and to enjoy the high life. So travel bans and asset freezes can be highly effective and clearly cause enough pain for some to engage in a powerful lobbying effort to end them.

This chapter also draws attention to overpaid bankers and CEOs and makes an unusual case: that here the market is finally starting to work, although only after a long delay. The pay of FTSE CEOs indeed appears to have fallen by 17% on average in the financial year 2016/17. And bankers' bonuses are less than half of their 2008 peak. Aggressive shareholder groups and the long-term effect of a sustained period of low yields have hit CEOs and bankers, while automation is affecting finance dramatically.

It has taken a long time for the market to work, but this seems to be the case with labour markets – that they work in aggregate surprisingly much more slowly than free-market zealots would wish. Because of the institutional constraints on pay and all the psychological factors associated with it, the labour market is one of those markets that clears remarkably slowly and often can take as long as a generation. Many of the effects of Mrs Thatcher's reforms didn't really affect the UK economy until after her departure as Prime Minister and came to fruition during the Blair years, more than two decades later. The benefits of the Clinton welfare reforms kept boosting the US economy until the late Obama years, when the problems of time limited welfare payments started to show.

Chapter 10 'Clogs to clogs in five generations' looks at a different factor: how long wealth survives. We have been very lucky to have been able to collaborate with the Sunday Times Rich List and have analysed its data to see how long wealth survives in a family after it has been made. The answer is much as ancient proverbs such as 'clogs to clogs in three generations' suggest – wealth disappears surprisingly fast. And wealth is increasingly new money and not inherited money. Studies by the Federal Reserve Bank of St Louis show the same effects in the US.

So the rich are a changing cast. Some do good for the world, others not. But the money disappears surprisingly quickly. Analysis of the impact of the top 1% needs to be aware of the fact that this group is a surprisingly rapidly changing set of people.

## Chapter 8
# WHO ARE THE SUPER-RICH?

THERE IS A FAMOUS ALLEGED SET OF QUOTATIONS FROM A DISCUSSION between the authors Ernest Hemingway and Scott Fitzgerald.[1] Fitzgerald is usually quoted as saying either 'The rich are different from you and me' or 'The rich are different from us.'

Hemingway is quoted as responding: 'Yes, they have more money.'

In fact the discussion never took place.

In 1925 Fitzgerald wrote a short story titled 'The Rich Boy' which was published in 1926 in *Red Book* magazine. This is the third paragraph:

> Let me tell you about the very rich. They are different from you and me. They possess and enjoy early, and it does something to them, makes them soft where we are hard, and cynical where we are trustful, in a way that, unless you were born rich, it is very difficult to understand. They think, deep in their hearts, that they are better than we are because we had to discover the compensations and refuges of life for ourselves. Even when they enter deep into our world or sink below us, they still think that they are better than we are. They are different.

This description of rich people is actually quite rude about those who have never had to work for their money.

Years later, Ernest Hemingway, who had a variable relationship with Fitzgerald that blew hot and cold, decided to mock those lines from 'The Rich Boy' in his short story 'The Snows of Kilimanjaro'. In his original version of this story, printed in the August 1936 issue of *Esquire* magazine, Hemingway wrote:

> The rich were dull and they drank too much, or they played too much backgammon. They were dull and they were repetitious. He remembered poor Scott Fitzgerald and his romantic awe of them and how he had started a story once that began, 'The very rich are different

from you and me.' And how someone had said to Scott, 'Yes, they have more money.' But that was not humorous to Scott. He thought they were a special glamorous race and when he found they weren't it wrecked him as much as any other thing that wrecked him.

Fitzgerald was not happy with this and did not respond with equanimity. He wrote both to Hemingway and to the celebrated editor Maxwell Perkins who edited both of their works and was employed by their publisher Charles Scribner and Sons.

Hemingway responded with a long and somewhat stream of consciousness sort of diatribe, offering no apology or even explanation, which did little to improve matters. But Perkins clearly did not want a confrontation between his two most important writers and decided to fix the problem. Using his editorial powers, he deleted the passage when he later reprinted 'The Snows of Kilimanjaro'.[2]

So are the rich really different and what do they do with all that money?

I wrote about this for the then relatively new group of high earners in the City of London and in commerce and industry in the first-ever issue of the magazine *Prospect* in October 1995,[3] and my conclusions were referenced in many of the news stories about this initial issue. It remains the only serious evidence-based study on the income, savings, spending and investment behaviour of high income earners in the UK. Its conclusions are therefore worth restating at length.

The analysis needs some context. In the UK, struggling to perform economically after the early stages of Thatcherism had seen a collapse in manufacturing and export-sensitive industry, the mid-1980s seemed bleak. The only positive signs had been the Thatcherite deregulation and the impact on the trade unions (who a few years earlier had seemed to be hell bent on wrecking the economy) of both high unemployment and the collapse of the miners' strike in 1983. But unemployment was still desperately high.

In the second half of the 1980s, however, as the old economy adjusted, a new economy came into place and, with lax monetary policy as the politicians bickered over whether to control the money supply or the exchange rate, the Lawson boom emerged that boosted asset values and the financial services industry in the City of London.

By the mid-1990s London was a fascinating economy. It had survived the recession, which had followed the Lawson boom, from the beginning of the decade. The greatest feature of the 1990s recession was the collapse in both the commercial and residential property markets from their inflated values in the Lawson boom as interest rates surged. Because of the historic importance of property in the London economy,[4] it took nearly a decade to work off the excess supply of commercial property in central London. But the economic history of London in this period was dominated by financial services following the 'Big Bang'.

As I explained in *The Flat White Economy*:

Oddly I was there at the beginning of the Big Bang. In a rare invitation to 10 Downing Street in the mid-1980s I had my longest ever conversation with Mrs Thatcher (to which my contribution was only three words ... 'Yes, Prime Minister'!) before she left me and cuddled up on a sofa with Sir Nicholas Goodison. Sir Nicholas was the then chairman of the Stock Exchange, the critical figure in the bonfire of regulations that created the Big Bang for London's financial service industry and that underpinned the explosion of financial service activity in London. Sir Nicholas was a very straight-laced figure who seemed to shrink further and further into the sofa as the Prime Minister flirted with him. Anyway, she had her wicked way with him – he acceded to her requests and the rest is history. I was amused that someone as important as a Prime Minister was prepared to use female wiles to get what she wanted.

Once I had clarified the statistics, it had become clear that since the Big Bang, London had had the sort of economic growth that had rivalled the mega growth in Far Eastern economies. I called it the 'Tiger Economy on the Thames'. London's growth continued until 2007; indeed for the entire period from 1997-2007 London's economy grew at an annual rate of 6.2% in cash terms. With inflation averaging perhaps 2% over the period this meant real GDP grew at an annual rate of over 4% – fast enough to rival Far East economies.

The growth was underpinned by the City of London. The number of so-called City Jobs rose from a plateau of 170,000 in the mid-1980s to a peak of 230,000 in 1989; collapsed to 190,000 by 1993 but it had recovered to over 350,000 by 2007. As the number of jobs increased, some of the financial excesses grew. City bonuses grew from about £1 billion in 1990 to a peak of £14 billion in 2008 before collapsing to £2 billion in 2011. The number of people getting million pound bonuses in the City rose from 30 in 2000 to 1,500 in 2007.

By 1995 the question of how high incomes were spent was not merely of prurient interest. As one commentator, William Wallace, wrote in the *Financial Times*: 'If a medium sized merchant bank [Barings] pays an annual bonus of £100m, we can assume that the sums received by senior City employees as a whole are now a significant factor in the economy of the south east – if not of the UK as a whole.'

There was no official information on the subject because the top income groups for government statistics generally covered a much wider range of incomes than the top salary earners alone. The government's General Household Survey at the time lumped together all those earning above £40,000, while the top category in the Inland Revenue Statistics included all those over £100,000 (for some items, over £50,000). Even the smallest of these groups – those on over £100,000 – represented as many as 95,000 income earners (0.37% of the total).

So with my then colleague Mark Pragnell I carried out a survey of those who we knew had high earnings. We defined earnings as pre-tax income including salary, bonuses, dividends and capital gains on shares in the companies in which the individuals work. Almost all respondents earned at least £500,000 per annum, but the strict qualifying level was a minimum average earning for the past three years of £350,000.

By extrapolating from the most recent Inland Revenue Statistics we estimated that 4,700 people earned more than £500,000 in 1994. This group accounted for about 1.1% of total personal incomes in the UK though they represented only 0.008% of the population, or one in 12,300. At the same time they accounted for 0.5% of UK consumers' expenditure and 2.3% of total tax and national insurance receipts: in other words each of them on average paid as much tax as 125 average taxpayers put together.

The next point of our investigation was to discover what all these people did for a living to earn this amount. The annual Labour Research survey of company reports for years ending in 1994 or early 1995 identified 187 directors paid over £500,000 per annum, of whom 58 earned over £1 million. This survey was based on the published accounts of public companies which are legally obliged to state directors' emoluments. As a result it could not be expected to include many of the high earners in financial services, the professions, small companies, sports and entertainment.

Scanning the *Sunday Times* list of the UK's 500 wealthiest people, it seemed plausible to assume that a further 250 people owning unquoted companies in industry and commerce were paying themselves salaries of

£500,000 or more. In addition we were informed that there are several hundred lawyers (mainly barristers) with earnings in this income bracket. We also calculated that there must have been at least 100 people in sports, media and entertainment who earn above £500,000 a year.

Yet it was clear that the bulk of those earning above £500,000 in any given year at the time when the article was written were likely to be working in the financial services sector. Our survey sample contains 77% from financial services and 11.5% each from industry and the professions. Probably this slightly over-represented the financial services sector, but not by much. A typical City firm then paid bonuses of perhaps one-third of pre-tax profits after deducting a notional return on capital invested (the 50% Barings payout was unusually high and of course the firm did not survive). This funded bonuses which would generate a total salary for a successful dealer of about one-quarter of his commission income.

Almost all top earners in financial services were traders in equity, bond and foreign exchange markets, particularly those dealing in derivatives. The second-largest group seemed to be fund managers, especially those in high-risk sectors. The rest were spread over a range of groups such as merger and acquisition experts, brokers of various types, and research advisers, such as investment strategists and even a handful of economists. Most successful firms also would have had a small number of senior managers who earned top salaries. Of course this has changed dramatically now with the highest earners in private equity, mergers and acquisitions, derivatives and fintech.

The Labour Research list of top industrialists was useful because it gave some indication of the volatility of high earnings. Only half (94 out of 187) of those included in the 1995 list would have made it for the previous two years; 39 out of the 132 in the Labour Research list published in 1993 no longer qualified for the 1995 list (this is a point made in Chapter 5: that many high incomes and low incomes are temporary, which causes distortions in measurement both of inequality and also of the progressivity of the tax system).

Indeed, a number of people on the Labour Research list of those earning more than £500,000 in 1994 whom we approached said that they did not qualify for our survey because their earnings had not been at the required level for the previous two years. Because earnings in financial services and small businesses are essentially more volatile than those in publicly quoted companies, even the indications from the Labour Research list may have understated the extent of the 'churn' in the top salary earners group.

So, just as the Institute for Fiscal Studies has argued that any snapshot of low earners in a given period will overstate the extent of poverty (as a result of including those for whom the low earnings are temporary), the number of high earners in a particular year will be greater than the number whose earnings are constantly high (which might be as much as 30-50% fewer).

Had the numbers of high earners risen? Other than during the early 1990s recession, the number of top earners in the UK had been increasing since the late 1970s. Several reasons were thought to be behind this. The background was then considered to be a global trend towards widening income differentials. Technology had increased the returns to skilled people, and the emergence of a world labour market for some of these skills had enabled them to translate these returns into high earnings. The UK had moved more rapidly than the rest of Europe towards becoming a market economy, and hence had been more exposed than the rest of Europe to the global labour market. It had also increased the volatility in many industries, so generating more 'shooting stars' with temporary high incomes.

The abolition of incomes policies and other controls in 1979 and the reduction of the top tax rate on earned income from 83% to 40% in 1985 meant that by 1995 high-fliers now concentrated less on perks, comfortable living and tax loopholes, and more on achieving very high pay. Whereas potential top earners used to go into tax exile, our survey indicated that the UK by 1995 might be attracting top earners from countries with higher tax rates.

There was, however, still a long way to go before returning to the income disparities of the pre-war era. In 1936 Lord Hirst, the then chairman of GEC, earned £100,000. To achieve the same after-tax spending power in 1995, he would have had to earn £1.9m – more than three times the pay of his then successor (although by the time that I was a member of the main board of the same company, by then renamed Marconi, the chief executive had been put on a long-term incentive package that in the first decade of the 21st century could have given him a payout of £20 million over about seven years. He eventually received a bit less than half that.)

With those earning more than £500,000 accounting for only 1.1% of total incomes in 1995, the idea that swings in their spending could have an important effect on the economy as a whole was probably exaggerated. Our evidence from top earners in the City indicated that the Barings bonuses were exceptionally high – so it would be misleading to scale up using them as a base.

But there were clearly areas of the economy on which this small group had a disproportionate effect. They controlled significant savings flows, for example. And although they were insignificant in relation to the economy as a whole, their spending power was likely to be critical to many of the individual markets in which it was deployed – such as the London property market – which may have had important knock-on effects elsewhere in the economy. Their spending may also have had 'demonstration' effects: affecting consumer behaviour in mass markets by establishing standards or fashions.

We sent out 400 detailed questionnaires and received 37 responses from people who met the earnings qualification. Clearly the sample was too small for it to be precisely representative and, because it was self-selected by those prepared to respond to a fairly intrusive questionnaire, there is a probable sample bias. But though we would caution against placing excessive weight on the precise numbers, the respondents covered a sufficient range of occupations, ages and backgrounds to give a good impressionistic picture of how top earners behave.

The survey respondents were all male, and their average age was 43. There was a preponderance of respondents from middle- and upper-middle-class backgrounds, but a sizeable representation described their background as working-class. Over two-thirds had been privately educated, but most of the rest had been educated at state schools. The great majority of top earners surveyed (77%) had college or university degrees.

Perhaps the most interesting characteristic of the respondents in 1995 was the high proportion with foreign connections. Just less than a third were citizens of some other country and nearly half the sample had parents who were not British citizens. While these proportions could be biased upwards in our sample because of the traditional British reserve towards talking about financial matters, these proportions were still a fascinating indication of the extent to which top jobs in the UK were now being taken up by those with cosmopolitan backgrounds.

Where did the money go?

From the responses to the survey, the top earners split their pre-tax income into roughly equal proportions between spending, investment and taxes. This compares with the national accounts figures for all income earners who spent most of their pre-tax income and invested only 7.6%.

Common sense would predict that the rate of investment/saving for top earners would be well above the average, but even so, the proportion revealed in the survey – which amounted to more than half of post-tax income – was remarkably high, accounting for 5.6% of national savings. It is possible that this proportion had been higher than usual in the early to mid-1990s because of economic uncertainty and weak property markets resulting from the early 1990s recession. Also the savings data would have been affected by the volatility of incomes to which I referred earlier. On the widely accepted basis that people's spending is based much more on long-term income than on temporary fluctuations, a sample of those earning a lot in an individual year would be likely to have a disproportionate share of income viewed as possibly temporary, which would have boosted savings above the long-run level for people with long-run incomes above £500,000.

Finally we looked at spending patterns. The most important finding was that the state of property markets was especially relevant to this group since nearly half its expenditure was on property compared with only a sixth for the population as a whole. This might seem counter-intuitive because one might have expected expenditure on 'necessities' such as housing to fall as incomes rise. But the top earners seemed to like buying property as a way of investing money. Just under half spent money on second homes, but the bulk of residential property expenditure was on the primary residence, including running costs and staff. Continuing expenditure on property by the high income groups may explain why central London property prices had fallen by only 2% from their peak in mid-1989 to mid-1995, compared with a 34% drop in house prices in general over the same period.

A second area of consistently high expenditure in absolute terms for the top earners was travel and holidays. Although the proportion of expenditure on travel for this group was only 4.8%, this was one of the main areas where most respondents spent significantly, £20,000 a year on personal/family travel.

A third area of distinctive behaviour was the purchase of antiques and works of art. Yet this was not a widespread phenomenon. For antiques, in particular, there was a correlation between the level of spending and background: those with an upper-middle-class background allocated 9.7% of their expenditure to antiques; those with a working-class background only 2.2%. For art, however, although the level of spending varied from person to person, social background did not seem a key determinant. Given their heavy expenditure on property, it is not surprising that art and antiques accounted for 13.4% of top earners' total expenditure – those properties need to be furnished. But spending on other collectables, such as classic cars, was only 0.3%. This indeed would have been lower than might have been recorded in the late 1980s before the classic car market fell dramatically around 1990.

Although top earners faced higher household expenses than the population as a whole, such expenses still accounted for a lower proportion of the total. Top earners spent 25.7% of their total expenditure on household expenses compared with a national average of 43.1%.

Glossy magazines sometimes create the impression that life for the rich is largely about lavish entertainment. This might have been so for those with inherited wealth in 1995, but the top earners who had to work for a living were more modest. They spent an average £11,000 a year on all entertainment – and some of this total included holiday spending. This was a sizeable amount, but it would not have been sufficient to pay for even one of the types of party that ended up in the gossip columns. Spending on entertainment varied with social background. Those born upper-middle-class spent about a quarter more on entertaining than those born working-class.

The proportion of expenditure on clothes was much less than the national average for this group (though the figure is probably an understatement because it did not include spending on clothes by spouses who received an allowance for the purpose). Here again there seemed to be some consistent variation in expenditure patterns/background. Those from a working-class background spent 65% more on clothes than those from an upper-middle-class background. The myth of the shabbily dressed English gentleman seemed to hold true.

There was considerable variation – no doubt as a result of different family and other circumstances – in expenditure on allowances and education for children and spouses. For those with dependent children, the average level of expenditure including education was £19,000.

About half the earners in the group provided a cash allowance for their spouse or partner. The average for those who did so was £42,000, but there was substantial variation. An interesting, unexplained group of 'others' received an allowance, typically of about £15,000 to £20,000. These might have been dependent relatives, but one respondent carefully wrote that his 'other' allowance was paid to a 'friend'. Had we stumbled across the going rate for a mistress? The figure seemed low – but this occupation, like others in the service sector, might have been part-time.

The top earners gave 2.3% of their income and 6.0% of their total expenditure to charities, a mixture of ad hoc, pre-committed and trust payments. This is much higher than people on average incomes, but still rather less than we expected. Nonetheless, more than half the group had some direct involvement with a charity. We estimated that the top earners accounted for between a third and a half of all payments to charities by private individuals.

Because those who worked in financial services generally had access to the low-cost dealings which might facilitate running a self-managed equity and bond portfolio, one might have expected top earners to be relatively sophisticated financial investors. And accordingly, the largest single share of top earners' financial investments in 1995 were in their personal portfolios – 15.9% of pre-tax income; about 40% of total personal investment.

Top earners invested what might at first have seemed a surprisingly large amount – £57,000 – in liquid assets such as bank and building society accounts. But one respondent specifically commented that his income was volatile and he thus deliberately adopted a very conservative investment strategy. Perhaps others were doing the same.

Such conservatism might explain why the top earners in the sample directly invested relatively small amounts in unquoted companies other than their own. Such investment amounted to only 4% of their total investment. If all top earners had invested similar proportions this would have amounted to about £100 million in total. Such a total would be surprisingly low given the extent of the tax advantages then available from investing in unquoted companies.

Top earners who had their own companies seem to have adopted a different spending and investment strategy from the others. They spent much less on property than the others (7% of pre-tax income rather than 19%) and invested much more in total. Of their investments, roughly half was income which was reinvested in their own company, but this was investment over and above the normal financial investments that were made in other types of assets. This sub-group also invested less in its equity and bond portfolio but about twice as much on average as the top earners in other unquoted companies.

Given the tax system and the income levels it is possible to calculate that these top earners were likely to pay about 45% of their income, on average, in income tax and national insurance contributions. Although the survey did not ask directly about tax, the residual between pre-tax incomes, expenditure and investment gave an implicit figure of 27% for tax deductions. This may seem low, but probably reflects the fact that some of the expenditure (especially that on property) is partly financed out of capital or borrowing. Given these factors, the implicit 27% for tax and other deductions emerging in the survey was probably consistent with an actual total tax payment in line with the calculated figure of 45% of pre-tax income. This suggests that the Inland Revenue has been largely successful in eliminating tax loopholes for this group. The top 1% of earners paid 15% cent of all income tax revenue (27% in 2015); the much smaller group of top earners (4,700) accounted for about one-ninth of that.

In their saving and spending patterns the rich were different in 1995. They saved and invested more and they spent much more on antiques, art and, especially, property. Although the incomes of the top earners considered here comprised only a small proportion of the UK total and their expenditure an even smaller proportion, the top end of the UK property market largely depended on their spending.

The mid-1990s top earners seemed a much more sober bunch than public stereotypes would suggest. They saved half their post-tax earnings, and when they did spend, it was mainly on investment goods. In relation to their incomes they spent relatively little on cars, clothes and entertainment. The only area where the 1980s image seemed to hold true is that the top earners in 1995 still spent heavily on travel. Perhaps they worked such long hours that they had no time for riotous living and used their holidays to make up.

No one has ever repeated our 1995 study so there is no direct comparison. But it is worth examining the evidence about today's rich to see how different they might be.

### The rich today
First, where are today's rich based?

A recent summary report, based on a survey of global multi-millionaires (so-called ultra high net worth individuals with assets worth more than $30 million) with more than one home suggested that the greatest concentration lived in London (Table 6).[5] But they are clearly a cosmopolitan bunch and even if based in global capitals such as London, New York, Hong Kong or Singapore have some kind of presence in other places.

Table 6. Where are the ultra-rich (worth more than $30 million) based?

| London | 22,300 |
|---|---|
| New York | 17,400 |
| Hong Kong | 14,800 |
| Singapore | 11,200 |
| Dubai | 8,200 |
| The Hamptons | 7,800 |
| Paris | 6,400 |
| Zurich | 6,200 |
| Geneva | 5,600 |
| Rio de Janeiro | 4,400 |

But a much more detailed report compiled by the estate agents Knight Frank suggested that New York had the advantage and that by 2026 both Beijing and Shanghai would have overtaken London.[6]

Not surprisingly the four top world international financial centres, London, New York, Hong Kong and Singapore dominate both lists. But what is fascinating is the number of places where there are now at least ten high net worth individuals. Already by 2016 there were 90 cities in the Knight Frank list that boasted that many and inspection suggests quite a lot of others that were not covered. There were at least 17 cities with more than ten high net worth individuals in Africa in 2016, on Knight Frank's calculations more than in any other region except Europe. While one suspects that the nature of their interest as estate agents means that they have overlooked many important areas around the world (why no Manchester? – the two football teams alone must account for many more UHNWIs than Addis Ababa, for example), the extent to which the wealth has spread is impressive.

### What do the rich look for in their property?
The current Mayor of London, Sadiq Khan, has coined two phrases which he thinks pick up a phenomenon of people who own property in London as effectively absentee landlords. The first is 'buy to leave' and he has commissioned the London School of Economics to investigate the habits of foreign buyers in the capital in a report. Khan has taken the line that London is open for business and that foreign investors are critical for this, but he is concerned about what might happen behind the closed doors of some of these apartments.

The second is 'Lights out London' a phrase that, for many, sums a problem with the capital's prime property market and its often absent owners. The phrase refers to the dark windows, complicated ownership patterns through a maze of offshore companies and very expensive facilities that remain unused as a result of super-rich owners living mainly elsewhere.

The two properties often cited as examples of this are One Hyde Park, just opposite Knightsbridge underground station and near Harvey Nichols and Harrods, and Kensington's Ashburn Place, where seven out of ten properties – in a street whose average property price is £2.8m and houses cost around £19m – are second homes.

The person who is reputed to know most about the top end of the London property market is a man called Dean Main, the founder of Rhodium, a London-based property management and concierge company part-owned by the Monaco royal family, who has carried out two studies of London's super-rich property market.[7] He manages more than £1.5bn of prime London property, including Northacre's No. 1 Palace Street, overlooking Buckingham Palace, and Finchatton's Kingwood just behind Harrods.

'That's our little niche – we only look after new-build super-prime. No one else offers the same level of service to residents,' says Main, who typically deals with boutique developments such as Glebe's The Mellier in Mayfair, where one of the five huge, lateral apartments recently sold for £15m. Rhodium is also working on two London schemes set to complete in 2020 where properties will range from £40m to £200m.

From his daily dealings with UHNWIs (ultra high net worth individuals), Main has a very different point of view to the picture painted by 'Lights out London'. Rhodium's research finds that 30% of owners of super-prime (£5m+) properties live in their London property full-time. Even owners who class their London home as a second residence spend at least 140 days a year there. 'There's a lot of negativity about super-prime owners not living in their properties, but they do. At this level of wealth, they travel a lot and they have multiple homes around the world, but these properties are still occupied – if not by the principal owner, then by their staff, or by friends and family. That's what keeps all these concierges busy,' says Main.

Most striking among the report's findings is the revelation of how much wealthy owners contribute to the local economy. The average owner of a £5-15m home in the Rhodium catchment area – which is mainly Kensington & Chelsea, and Westminster boroughs – spends £2.7m a year in 'lifestyle' household expenditure in the London area (this does not include base expenditure like purchase prices or mortgages). For owners of £15m+ homes, their annual spending totals about £4.6m.

'It's incredible how much they spend. They buy lots of luxury goods and cars, and we know that big business tycoons employ a huge number of people because we help many of them find office space and recruit staff,' says Main.

What surprises him is how young the super-rich are these days: 'I assumed tycoons would be a lot older, but the levels of wealth that people in their 40s have is extraordinary. They account for 42% of super-prime owners. A decade ago, that would have looked very different.'

There is an even younger tranche: the city's super-rich students, of the sort likely to be among the residents of Lodha UK's Lincoln Square in Holborn, close to the LSE and King's College London. 'Study' was the reason given by 45% of respondents as their reason for living in London. 'We have £30m apartments with students in them. Their parents see London as the best place in the world to educate their kids, then they return home to Russia or wherever,' Main comments.

As a result, the concierges in prime developments are getting used to dealing with a new breed of request. 'Restaurant recommendations have traditionally been the main request, but now concierges tell me they are asked about the best nightclubs and private members' clubs, or entry to the biggest football matches, fashion events or art exhibitions. These super-rich students don't just want tickets. They want exclusive access or a preview before anyone else, and a chauffeur to take them there and back.'

In recent years the UK government has tried to increase the level of taxation on the super-rich and as a result the super-prime property market is now struggling. Sales of new-build flats in London's luxury market were down by 57% by the end of 2016 compared with the previous year, according to property advisors London Central Portfolio (LCP). Increased stamp duty is mainly to blame, with many buyers having rushed to purchase before the rates changed in April 2016. Other 'aggressive tax hits' on foreign ownership have also taken their toll, say LCP.

But the fall in sterling post-Brexit has brought about an upside for dollar buyers – not just Americans, but those from dollar-denominated Asia too. 'If you have a certain amount of money, you will have a home in London,' says Main. The super-prime market's stagnancy is also piling the pressure on developers to find a winning formula that will seduce a reduced pot of potential buyers – which is where Rhodium comes in.

'We work with developers from the planning stage and stay on indefinitely once the residents have moved in,' says Main, who will advise developers on everything from service charges (two developments in London have now gone beyond an astronomical £20 per sq ft) to pool lengths and layouts (put the Jacuzzi beside the pool; residents don't like having to walk into a separate room) and why they should have a reformer machine in their residents' gym (Pilates is big at the moment).

Technology is another issue for the super-rich. 'Clients tell us they want things simpler. They miss their remote controls.' And crucial to the success of a prime new development is finding the right concierge. 'We look all over the world. It can take us a year and many are ex general managers of the world's top hotels,' says Main.

Where, until recently, the concierge hid in a back room, now they are front of stage. They are 'exceptionally well paid', says Main, 'and get big performance-based bonuses on top. There are always issues in the first year or two of a new development, and a concierge's success depends on how well they deal with complaints. Our clients just want problems fixed. They want exceptional, hotel-standard service in their home, all the time.'

Looking at some of the other characteristics of the super-rich, it does appear that there are at least three groups. Many European super-rich have inherited their fortunes. Many in the emerging economies are the first generations to break into this group and have done so on the back of globalisation in some way. While in the US much of the wealth is new and is based on tech or on the financial economy.

Data analysis shows that the super-rich in the United States are more dynamic than in Europe.[8] Just over half of European billionaires inherited their fortunes, as compared with one-third in the United States. The median age of a company of a European billionaire is nearly 20 years older than that of an American billionaire.

Traditional sectors explain more than half of the rise in wealth in Europe; the financial sector and technology-related sectors together are largely responsible for the rise in US wealth.

There is some evidence that returns to the super-rich are higher in the United States than Europe, as not only is the number of US billionaires expanding rapidly, but US billionaires are also getting richer on average over time, especially when wealth is connected to resources, nontradables or finance.[9]

The most closely related paper to this work is by Kaplan and Rauh, who use the World's Billionaires lists from 1987, 1992, 2001 and 2011 to compare US billionaires with billionaires in the rest of the world. They assess US and non-US billionaires in three areas: self-made versus inherited wealth, income level of billionaires' families, and industry. They argue that the composition of US billionaires supports the importance of skills-biased technological change – and subsequent development of tech 'superstars' who are increasingly likely to have made their own fortunes – as a contributor to increased income inequality in the United States. However, this same phenomenon is not present in the data for rest of the world.

## Conclusion

The analysis in this chapter of how the super-rich behave suggests that even those who travel around the world pass through quite a lot of spending into the locations where they have property. Whether this offsets the negative impact of their spending on positional goods is an interesting question.

It is also clear that the super-rich are a changing cast, a subject which is investigated in greater detail later.

*Chapter 9*

# THE UNDESERVING RICH

## Introduction

A LTHOUGH TYPE 1 INEQUALITY MAY ACCOUNT FOR ONLY ABOUT A FIFTH of the recent growth in inequality, it is still important. First, a fifth is a significant proportion. But secondly, the growth of inequality from the abuse of power has a more than proportionate influence on public opinion because it is generally very public. This type of inequality is obvious and because of that often makes people think that it is the only type (hence, perhaps, the mass sales of Piketty's book). And as a result it encourages an approach towards inequality and to anti-inequality policy which can be based on misleading assumptions and can often be counterproductive.

It is important therefore to be aware of this source of inequality and, to the extent that it is possible, remove it. Obviously, since much of this involves the abuse of power by those who typically combine wealth with political connections, fixing the problem is not a trivial task. But pointing the finger and causing embarrassment helps. And when it becomes clear that people in power have abused it, it is often possible through democratic processes (where they exist) to make progress in undoing the abuse. Obviously it is much easier for democracy to work where there are competing political parties of essentially moderate views who do not seek to abuse power by trampling on the rights of minorities (even the rich).

The title of this chapter, 'The undeserving rich', echoes the Victorian concept that there were two types of poor people, the deserving poor and the undeserving poor.[1] The deserving poor were those who were poor through no fault of their own, because of illness, accident, family circumstances, age or through bad luck such as a factory closure in their town. They were contrasted with the undeserving poor who were poor because they were feckless, lazy or drunk. The distinction, especially when made by someone who is much better off or who has been lucky in life, seems invidious and distasteful.

But for rich people there is a real distinction to be made between those who have contributed to society as part of the process of getting rich, whom we can call the 'deserving rich', and those who have extorted their wealth as a transfer from the rest of society, who are pretty clearly the 'undeserving rich'. Obviously the real world is much more complicated than these simple stereotypes and most of the rich are partly one and partly the other. But the stereotypes are useful for explaining the issues.

Many wealthy entrepreneurs have become wealthy through developing products and services that are worth multiple times more to society than the amount that the entrepreneurs receive in return. The gap comes from knowledge spillovers, from knock-on and multiplier effects and of course from both income and other taxes paid not only by the tycoons but also emerging from the economic activity generated by their products and services. These entrepreneurs can be seen as the deserving rich, since society benefits very much more than they do. Even if, from an equality point of view, one might think they earn too much, it is still likely to be the case that if the deserving rich were driven away, society as a whole (and almost always the poorest in society) would be worse off as a result of their departure.

The 'undeserving rich' reflect a range of different sets of circumstances. Their income and wealth are a diversion from the rest of society from a sort of zero-sum game, and to the extent that they are well-off, other people are less so. Moreover their very actions, through abuse of monopoly or other power, tend to have negative knock-on economic effects which reduce growth. So not only do they 'steal' an excessively big slice of the cake, but their very actions make the total cake smaller than it otherwise would be. In reality it is a negative-sum game.

The chapter focuses on four particular areas where Type 1 Inequality from exploitation seems to have the most adverse consequences, creating different categories of 'undeserving rich'.

First is so-called crony capitalism (actually why capitalism gets blamed for something which has nothing to do with capitalism beats me – conspiracy theorists could conclude that it is an attempt by the left to abuse language to make surreptitious political points), where corrupt politicians and civil servants provide unfair privileges to their friends – this should really be called simple cronyism.

Second are the fat cat businessmen, who have been inflating their own salaries over the past 40 years in the real value of executive pay, especially in Anglo-Saxon economies.

Third are the overpaid bankers, where I argue that bad regulation (often set up by apparently left-wing politicians such as Gordon Brown and the Clintons) and market failure have led to overpay for bankers and the exploitation of consumers. I look specifically at one of the more successful teams of investment bankers, Goldman Sachs, to show how they have consistently broken laws all around the world to help them make money and how they have abused their links with politicians to protect themselves and (to some extent) do down their direct rivals.

Finally we also have a separate example of tech billionaires. In most cases these have certainly added to the wealth of nations and should not be treated as undeserving in the normal sense. But some have managed to do rather better from sustaining monopolies than would seem appropriate. Moreover, while it would be fair to say that in most cases the good they have done so far substantially outweighs the bad, the amount of damage they do (sometimes inadvertently) is growing.

### 'Crony capitalists'

The most glaring example of the undeserving rich are the classic protection racketeers who force local businesses to pay up under duress (see *The Godfather Part II* for a demonstration of how it works). The first-round effect of this is simply to transfer cash from businesses to the racketeers who prey on them. Oddly, the initial results may not actually be anti-egalitarian, depending on the relative wealth of the businessmen and the racketeers. But the second- and third-round effects are definitely anti-egalitarian. First, business development in the local area is reduced, reducing employment opportunities and ultimately pushing down wages. Second, local monopoly power is increased as the local (protected) businessmen push up prices. And often potential competition, which might encourage them to hold down prices, is scared off by the protection racketeers. So ultimately the least well-off in the local area suffer from a toxic package of lower wages, reduced employment opportunities and higher prices. Not a great result for them.

Less obvious, but in many cases more costly to society, are crony capitalists who amass wealth through backstairs deals with governments to sell them state assets on the cheap, give them lucrative mineral concessions at below market value, give them special tax or regulatory concessions, or in some other way allow them in effect to steal assets either from the public or from the rest of the private sector. To do this they generally need a climate where the rule of law is less than perfect. Also they tend to work hand in glove with corrupt civil servants or politicians. Some of the worst are politicians themselves.

The example about which I know a little, since I went to kindergarten with the person accused (his father's driver drove us there), is the case of the man who was Malaysian Prime Minister at the time when the book was being written, Najib Razak. He has since been voted out of office in an election despite doing what he could to ensure that he could stay in power.

According to the *Wall Street Journal*, global investigators believe more than $1 billion entered Najib Razak's personal bank accounts, much of it from the state investment fund 1MDB.[2] Both Najib Razak and 1MDB deny wrongdoing and the investment fund claims to be cooperating with investigations.

If the claims are true, essentially Najib Razak dipped his hand(s) into the till of the state investment fund intended for the pensions of the people of his country in order to enrich himself, and did so on an enormous scale. If the allegations are proved, what we are looking at is straightforward theft of a kind that makes the pension funds of ordinary people in Malaysia significantly worse off while enriching the former Prime Minister himself. It is hard to see any moral justification for this. I wrote before the election that as Malaysia is a democracy it would be relatively easy to stop it: Malaysians could stand up to the pressure from Najib Razak and his colleagues to keep voting for him and overturn him in an election. This has subsequently happened and the new government has launched various investigations and stopped the former Prime Minister from leaving the country though pictures have emerged of bags already packed, some stuffed with cash. This is a fast-moving situation and no doubt it will have developed further by the time this book is published. But the key point here is what has been illustrated by the election result. When there is democracy and the electorate have a choice, the most potent threat against corruption is the likelihood of loss of power by being voted out in an election.

But if the corrupt politician is too worried about the consequences of losing office to hold a free and fair election, the pressure for regime change has to happen either through internal pressure (and the Arab Spring shows how that might backfire) or through international pressure.

I think that rather than encourage violence on the streets, it is generally better for the international authorities to put economic pressure on the relevant individuals. Globalisation has greatly increased the impact of economic sanctions which do appear to build up considerable pressure on non-cooperating governments. International authorities can impose both financial sanctions and travel bans both on corrupt politicians and in relevant cases on their family and close associates to stop them travelling to their countries without first appearing in court to answer the charges of theft.

Probably the worst examples of crony capitalism concern some of the privatisations in Eastern Europe in the 1990s. What happened was described in detail by the well known economic adviser Jeffrey Sachs:[3]

> I believed that Russia's privatization should be quick but transparent and law-based. Care should be taken to prevent corruption. This was not done. The privatizers went ahead outside of transparency and the law. Corruption and insider dealing were rampant.
>
> I believed that the large natural resource companies should remain in state hands. This was to ensure that the Russian Government got the revenues from the production of metals, hydrocarbons, and other valuable commodities. This was not done. The natural resource sector was corruptly privatized, giving rise to the new oligarchy ...
>
> During my final trip to Moscow in early 1995, the infamous 'loans-for-shares' deal was just getting underway. This deal involved a massive and corrupt transfer of natural resource enterprises to the Government's cronies, disguised as a collateralized loan to the Russian Government by Russian banks. The arrangements were blatantly corrupt from the start. I spent my final visit in Moscow visiting Western officials to warn them about what was happening. I felt that my antennae were pretty sound at that point, and that my perspective would be helpful to head off a disaster. I was stunned by the obtuseness of the response, from the IMF, an OECD visiting mission, and later from very senior U.S. officials, including Larry Summers (both before and after working with the Clintons).
>
> Nobody wanted to look closely at the abuses, and certainly nobody wanted to blow the whistle. Most close observers believe that the hyper-corruption surrounding the massive giveaways of the oil and gas sectors was linked to the campaign financing for President Yeltsin's re-election. Tens of billions of dollars of natural resource assets were given away, and hundreds of millions were collected in return as campaign contributions. It was a pretty lousy and inefficient way to finance an election campaign, but such a linkage perhaps ex-

plains the remarkable reticence of the U.S. Government in responding
to this flagrant corruption – a level of corruption that easily outpaces
anything seen in other parts of the world in recent years.

The most quoted scholarly article on the subject is by Black, Kraakman
and Tarasova and describes the acquisition of the Russian oil company
Yukos:[4]

> Bank Menatep (controlled by kleptocrat Mikhail Khodorkovski) ac-
> quired Yukos, a major Russian oil holding company, in 1995. For
> 1996, Yukos' financial statements show revenue of $8.60 per barrel
> of oil – about $4 per barrel less than it should have been (This assumes
> that Yukos exported roughly 25% of its production, at world prices
> of around $18/barrel, and sold the balance at domestic prices of
> around $10.50/barrel).
>
> Khodorkovski skimmed over 30 cents per dollar of revenue
> while stiffing his workers on wages, defaulting on tax payments, de-
> stroying the value of minority shares in Yukos and its production sub-
> sidiaries, and not reinvesting in Yukos' oil fields. It's doubtful that
> running Yukos honestly could have earned Khodorkovski a fraction
> of what he earned by skimming revenue, let alone offshore and tax-
> free. He made a rational, privately value-maximizing choice. Even if
> running Yukos honestly was the best long-run strategy, Khodorkovski
> might have preferred present profit over future uncertainty. Besides,
> skimming was a business that he knew, while oil production was a
> tough business that he might fail in.

It is important to note that most of these reported abuses took place
under governments that preceded the present government, and President
Putin jailed Mikhail Khodorkovski for his involvement in Yukos.

Politicians who steal money from their country don't just impoverish
their people through the amount they steal but do so to a much greater
extent by discouraging savings, investment and enterprise. Other than
the minerals sector, the Russian economy has developed surprisingly
slowly since the end of communism, and corruption and crony capitalism
have almost certainly been the main inhibitors to inward investment.
Cebr and Global Construction Perspectives in their World Economic
League Table 2018 show the Russian economy falling from the world's
eighth largest in 2012 to the seventeenth largest in 2032.[5] And this at a

time when the economy ought to be diversifying and climbing up the league as it recovers from the ravages of Communism.

A good example has been the approach taken by the Russians to their biggest inward investor, the UK-based oil company BP. The current CEO of BP, Bob Dudley, headed the BP joint venture in Russia. In 2008, when he was CEO of TNK-BP, the joint venture between BP and a group of Russian billionaires:

> Dudley faced a stream of lawsuits and tax probes: administrative bullying, Russian style. He couldn't even get his work visa renewed.
>
> In July of that year, he fled Moscow, saying in a bitter statement that he'd suffered 'sustained harassment' by Russian authorities and his partners. He told the U.S. ambassador at the time that he thought then-Deputy Prime Minister Igor Sechin was behind the attacks, according to a U.S. embassy cable released by WikiLeaks.[6]

Not surprisingly, Russia has hugely underperformed in attracting inward investment and so is growing its economy much more slowly (indeed the latest data suggests decline) than the tiger economies in Eastern Europe, such as Poland and the Baltic states.

Although at low levels corruption may appear to oil the wheels of capitalism, it is difficult when corruption takes hold for it not to inhibit growth and in extreme cases bring economic growth to a halt. The consequences of underperforming economies mean that, especially when the corrupt have access to wealth from mineral exploitation, the poor suffer much more than the rich. So the poor in the country suffer a double burden; not only is their own potential wealth stolen from them, but they suffer the additional impoverishment resulting from slow or negative growth.

## Overpaid chief executives

The next group of 'undeserving rich' are overpaid senior corporate executives. Because what senior executives produce is a joint product with other employees and with investors, it is not easily possible to determine their individual marginal product. Because senior executives are the most visible to investors, it is tempting for the investors to offer mouthwatering incentives to these executives to try to ensure that they align their interests with those of the investors.

Again I have some relevant firsthand experience. When I was on the main board and on the remuneration committee of Marconi plc, we came under some criticism for the huge potential incentives that might be available to the senior management team.[7] I make no apology for my own actions since we created about £5 billion in added value for the investors, bondholders and especially the pension fund while I was on the board and indeed the shares of the company rose by £46 million on the day when it was announced that I was joining the board.

The value add that we created (much of which was transferred to the company pension fund) was more than 100 times the amount paid out in incentives because much more value was created than taken out by this board and senior management. The generous incentive scheme was in place when I joined the board and although in an ideal world the incentives would have been much less generous (I'm sure the behaviour would have been much the same even had the incentives been half or less), there was nothing to be gained (other than paying out much more in legal fees) from trying to unscramble the eggs. In the end only slightly less than half the potential payouts were in fact paid out. The bulk of the company was sold to Ericsson AG. The rump was sold to The Pension Corporation.

This experience showed me some of the flaws in the system.

Pay was based on the advice of remuneration consultants. Remuneration consultants showed the rates of remuneration in comparable businesses. Remuneration was typically composed of three parts – a base salary, a short-term incentive payment based on current-year performance (normally profits) and a long-term incentive payment, normally based on the change in share price.

It was standard to aim to be in the top quartile. But if everyone wants to be in the top quartile, it must inevitably lead to a continued ratcheting up of senior executive pay regardless of the circumstances. The system did not lend itself to careful calculation of the exact contribution made by the individuals. Actually the individuals concerned in the particular example of Marconi plc did a pretty good job in extremely difficult circumstances. They worked amazing hours and, even though they paid themselves well, they were extremely tough on other potential areas of potential executive reward such as perks.

Looking at the US, Figure 7 shows how CEO pay ratcheted up until 2002, though it fell back afterwards (and now is rising again). Pay trended downwards from 2002 to 2010 but has since risen again to new peaks.

Figure 7. CEO remuneration in the US (in millions of $)

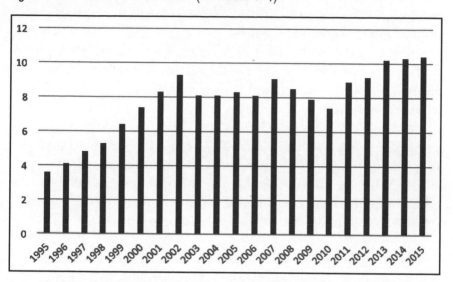

*Source: Equitar, CEO Pay Trends 2016. Sample includes CEO compensation of companies listed in the S&P 500 Index. CEO Compensation Data Spotlight David Lacker and Brian Tayan Stanford Graduate School of Business Corporate Governance Inititative.*

In theory it ought to be possible to pay CEOs less than the remuneration consultants recommend. In practice, however, the market works fairly inefficiently, and it is hard to have a reasonably happy CEO if you clearly pay him or her less than their peers.

Moreover, the number of people sufficiently well known to be credible for major corporate appointments is limited. Particularly in the US and the UK where the shares of major companies are traded on the markets and owned by financial institutions, these people have to be credible to external investors and therefore need to have some reputation. The Catch-22 is that the only way to obtain this reputation and the relevant experience is either to do the job or a job very close to the top job in a company. This limits the potential pool of talent to a rather smaller pool than those who probably would actually be capable of doing the job.

In addition, there is huge pressure on CEOs to accept high pay. They are not considered to be 'serious' unless they have negotiated very large packages for themselves. It is partly about bragging rights, partly a demonstration of their negotiating abilities. Also their own pay drives what they can pay subordinates; if they are paid a lot, they are able to compete for the best subordinates by paying them a lot. Executive pay is still a relatively small proportion of corporate income and expenditure and if top executives can demonstrate relatively small proportionate improvements in corporate results they can show to investors that their high remuneration is on balance justified.

However, there is bound to be a group of potential CEOs available who, if they knew how to present themselves, would be able to offer themselves at lower rates of pay.[8] For example, the leaders of the second-largest retailer in the US, Costco.[9]

Costco's CEO was paid $699,810 in 2015, plus a $188,800 bonus and stocks worth about $5,322,962 based on the company's performance. His predecessor, Jim Singegal, was paid even less – $325,000 a year in 2011. Mr Singegal was one of the founders of the firm and of course benefited from his shares and dividends, and he recruited Craig Jelinek, the current CEO, from within. To quote Bloomberg:[10]

> Costco has a $55-a-year membership fee and large warehouses stocked floor to ceiling and has grown 39 percent while its stock price has doubled since 2011. Despite the sagging economy and challenges to the industry, Costco paid its hourly workers an average of $20.89 an hour in 2013, not including overtime (vs. the minimum wage of $7.25 an hour). By comparison, Walmart said its average wage for full-time employees in the U.S. is $12.67 an hour, according to a letter it sent to activist Ralph Nader.

The Costco model seems to work, though it probably would have more difficulties had the company gone to the open market to recruit a CEO. The company lives frugally with posters decorating the wall rather than art, false wood tables at its headquarters and no PR staff. My own company, Cebr, has the same approach, using copies of the pre-race posters for the Monaco Grand Prix in the 1930s as wall decoration, purchased at €15 each (the frames cost more). Some of these are by artists that went on to achieve some distinction. The fun of Monaco Grand Prix posters is that by tradition the race poster has a representation of the previous year's winning car as the focal point of the picture.

In 2015 CNN Money named Craig Jelinek its CEO of the year:

> It was a terrible year for retail stocks. Nearly every major brick-and-mortar chain got bowled over by Amazon. But not Costco. Its stock rose more than 15% and is near its all-time high.

And those bargains! The low prices are what makes Costco Amazon-proof.

Costco continues to give its members huge deals for bulk items that make the $55 annual fee worth it. More than 90% of Costco shoppers renew their memberships.[11]

The fact that there are increasing examples of companies where the CEOs decline to be overpaid means that it might be time for a shareholders' revolt against overpaid CEOs. Indeed there are clear signs that this is happening in the UK, with evidence from Berkeley Homes, Reckitt Benckiser, Hiscox, Tesco, AstraZeneca, HSBC, Ocado, Anglo American, Foxtons, Paddy Power, Persimmon, BP and Smith & Nephew from 2015-17. There seems to be less evidence in the US, but trends like this tend to spread internationally.

Although it is possible for governments to try to legislate over boardroom pay, it is difficult to do so effectively without risking some damage to the corporate sector. The law tends to be extremely inflexible when applied to details of corporate management such as pay and often yields perverse results.

In my view it is better to encourage shareholders to act in what is, after all, their own interest to ensure that corporate earnings are received by the relevant investors rather than the boardroom fat cats. Once investors get used to this, they are unlikely to support main board directors who regularly allow overpaid executives. And in turn these directors will pass the pressure back down the line. The process of getting executive pay right is likely to take time, but a market-determined outcome will probably do much less damage to the economy and to growth and hence to the incomes of the poorest in the country than a heavy-handed approach from government.

### Bankers and others in the financial services sector

It is easy to treat bankers as the undeserving rich. An article in the *New York Times* in October 2013 was headlined 'Bankers have done more damage than Mobsters'.[12] This is an exaggeration. But it is interesting that the issue even has to be asked. Bankers' pay levels have created an atmosphere of antagonism to wealth creation and in that sense done serious damage to a system that is integral the functioning of the economy.

Why is pay in the financial services sector so high?[13]

Probably the best analogy is that of the waterfall. If you stand near a waterfall you get sprayed even though the water is not actually falling on you. When I drove my classic Aston Martin around the US in 2013 I visited the Canadian side of Niagara Falls (for the first time since 1968) and even covered with a cape got very wet from the spray. In the same way when there are large sums of money passing round you, very small percentages slipping into your hands can make you very rich. And often there is a temptation to use these small percentages to incentivise efficient and entrepreneurial activity.

Starting with traders, it is easy to quantify exactly how much a trader makes for their company. In addition decisions need to be made quickly and accurately. To do so it makes sense to attract the best talent. The work is hard, very high pressure and stressful. Of course the markets are essentially a zero-sum game in the first instance so there is no initial net gain to society, though the liquidity provided by markets has its own value in enabling businesses and financial instruments to have a value so that they can be collateralised.

Although individual markets are zero-sum games, the benefits to society from these markets reflect two factors:

(1) They generate a lot of tax revenue as spin-off.

(2) The liquidity they generate allows improved allocations of resources in the overall economy.

But the danger is that highly paid and over-incentivised staff distort corporate priorities and ethics and are encouraged to abuse market power and disobey laws.

Ultimately, as in an enormous casino, huge amounts of money get moved around in the financial markets (Forex markets, for example, trade $5.1 trillion per day according to the 2016 BIS triennial forex trading survey[14]). This is almost exactly 100 times larger than world cross-border trade (annual world trade in 2015 was $18.5 trillion). Not surprisingly, fractions of percentages leak out which translate into mind-bogglingly large salaries. The problem is not so much a classical market failure but more that management focuses on the bigger issues. If salaries are small in relation to potential earnings, minimising salaries tends not to be the focus of management attention.

The basis of the overpay in the financial services sector is a mixture of factors. For many years the convention in fund management was to pay approximately a 1% management fee. Only now, with yields bid right down, is this starting to change. But for much of the period from 1980 to 2010 fees tended to rise.

In the US, fees for active management have had an interesting history. Investment management was once considered a loss leader, but when pension funds first mushroomed as 'fringe benefits' during the post–Second World War wage-and-price freeze (itself evidence for the impact of the law of unintended consequences when governments get involved with trying to set pay), most major banks agreed to manage their assets for no explicit fee, given the then fixed-rate brokerage commissions that were at the time conventional.

In the 1960s, a few institutional brokerage firms had investment management units that charged full fees (usually 1%), but even then they normally offset those nominal fees entirely with brokerage commissions.

When the Morgan Bank took the lead in charging fees by announcing institutional fees of one-quarter of 1% in the late 1960s, they were expected to lose business but did not in fact do so to any significant extent. Then fees started to edge up on the basis that the right manager could provide enough additional yield to offset the fees. Even today, despite the logic that says that only a proportion of managers can 'beat the market', both individual and institutional investors typically expect their chosen managers to produce significantly above-market returns. Obviously it is absurd to expect that everyone should generate above-average yields.

But especially during the great bull market from the mid-70s to the early 2000s compound yields were double-digit (the S&P yielded 10.8% compound from 1973-2010, the FTSE yielded 15.7% from 1975-2002) and these easily offset management and other fees. Meanwhile, although inflation eroded these gains in the first few years of this market, the impact of the adjustment to a low inflation environment meant that interest rates fell, asset values rose and returns rose even as inflation was falling. Obviously this was going to come to an end eventually, but by an accident of history, the ultra low interest rates driven by the high Chinese savings ratio reemerged in the late 2000s and forced asset values up again at a time when all the other economic fundamentals would have been pushing them down. As a result the pressure to reduce fees from falling yields was partly short-circuited.

From 1980 to 2006, the financial services sector of the United States economy grew from 4.9% to 8.0% of GDP. A substantial share of that increase was generated from increases in the fees paid for asset management. Despite the economies of scale that should be realisable in the asset management business, the asset-weighted expense ratios charged to both individual and institutional investors actually rose over time during that period.

If we exclude index funds (an innovation that has made market returns available even to small investors at close to zero expense), fees have risen substantially as a percentage of assets managed. One could argue that the increase in fees charged by actively managed funds could prove to be socially useful, if it reflected increasing returns for investors from active management or if it was necessary to improve the efficiency of the market for investors who availed themselves of low-cost passive (index) funds. But neither of these arguments can be supported by the data.[16]

However, the world is moving on. High fines and falling fees are forcing attention on staff costs in a world of low yields. Meanwhile automation is making available a regulatory-compliant product at a fraction of the cost of staff who might easily not just be guilty of regulatory infractions but might cost financial institutions considerable amounts of their capital base in trading errors and fines.

Meanwhile, the persistence of low yields and low returns (in stark contrast to Piketty's belief that risk-free yields would comfortably exceed growth and hence allow the capitalists to accumulate wealth rising in relation to GDP) will eventually (when asset prices have priced in the likely persistence of low yields which is probably a position that either has been reached or will be soon) mean that the returns from investments in the market will be low. In these circumstances it is inevitable that there will be substantial downward pressure on fees.

Vanguard is now the second-largest asset management fund in the world. Set up and run by John Bogle, Vanguard runs $4 trillion of assets. Bogle was the first to set up a passive (index tracking) fund. But what is peculiar about Vanguard (who when they set up their first UK fund in May 2017 charging only a 0.3% management fee caused the share prices of the main competitors to drop by nearly 10%) is that the fund is a mutual and is owned by those whose assets it manages. Vanguard's costs are 12 basis points (0.12%).

Vanguard points out that even a modest 1% fee would mean that over 30 years – the typical life of a pension scheme – 22% of the assets would move from the fund owner to the manager, leaving the investor with only 78%.

Bogle points out that a disproportionate share of the gains in financial markets has benefited the asset manager compared with the investor:[17]

> The remarkable growth of mutual fund assets has served the owners of fund management companies bountifully, but it has bypassed the owners of mutual fund shares. All of the economies of scale in investing – and more – have benefited fund managers. None of these economies were shared by fund investors.
>
> Can that allegation really be true? Let's look at the record. During 1951, the year that I joined the industry, fund assets were $3 billion, the asset-weighted expense ratio was 63 basis points; and total expenses were $20 million ($187 million in today's dollars). As the industry grew, dominated by equity funds in those early years, the asset-weighted average expense ratio actually declined, to 55 basis points. But then the rise began. By 1980, equity fund expense ratios had risen 120% to 121 basis points, double the 1951 level.
>
> In 1980, equity fund assets were $44 billion. By 2016 these assets had soared to more than $8 trillion. Expense ratios of actively-managed funds had declined to 84 basis points, still 53% above the 1960 level. With the growth of lower-cost bond funds, the industry-wide asset-weighted expense ratio for long-term funds is now at 68 basis points, almost 25% above the 1960 level. With total fund assets averaging $17 trillion in 2016, fund advisory fees and operating expenses come to a total of $110 billion per year – 5,600 times the 1951 level of $20 million in an industry whose assets grew by 5,400 fold. Economies of scale for fund investors – zero.
>
> The industry's huge revenue growth has been a bonanza for the owners of fund managers. Just look at the returns on the stocks of publicly held fund managers. Over the past two decades alone, the shareholders of the three largest publicly-owned fund managers have enjoyed annual returns averaging 13%, almost double the annual return of 7.7% on the S&P 500 Index, a return earned by remarkably few mutual funds. Cumulative returns: fund managers +1167%, S&P +339%. More than triple. Wow!
>
> But the owners of mutual funds – those whose hope and trust have built this giant industry – are paying their active equity managers at a rate that has increased by 53% since 1960. Given those enormous increases in our industry's asset base, one can only wonder how this dichotomy could have taken place.[18]

In turn this downward pressure on fees will lead to downward pressure on pay which is broadly proportional to the corporate earnings in the sector.

In addition, as mentioned above, it is now possible to pursue an investment strategy of 'buying the market' or investing in indexed funds that are managed automatically and that enable investors to obtain virtually (minus a very small amount) the market yield. It is likely that such indexed or tracker funds will become dominant and will be available at very low fees. This will further ratchet down fee income and hence salaries and bonuses.

In many ways the hedge fund philosophy of charging high prices for asset management for what is claimed to be exceptional performance has been found wanting. The high prices were real but the exceptional performance was not.

This was proved by the results of a classic challenge to the hedge funds by the famous investor Warren Buffett. To quote from Investopedia:[19]

> In 2008, Warren Buffett issued a challenge to the hedge fund industry, which in his view charged exorbitant fees that the funds' performances couldn't justify. Protégé Partners LLC accepted, and the two parties placed a million-dollar bet.
>
> Buffett has won the bet, Ted Seides wrote in a Bloomberg op-ed in May. The Protégé co-founder, who left the fund in 2015, conceded defeat ahead of the contest's scheduled wrap-up on December 31, 2017, writing, 'for all intents and purposes, the game is over. I lost.'
>
> Buffett's ultimately successful contention was that, including fees, costs and expenses, an S&P 500 index fund would outperform a hand-picked portfolio of hedge funds over 10 years. The bet pit two basic investing philosophies against each other: passive and active investing.

It is noteworthy that in the UK (Edinburgh actually), Standard Life (now Aberdeen Standard Life) chairman Sir Gerry Grimstone (a former civil servant) has claimed that the pay structure of top executives working in the UK's financial services industry is 'too high'.[20] The statement came after more than a fifth of the company's shareholders voted against its 2015 remuneration report. Grimstone said that the voting trend sends out a message that pay structures have started to shrink and will continue to do so further. At the insurer's annual meeting – held for the first time in London on 4 May 2016 – 22.3% of its shareholders voted against pay deals for board executives.

It is likely therefore that the prediction here – that the trend has turned for pay in the financial services sector, will be supported as low yields and automation support the downward pressure. Whether pay will fall to the right level is not at all clear. But it will almost certainly fall significantly.

There is a separate issue about whether an investment management market of passive index tracking funds can really exist. Since the indices emerge from active trades it is arguable that passive funds with their low costs piggyback and are free riders on the back of the active fund managers.

My guess is that active managers will manage to get their fees down to points where there will be a market with some investors paying low fees for passive fund management and others paying more (but still a lot less than today) for active management. But one cannot guarantee that this will be a stable equilibrium.

## Goldman Sachs

The City of London used to be filled with so-called gentlemen whose 'word was their bond', though, having had reasonable access to the UK upper middle classes from public school through Oxford to a senior post at the CBI, I'm always cautious of the claims that 'gentlemen' do not break their word – there are plenty of counter-examples. History shows far too many 'gentlemen' stockbrokers who, even before the emergence of hedge funds, made good money on their private accounts and lost money for their clients while charging them for the privilege.

There is no doubt, however, that they were very aware of which forms of behaviour were acceptable and which might lay them open to social sanctions. After the big bang the market changed its nature. Outsiders entering the market, often from abroad, made social sanctions irrelevant. And because the sums involved were so large, some of the attitudes of putting clients' interests first became frayed.

The firm that has been most criticised for pursuing its own interest at the expense of its clients is Goldman Sachs. I set out the charge sheet below. But the problem with Goldman is not just the offences but also the combination of its aberrant behaviour with the use of political connections. The current Governors of the Bank of England and the European Central Bank are Goldman alumni. When Steven Mnuchkin was confirmed as President Trump's Treasury Secretary, three out of the past four US Treasury Secretaries had been Goldman alumni. Wikipedia has a two-page list of Goldman alumni in public positions around the world.

The latest Goldman alumnus to achieve high public office is Malcolm Turnbull, Prime Minister of Australia.

Goldman has developed a speciality in linking with centre-left politicians rather than simply confining their attentions to the Republicans and Conservatives who are normally closest to the financial services sector. In the US their links with the Clintons especially were subject to Wikileaks exposure, the results of which possibly derailed Hillary Clinton's bid for the White House.

In the UK, the former Labour Chancellor and Prime Minister Gordon Brown was very close to Goldman, with the Goldman economic adviser Gavyn Davies moonlighting for him while his wife ran Brown's office.[21] Goldman has also worked closely with the left-wing newspaper the *Financial Times*, which despite its fulminations against capitalist excesses has rarely drawn specific attention to Goldman Sachs despite that company's track record.

Yet the charge sheet against the company is a long one:

## Before the financial crisis

- Robert Freeman, head of arbitrage at Goldman, was implicated in an insider trading scandal and in 1989 pleaded guilty to one count of fraud.
- In the early 1990s, Goldman was investigated by Britain's Serious Fraud Office for its links with controversial media magnate Robert Maxwell.
- In 2002 it was fined $1.65 million by the industry regulatory body NASD (now FINRA) for failing to preserve e-mail communications.
- In 2003 it paid $110 million as its share of a global settlement by ten firms with federal, state and industry regulators concerning alleged conflicts of interest between their research and investment banking activities.
- That same year, it had to pay $9.3 million in fines and disgorgement of profits in connection with federal allegations that it failed to properly oversee a former employee who had been charged with insider trading and perjury.
- In 2004 Goldman was one of four firms each fined $5 million by NASD for rule violations relating to trading in high-yield corporate bonds; Goldman also had to make restitution payments of about $344,000.
- In 2005 the US Securities and Exchange Commission (SEC) announced that Goldman would pay a civil penalty of $40 million to resolve allegations that it violated rules relating to the allocation of stock to institutional customers in initial public offerings.

- That same year, it paid a fine of $125,000 to NASD for violating rules relating to the sale of restricted securities during initial public offerings. Shortly thereafter, it was fined $140,000 by NASD for late and/or inaccurate reporting of municipal securities transactions.
- In 2006 Goldman was one of 15 financial services companies that were fined a total of $13 million in connection with SEC charges that they violated rules relating to auction-rate securities. In another case relating to auction-rate securities brought by the New York State Attorney General, Goldman was fined $22.5 million in 2008.

## Goldman in the 2008 financial crisis

When the financial crisis erupted in 2008, Goldman Sachs and Morgan Stanley were forced by federal regulators to convert themselves into bank holding companies and become subject to oversight by the Federal Reserve Bank. But their main competitors were put into a much worse position – the purchase of Merrill Lynch and Bear Stearns by commercial banks (Bank of America and JPMorgan Chase, respectively) while Lehman Brothers was allowed to collapse. It is important to note that had this not happened both these businesses are quite likely to have gone into bankruptcy. Moreover, had Goldman Sachs not converted from a partnership in 1999, if they had gone bankrupt the 221 individual partners would have been liable.

Goldman also propped itself up by negotiating a deal in which Warren Buffett's Berkshire Hathaway invested $5 billion in the firm in exchange for a 10% stake. Buffett's holding took the form of preferred stock paying a generous 10% dividend. Goldman also received $16 billion from the federal government's Troubled Assets Relief Program (TARP) some of which was paid on to counterparties.

During this period, Goldman profited from subprime mortgages through its ownership of Litton Loan Servicing, which it sold in 2011 in the wake of numerous abuse allegations.

The forced restructuring of Wall Street took place largely under the direction of Treasury Secretary Hank Paulson, who left Goldman in 2006 to take the post at the request of President George W. Bush (having masterminded the conversion from a partnership to a limited liability bank).

Although Paulson was required to liquidate his Goldman holdings before moving to Treasury, his actions during the 2008 crisis were heavily criticised as working to the benefit of his former firm. Chief among these was the allegation that he allowed Lehman Brothers to collapse while taking pains to bail out insurance giant A.I.G., which had extensive dealings with Goldman and which used its federal support to pay off its obligations at 100 cents on the dollar. In the case of Goldman, this amounted to $12.9 billion.

The tendency of Paulson to recruit other Goldman alumni for his crisis team at the US Treasury prompted the nickname 'Government Sachs'. It later came out that Paulson was in frequent contact with Lloyd Blankfein, his successor at Goldman, during the height of the crisis.

During this difficult period, ProPublica and the *Los Angeles Times* put more pressure on Goldman by revealing that the firm had advised some of its big clients to place investment bets against California bonds right after collecting hefty fees from the state for underwriting some of those bonds.

Goldman chafed at the limitations on executive compensation that were part of TARP and successfully pushed for permission to repay the federal loan, while it and other banks continued to enjoy essentially interest-free borrowing from the Federal Reserve.

In May 2009 Goldman agreed to provide about $50 million in relief to holders of subprime mortgages in Massachusetts to remove itself from the state attorney general's investigation of abuses relating to the origination and securitisation of subprime loans.

Blankfein initially responded to the criticism by making the far-fetched claim that Goldman was doing 'God's work'. When that did not go over well, he issued an apology for the firm's mistakes and vowed to spend $500 million to help thousands of small businesses recover from the recession. That did little to rectify the situation. In the 10-K filing it issued in March 2010, Goldman added to the usual risk factors 'adverse publicity', which it said could 'adversely impact the morale and performance of our employees, which in turn could seriously harm our businesses and results of operations'.

## Goldman after the financial crisis

- In April 2010 the SEC accused Goldman of having committed securities fraud when it sold mortgage-related securities to investors without telling them that the investment vehicle, called Abacus, had been designed in consultation with hedge fund manager John Paulson (no relation to Hank Paulson), who chose securities he expected to decline in value and had shorted the portfolio. The Goldman product did indeed fall in value, causing institutional customers to lose more than $1 billion and Paulson to make a bundle. Paulson was not charged, but the SEC did name Fabrice Tourre, the Goldman vice president who helped create and sell the securities. (A federal jury later found him guilty of deceiving investors.)

- Goldman initially defended its actions and claimed that it lost money on Abacus, but a Senate subcommittee later released e-mail messages between Goldman executives discussing how they expected to make 'serious money' by shorting the housing market. The uproar continued as evidence emerged that Goldman had devised not one but a series of complex deals to profit from the collapse of the home mortgage values. A group of Goldman officials, including Tourre, appeared before that Senate subcommittee and were questioned for ten hours. A couple of months later, Goldman executives were grilled by the Financial Crisis Inquiry Committee, whose chairman Phil Angelides suggested that the firm had helped drive down mortgage securities prices in order to benefit from its short position.

- In July 2010 the SEC announced that Goldman would pay $550 million to settle the Abacus charges. That sum included a payment of $300 million to the US Treasury and a distribution of $250 million to investors who had suffered losses in the deal. The settlement also required Goldman to 'reform its business practices' but did not oblige the firm to admit to wrongdoing.

- The Abacus scandal also led to a £17.5 million fine imposed by Britain's Financial Services Authority and a federal investor lawsuit that is pending.

- In November 2010 FINRA fined Goldman $650,000 for failing to disclose that two of its registered representatives, including Fabrice Tourre, had been notified by the SEC that they were under investigation.

- In March 2011 the SEC announced that it was bringing insider trading charges against former Goldman director Rajat Gupta. He was accused of providing illegal tips, including one about Warren Buffet's $5 billion investment in Goldman in 2008, to hedge fund manager Raj Rajaratnam. (Gupta was later convicted and sentenced to two years in prison.)

- In September 2011 the Federal Housing Finance Agency sued Goldman and 16 other financial institutions for violations of federal securities law in the sale of mortgaged-backed securities to Fannie Mae and Freddie Mac. In August 2014 the agency announced that Goldman would pay $3.15 billion to settle its role in the case (through bond repurchases).

- In March 2012 the Commodities Futures Trading Commission announced that Goldman would pay $7 million to settle charges that it failed to diligently supervise trading accounts in the period from May 2007 to December 2009. Later that year, the CFTC fined Goldman $1.5 million for failing to properly supervise a trader who fabricated large positions to try to cover up losses.

- Also in March 2012 a Goldman executive director named Greg Smith published an op-ed in the *New York Times* announcing his departure from what he called a 'toxic and destructive' environment at the firm, saying he could 'no longer in good conscience identify with what it stands for'.
- In April 2012 the SEC and FINRA fined Goldman $22 million for failing to prevent its employees from passing illegal stock tips to major customers.
- In July 2012 a federal appeals court rejected an effort by Goldman to overturn a $20.5 million arbitrator's award to investors in the failed hedge fund Bayou Group who had accused Goldman of helping to perpetuate a Ponzi scheme.
- That same month, Goldman agreed to pay $26.6 million to settle a suit brought by the Public Employee's Retirement System of Mississippi accusing it of defrauding investors in a 2006 offering of mortgage-backed securities.
- In September 2012 the SEC charged Goldman and one of its former investment bankers with 'pay-to-play' violations involving undisclosed campaign contributions to then Massachusetts state treasurer Timothy Cahill while he was a candidate for governor. Goldman settled its charges by agreeing to pay $12.1 million in disgorgement and penalties.[22]
- Some good news for Goldman came in August 2012, when the Justice Department decided it would not proceed with a criminal investigation into the firm's actions during the financial crisis and the SEC dropped an investigation of the firm's role in a $1.3 billion subprime mortgage deal.
- In January 2013 the Federal Reserve announced that Goldman and Morgan Stanley would together pay $557 million to settle allegations of foreclosure abuses by their loan servicing operations (Goldman's share was $330 million).
- In March 2013 the Fed cited 'weaknesses' in Goldman's capital plan and ordered it to submit a new proposal.
- In December 2014 FINRA fined Goldman $5 million as part of a case against ten investment banks for allowing their stock analysts to solicit business and offer favourable research coverage in connection with a planned initial public offering of Toys R Us in 2010.
- In April 2016 the Justice Department announced that Goldman would

pay $5.06 billion to settle allegations relating to the sale of toxic securities between 2005 and 2007.

* In August 2016 the Federal Reserve imposed a $36.3 million penalty on Goldman in connection with a case involving a leak of confidential government information.

## Goldman and the Greek crisis

The euro crisis has been a major drag on the European economy in recent years. The Eurozone has grown at less than half the rate of growth of the world economy since the crisis started six years ago. And some parts of Southern Europe, including the weakest member, Greece, have faced catastrophic declines in GDP. Greek GDP has fallen by 26.5% since the crisis started in 2008. Yet, had it not been for Goldman Sachs, Greece would never have joined the euro. And yet their actions exacerbated the crisis once it emerged.

In 2001, Greece was looking for ways to disguise its mounting financial troubles. The Maastricht Treaty required all eurozone member states to show improvement in their public finances, but Greece was heading in the wrong direction. Then Goldman Sachs (led by the current CEO, Lloyd Blankfein) arranged a secret loan of 2.8 billion euros for Greece, disguised as an off-the-books 'cross-currency swap' – a complicated transaction in which Greece's foreign-currency debt was converted into a domestic-currency obligation using a fictitious market exchange rate.

As a result, about 2% of Greece's debt magically disappeared from its national accounts. Christoforos Sardelis, then head of Greece's Public Debt Management Agency, later described the deal to Bloomberg Business as 'a very sexy story between two sinners'.[23] For its services, Goldman received a pretty hefty payment of €600 million ($793 million), according to Spyros Papanicolaou, who took over from Sardelis in 2005. That came to about 12% of Goldman's revenue from its giant trading and principal-investments unit in 2001 – which posted record sales that year. The unit was run by Blankfein.

Then the deal turned sour. After the 9/11 attacks, bond yields plunged, resulting in a big loss for Greece because of the formula Goldman had used to compute the country's debt repayments under the swap. By 2005, Greece owed almost double what it had put into the deal, pushing its off-the-books debt from €2.8 billion to €5.1 billion. In 2005, the deal was restructured and that €5.1 billion in debt locked in. Perhaps not incidentally, Mario Draghi, now head of the European Central Bank and a major player in the current Greek drama, was then managing director of Goldman's international division.

Greece wasn't the only sinner. Until 2008, European Union accounting rules allowed member nations to manage their debt with so-called off-market rates in swaps, pushed by Goldman and other Wall Street banks. In the late 1990s, JPMorgan enabled Italy to hide its debt by swapping currency at a favourable exchange rate, thereby committing Italy to future payments that didn't appear on its national accounts as future liabilities.

But Greece was in the worst shape, and Goldman was the biggest enabler. Undoubtedly, Greece suffers from years of corruption and tax avoidance by its wealthy. But Goldman wasn't an innocent bystander: It padded its profits by leveraging Greece to the hilt – along with much of the rest of the global economy. Other Wall Street banks did the same. When the bubble burst, all that leveraging pulled the world economy to its knees and did even more damage to Greece.

Even with the global economy reeling from Wall Street's excesses, Goldman offered Greece another gimmick. In early November 2009, three months before the country's debt crisis became global news, a Goldman team proposed a financial instrument that would push the debt from Greece's healthcare system far into the future. This time, though, Greece didn't take the deal, partly because its finances were under much closer international scrutiny.[24]

The consequence has been far reaching. Greece has been mired in poverty since the crisis started. The number of people in work in Greece fell by a fifth from 4.6 million in 2009 to 3.5 million in 2015. GDP has declined since 2008 by 26.5% by 2014. While it is not possible to claim that some of these problems would not have emerged had the Goldman deal not allowed Greece to join the euro, they have been substantially exacerbated by the deal and euro membership.

It is hard to believe that a business that has been implicated in so many crimes as Goldman Sachs is still allowed to operate. Although it is not possible to prove the use of undue influence, it is hard not to suspect that conclusion.

Although many political parties have been involved, a peculiar speciality of Goldman has been to associate with left-of-centre politicians such as the Clintons in the US and the Tony Blair and Gordon Brown administration in the UK. Since most in the financial markets are ideologically right of centre, Goldman has been clever in spotting a market opportunity by associating with left-wing politicians ignored by other operators in the financial markets.

This has been in many ways the most shocking example of the abuse of position and power generating Type 1 Inequality. And possibly one of the most heinous aspects of it has been that Goldman has appeared to be aided and abetted by the types of left-of-centre politicians who rail against inequality in their speeches while encouraging it by their own actions.

My beef against this behaviour is twofold. First, I am shocked by the hypocrisy. But secondly I am worried by the way in which this behaviour undermines support for a capitalist system that has come close to performing miracles in reducing poverty. I believe that the behaviour of Goldman is cutting off the branch on which we all sit. And those who will ultimately suffer most will be those who have been brought out of poverty by the combination of capitalism and globalisation.

### How do you solve the problem of excess pay among bankers?

It is likely that eventually the markets will work. These days for many bankers the message on bonuses is 'Your bonus is not getting sacked'. Bonuses in London have collapsed from £12 billion in 2008 to around £4 billion today. Salaries have risen partly to compensate but by nothing like as much.

I don't believe that banking can really work without a culture of ethical behaviour. You leave your money in what you hope is a safe place and hope to get it back, having been ethically invested in the interim.

There is a point in the cult film *Leon* (1994) where Tony, the local Mafioso, tells Leon, the illiterate killer with a heart of gold, that leaving the money with him is much better than a bank (of course all the while he is arranging for Leon to be killed with no dependents so that he can steal the money):

> TONY: Hey, it's your money. I mean, I'm just holding it for you, like a bank. Except better than a bank, 'cause you know banks always get knocked off.
>
> No one knocks off old Tony.

I think it is fair to say that bankers are still better at looking after money than mobsters. But it is a sad reflection that the question has even to be asked.

When I was young local bankers were considered to be part of a quartet of professional people with accountants, lawyers and doctors.

What being a professional person meant was putting your client's interest above your own.

Sadly in modern times standards have slipped. I think most doctors at least in the UK still act professionally, though their governing bodies sometimes act like the worst kinds of trade unions and some of the abuse that these bodies and their representatives dish out to those whose research does not support some of their preferred positions is not consistent with professional behaviour.

Lawyers and more especially accountants are somewhere in the middle, some behaving ethically and some not.

But few would sensibly trust bankers to put their client's interests before their own, though ironically the evidence that people stay with banks longer than with their spouses suggests that a surprisingly large group do in fact give their banks substantial trust despite all the evidence that this is not deserved.

When I was a schoolboy I noticed that most of my classmates who went into banking were those who had been rejected by the military, the alternative destination for public school D streams. Since then I have been careful to keep my bank accounts in healthy overdraft. I really didn't see why I should risk my money with them. But oddly the D streamers made fairly good bankers – they played sports and often compensated for their intellectual weaknesses by becoming quite good judges of character, an attribute which is very much what you need in most forms of banking. In many ways they were very much better than their more computer literate and allegedly better educated successors.

But leaving your money to bankers requires long-term trust which is not really possible without being able to rely on ethical behaviour. While some forms of ethical behaviour can be enforced by regulation, there is some correlation between heavy enforcement and bad behaviour. Over-regulation of bankers can actually prevent ethical behaviour because people use the regulation as a crutch and as an alternative to making their own ethical decisions.

The return of UK banking supervision to the Bank of England in 2010 after Gordon Brown and Howard Davies's disastrous setting up of a separate Financial Services Authority in 1997 has been the first step in restoring confidence in the bankers in the UK. When the Bank of England did the job, fully grown-up men had sleepless nights in anticipation of the Bank's annual visit. When the FSA did the job, it became a box-ticking exercise and no one found them scary. But more still needs to be done.

The next step is to enforce a general duty of customer care for the financial services sector. There should be a flexible code of practice, regularly updated, spelling out what this means.

I would apply rough justice to banking supervision where boards whose staff are guilty of ethical violations or who have to be bailed out are penalised with lifetime bans from working in financial services.

I suspect that that might be sufficient, but Hephzi Pemberton, co-founder of Kea, a leading recruitment and remuneration consultancy for the financial services sector, argues that preventing highly incentivised salaries from leading to unethical behaviour means that the whole chain of command who have signed off on the bonuses have to have their career at risk when ethical problems emerge.

My current view is that is taking things too far, and I would start with the boards. Having served on a plc board, my experience suggests this would be sufficient. Board members tend to be older and tougher and near the end of their careers, and will work hard to ensure their careers don't end in disgrace (though their remuneration will have to rise substantially to make this work). They are the legal guardians of their companies who have both the power and the responsibility. But I could easily be wrong, and if acting with boards alone doesn't work then Ms Pemberton's approach is the next step.

Ultimately, however, the Bank of England has to be the ethical guardian of the financial services sector and has to build a climate where people don't dare to behave unethically.

## Tech billionaires

Many tech billionaires have greatly added to prosperity by generating new businesses and ways of doing things that have lowered costs and added to opportunities, many of which do not get properly measured in official statistics for either measurement or definitional reasons. But the economics of tech (see Chapter 11) means that there is a tendency towards monopoly which could in some cases permit exploitation.

An example of where inequality might appear to be caused by exploitation is Carlos Slim, from 2010 to 2013 the world's richest man, who made his money from having a near monopoly of the Mexican phone industry. In 2013, of his $50 billion fortune, it is estimated that $49 billion was from his shares in Telmex and America Movil.[25] His market share for Mexican fixed line telephony in 2014 was 80% and for mobile 70%. In March 2014 the Federal Institute of Telecommunications

(IFT), Mexico's then new autonomous regulatory body, declared Slim's companies 'preponderant' or market dominant, and Mr Slim started proceedings to sell off his holdings in the telecom sector.[26] The type of anti-monopoly policy common in most mature economies would have forced more competition on Mr Slim's phone companies, lower prices, lower profits and less wealth. The conspiracy theory might well explain how such anti-monopoly policies only started to be applied in his case relatively recently.[27]

In Chapter 13 we look more closely at how to handle competition policy in the tech sector, starting from the position that this is a particularly complicated issue.

## Conclusion

This chapter has looked at some areas where market failure or government policy has directly boosted inequality. This is the Type 1 Inequality from so-called exploitation. The areas contrast – the racketeering and corruption shown from the *Godfather* through the former Malaysian Prime Minister to the gangster economy in the initial stages of post-communist Russia show a very obvious type of exploitation. These need political action to be reversed.

The unnecessarily high levels of pay for top executives and for bankers seem to result mostly from the use of comparative yardsticks for measuring remuneration and from the fact that the absolute amounts are small in relation to the amounts changing hands. There is a reasonable hope that these might reverse themselves as shareholders become more activist, but it is early days yet. The operation of Goldman Sachs, which mixes political influence with activities that sometimes spill over into market rigging, is a mixture of both. My instinct would be to revoke their banking licence, though it may be difficult to find a good legal justification for doing so since the April 2016 settlement with the US Federal Government.

It is important to limit these excesses where political power is abused to increase inequality. As we will see in future chapters, there are enough forces promoting economic inequality from largely unavoidable global forces such as technology and globalisation not to have to add to it further from unnecessary government action and the abuse of political power. Hopefully, by casting a light on some of the examples, this chapter will help political forces to emerge that diminish this type of inequality.

## Chapter 10

# CLOGS TO CLOGS IN FIVE
# GENERATIONS – NOT THREE

## Introduction

THE DATA IN CHAPTER 5 ABOUT THE TRENDS IN INEQUALITY ESSENTIALLY updates the information contained in the Piketty and Milanovic books and elsewhere and assesses their conclusions critically. The conclusions in Chapter 5 relate to shares of the top 1 and 10% for income and wealth as well as the Gini coefficients. This chapter looks at a completely different issue – the stability of the positions for those with the highest levels of wealth.

After all, in a theoretically extreme case, if everyone had a chance of being rich for a period in their lives, it wouldn't matter so much if at any point in time there was a wide distribution of income and wealth. Because, a bit like a lottery where everyone won at some point, we would just wait until it was our turn to win. Of course in the real world it is clear that plenty of people are never going to be rich. But there is a difference between a situation where income (and more especially wealth) always goes to the same group of well-off people and one where the cast of well-off is constantly changing.

## Old sayings

Many cultures have their equivalent saying of the Lancashire saying 'Clogs to clogs in three generations', meaning that wealth rarely survives three generations.[1] Typically the first generation earns the wealth, the second generation benefits from it and the third generation squanders it.[2] In Japan the expression is 'Rice paddies to rice paddies in three generations.' The Scots say 'The father buys, the son builds, the grandchild sells, and his son begs.' In China, 'Wealth never survives three generations.'[3] The Americans say 'Shirtsleeve to shirtsleeve in three generations', attributing the phrase to Scots-born industrialist Andrew Carnegie.[4]

A US study by Merrill Lynch's private banking arm this year found that, in two out of three cases, family wealth did not outlive the generation following the one that created it. In 90% of cases, it was exhausted by the end of the third generation – illustrating the 'clogs to clogs' adage.

Knowing these sayings, economists have tended to assume that persistence of wealth has not been a major economic issue.

## The Bank of Italy study

But the economics world was taken by surprise when two economists from the Bank of Italy, Guglielmo Barone and Sauro Mocetti, managed to discover some newly digitalised tax data for Florence from 1427 that purported to show a remarkable continuity and persistence in family wealth for the city and surrounding area.

The study compared tax records for family dynasties (identified by surname) in Florence in 1427 and 2011. Its conclusion was unexpected: 'When regressing the pseudo-descendant's earnings on pseudo-ancestor's earnings, the results are surprising: the long-run earnings elasticity is positive, statistically significant, and equals about 0.04' (ancestors' earnings were estimated on the basis of occupation/skill groups). The descendant of a family at the 90th percentile of the earnings distribution instead of the 10th percentile in 1427 entails 'a 5% increase in earnings among current tax payers' (after adjusting for age and gender). The intergenerational real wealth elasticity is significant too and the magnitude of its implied effect is even larger: the 10th-90th exercise entails more than a 10% (in fact 12%) difference today.

Looking for non-linearities using transition matrices (a statistical test), they found some evidence of a glass floor that prevents the upper class from 'falling down the economic ladder ... for those originating from the lower class (in terms of earnings), there are fairly similar opportunities to belong to one of the three destination classes (categorized as lower, middle and upper). For those coming from the upper class, in contrast, the probability of falling down to the bottom of the economic ladder is relatively low.' A similar 'glass floor' was observed for the wealth transition matrix; moreover, in this case there also appears to be a 'sticky floor': more than two-fifths of descendants from the lower class remain there after centuries.

The results are fascinating, but of course difficult to replicate elsewhere. The homogeneity of Italian society over this period is unlikely to be repeated in many other places; the ability to identify people by name is also less easy in most other societies. It is important also not to exaggerate the conclusions – they show a statistically significant influence from the wealth of the ancestor, but the relationship is not a very strong one. Only about 4% of the earnings for those in the study are explained by their ancestry – and therefore 96% by other factors. Still, even the 4% is a surprise over such a long period.

Italy has been a remarkably static society, particularly compared with the Anglo-Saxon world. Much of the wealth has been in property, and property ownership in Italy has changed hands very much less than has been traditional in many other countries because of exceedingly high transactions charges.

## The St Louis Federal Reserve study

Since this study other central bank economists have applied themselves to the same issue (and indeed many had looked at the issue earlier as well). The St Louis Federal Reserve bank economists George-Levi Gayle and Andrés Hincapié looked at the Panel Study of Income Dynamics data from the US from 1968 to 2013.

The results are fascinating and seem plausible. First, it takes about five generations (about 125 years) in the US for the influence of your ancestry on your income to diminish to less than 5%. This compares with Florence where the Bank of Italy study suggests it took roughly 700 years.

The intergenerational elasticity of earnings in the US is 0.4% and that of wealth is 0.38%, meaning that a 10% difference in parents' incomes will lead to a 4% difference in offspring's incomes and a 10% difference in parents' wealth a 3.8% difference in offspring's wealth. Unfortunately the data on which this is based excludes those with zero or negative wealth who comprise about a fifth of households. So the authors of the study have also looked at the parents' and offspring's rank in the income and wealth distributions. These show surprisingly low correlations of 0.3 for wealth and 0.4 for income. They also show that earnings seem to be 33% more persistent than wealth – which supports the concept that education and human skills are more important than wealth per se and is relevant to the 'superbabies' concept described later in this chapter.

## The Sunday Times Rich List data

Partly because I had access to some valuable data on the rich both in the world economy and in more detail in the UK through my connections with the *Sunday Times*, we tested the academic conclusions against this real life data.

The Sunday Times Rich List is a list of the 1,000 wealthiest people in the UK and the 250 wealthiest people in Ireland prepared by the UK *Sunday Times* newspaper. In addition the paper collects data on the 50 wealthiest people in the world. The series has been in existence since the 1980s. The data is collected carefully by a team of investigative journalists who carefully research the wealth of each individual on the list.

We have examined this data very carefully to understand how the cast of the very wealthy changes over the years. In 2016 to enter the world's wealthiest 50 one needed a wealth of £12.6 billion; to be in the UK top 1,000 the entry level was £103 million, while to enter the Irish top 250 one needed wealth of £42 million.

For our analysis:

- The basic technique of the Florentine study is used – the earliest Sunday Times Rich List data is compared with the latest.
- Individual names are checked for origin and those in the most recent list for relationships with those in the older list.
- Where rich people have entered the UK from abroad, they have been allocated to a separate category.
- Income sources have been categorised, refining the *Sunday Times* categorisation.

The first analysis is of the global rich list. What it shows is that more than half (56%) of those in the global rich list in 2016 were not in (or were not descendants of those in) the 1999 global rich list. This is shown in Figure 8. So in less than one generation (about 25 years) more than half those in the global rich list drop out.

This compares with the top 50 for the UK (Figure 9) which shows that only 46% of those in the top 50 list in 2016 were not in the top 1000 in 1998. Moreover, of the 46%, 12% migrated to the UK during this period and so might possibly also have been on the list had they been in the country. Meanwhile, the bottom 50 of the top 1,000 show, as might be expected, that the majority are new entrants to the list between 1998 and 2016. Only 14% of the bottom 50 in the top 1,000 in 2016 were in the top 1,000 in 1998, though a further 8% had migrated to the UK during the period and might possibly have been on the list had they been in the UK.

Although the level of churn in the UK list is slightly less than that in the global list, it is still significant – nearly half in much less than one generation.

Figure 8. Entrenchment in the global rich list 2016 (top 50)

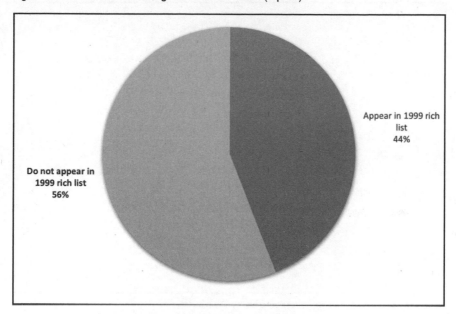

*Source: Cebr analysis of Sunday Times Rich List.*

Figure 9. Entrenchment in the UK rich list 2016 (top 50)

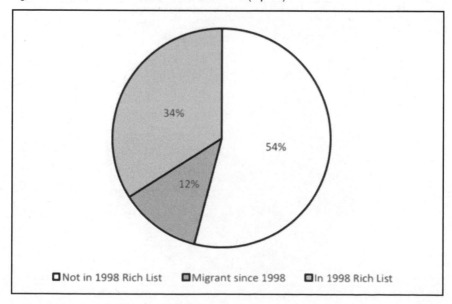

*Source: Cebr analysis of Sunday Times Rich List.*

Figure 10. Entrenchment in the UK rich list (top 1000)

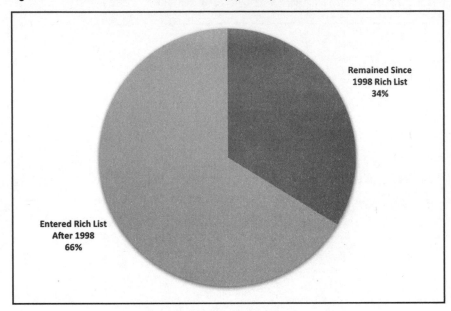

*Source: Cebr analysis of Sunday Times Rich List.*

Figure 11. Sources of wealth in the global rich list, 1999

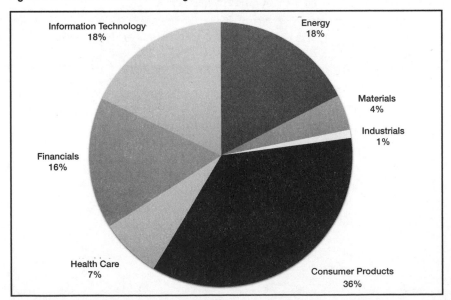

*Source: Cebr analysis of Sunday Times Rich List.*

Figure 12. Sources of wealth in the global rich list, 2016

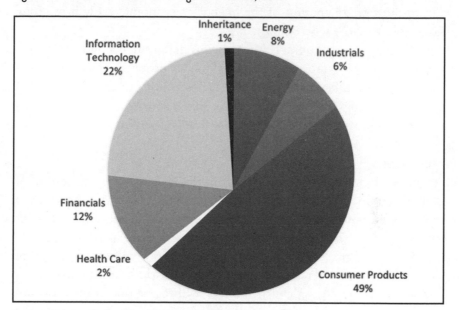

Source: Cebr analysis of Sunday Times Rich List.

Figure 10 shows the degree of entrenchment for the whole UK top 1,000 rich list, showing that only 34% of the people and families in the Rich List in 2016 were on the list in 1998. Although the top 1,000 are just a subset of the very richest people, this does support (though not prove) the conjecture that in a country like the UK, the very rich are a changing cast of people.

The next analysis, in Figures 11 and 12, shows the changing sources of wealth for the global top 50. It is interesting to see how the largest single category is consumer products in both 1999 and 2016. But the role of consumer products is significantly larger in 2016. Meanwhile the importance of oil and mining barons has reduced from 22% to 8%. Tech has grown as the main source of wealth for the global top 50 from 18% in 1999 to 22% in 2016. Both the last two results might be partly a function of the state of the cycle for the oil, commodities and tech sectors.

The equivalent analysis for the UK shows an extraordinary concentration of wealth on property. UK property prices have risen dramatically over the period, catalysed by tight planning regulation. This has almost certainly added to inequality and the data supports one of the themes of this book – that one of the causes of inequality in many countries is high and rising property values driven by tight planning regulations.

A causal analysis of wealth in Hong Kong shows a similar result – a disproportionate amount of the benefit of economic growth in Hong Kong goes to those who own the land.

All this analysis is important. It means that a surprisingly small proportion of wealth is inherited – a much greater proportion is created. Although it often takes more than one generation to create wealth, with the fortunes being made in e-businesses this is starting to change and increasing proportions of the rich list are first generation.

### 'Superbabies'[11]

I mentioned above that the results from the Federal Reserve Bank of St Louis indicate that generations pass on levels of earning more than wealth. One potential cause is homogamy which generates Type 4 Inequality. This is the tendency for people to seek out partners similar to themselves. Its prevalence has increased sharply with the growth of women going to university since the Second World War. As universities stopped being largely male institutions they became one of the most important places for people to meet their future partners. An article in the *Independent* reports on research on this in the US:[12] 'Dan Kopf of the blog, Priceonomics, analysed US Census data and found that the percentage of Americans who marry someone within their own major is actually fairly high.'

Moreover, 71% of college graduates in the US marry other college graduates.[13] And there are many studies showing how poverty and parenting can interact to make it extremely difficult for social mobility to emerge.[14] It is important to note here that pointing out that poverty and less good parenting are correlated is not to imply a moralistic view. Indeed, on any measure of results achieved in relation to resources available, the achievements of many parents in poverty can often be seen as not far short of miraculous. But they are frequently struggling against heavy odds. It is also important to note that this analysis is not meant to be an argument against women going to university; logically it could just as much be an argument against men going there.

One of the consequences of tertiary co-education is that men and women increasingly meet immediately after leaving home and hence partner people of similar background and education. So those with the highest IQ have partners with equally high IQ. The result is 'superbabies'. Quite apart from their genetic inheritance, they have parents with strong parenting skills. The combination entrenches a meritocracy and is hard to shake off, even though this book contains evidence that for-tunes tend eventually to dissipate through consumption running ahead of income for the inheritance generations. Even so, it still takes five gen-erations for a fortune largely to disappear! And with 'superbabies' this process may weaken.

It used to be thought that equality of opportunity would solve most problems of inequality. But even in a system where state provision tries to equalise opportunity, differences in opportunities for children emerge from the different parenting skills of the parents. Belsky in an oft-cited work shows how the expected differences in background affect parents' skills in bringing up children.[15] Shaw shows how differences in parenting skills affect how children develop.[16]

When my father went to Edinburgh University during the war, very few women went to university unless they planned to be teachers.[17] Even when I went to Oxford in 1969, Oxbridge undergraduate colleges were single sex and the number of women at my university was about a fifth of the number of men. Our amateur attempts to create de facto coedu-cation consisted of climbing over walls and through windows. But this has changed and at most universities in the UK now there are roughly equal numbers of women and men. The US (and most universities in the UK) were well ahead of Oxford and Cambridge as were many Continen-tal European universities.

Nowadays most universities worldwide, other than in some emerg-ing economies, coeducate women and men. Huber and Fieder comment: 'We find a very high prevalence of educational homogamy in all investi-gated countries irrespective of the women's education. In almost all cen-suses, peak sample sizes occurred in homogamous and minimum sample sizes in the most heterogamous mating patterns, particularly in the high-est and lowest educated women.'[18]

This is important because for those people who go to university, this is often their first time away from home and there is a considerable chance, given the ages at which they go to university, that they will meet their future partners there. One of the consequences is that the children of those at the best universities have two parents who are superbly equipped to bring them up. So apart from inheriting intelligence (the lat-est studies say that between 40% and 75% of intelligence is inherited[19]) their children benefit from highly competent parents as well. So they get the best nutrition, exercise, early schooling[20] and of course intelligent conversation at an early age.

We are creating a generation of 'superbabies' who are likely to hoover up many of the key opportunities. The only way to handle the increasing impact of this is to work hard at leaning into the wind to provide opportunities for those whose background is disadvantaged, especially in education. The best teachers need to go to the worst schools – though that is much easier to say than to make happen.

## Conclusions

The conclusions of both the St Louis Fed study and the Sunday Times Rich List study suggest that in Anglo-Saxon countries at least, wealth is transferred much faster than in Florence. The Fed study shows that after as few as five generations, the transmission of wealth is such that only 5% persists. So clogs to clogs does happen, only it takes five generations, not three.

Obviously part of this reflects inheritance taxation, yet in the US the tax exemption for inheritance tax at federal level is $5.45 million per person (so if assets are jointly owned the effective allowance could be $10.9 million) though in about half the states there are additional local estate or inheritance taxes. Note that these tax exemptions are for US citizens only – if you are foreign the limit is only $60,000 so if you are foreign and near the end of your life, the US is to be avoided. The rate of tax on more than roughly $1 million of taxable inheritance is 40%.

Most of the failure of wealth to persist, however, must reflect the fact that inherited wealth tends to discourage earnings and to encourage consumption. Clogs to clogs in three generations is surprisingly close to the truth.

But the more important part of the St Louis study is that incomes persist much longer than wealth. This is important because it tells us that the benefits of culture and education which get passed through generations are much more persistent than wealth itself.

The way in which the best educated create 'superbabies' with the best nutrition, education and parenting also emphasises the need to reform education so that the best teachers go to the schools with the most disadvantaged pupils.

# PART IV
## Fixing the Problem

THIS FINAL PART of the book looks at what can be done to reduce excess inequality and make Western societies more equal, while continuing to reduce poverty.

It starts with Chapter 11 'Elephants, camels and spitting cobras: what happens next?', an impressionistic projection into the future, drawing attention to the likely trends in inequality over the next quarter century. Obviously any such projection must be subject to huge margins of error – the fact that I have a reasonable forecasting track record before is no guarantee that these particular highly impressionistic forecasts are correct!

Whereas the rise in inequality in the West was attributed in Part III largely to the impact of globalisation and financial capitalism, with an element from Piketty-type exploitation, it looks as though the rise in inequality over the next quarter century is more likely to be caused by different phenomena: the impact of technology, the impact of 'superbabies' and the global power of the tech monopolies. It is hard to tell how much these will affect inequality. The first industrial revolution reduced the relative wages of manual employees, particularly those with skills. But since then technological advance has largely been associated with growth and better employment opportunities. It is all too easy to see which jobs will disappear from technology; much less easy to see which jobs will be created. So, even if it seems likely that technological progress will increase inequality, the scale of this effect is uncertain.

After the projection into the future, I look at various policy options.

First, education (Chapter 12 'Education, education, education – and education'). Without a more even spread of education there is little chance of stopping inequality rising. Even with a successful spread of good education to all groups, preventing an increase in inequality will be tough and will require a range of other measures.

Second (Chapter 13 'Saving capitalism from itself'), the excesses of capitalism need to be brought under control. I'm reasonably optimistic that the market will start to deal with many of the excesses of financial capitalism that have been so prevalent over the past 40 years, but it will be important to keep an eye on the extent to which this is happening.

I would like to see bankers and other professional advisers who act in an unprofessional way, putting their own interests ahead of those of their clients, suffer rather more severe sanctions than happens at present, with firms losing their operating licences and people being banned from doing business or, in serious cases, jailed. But the bigger task over the next quarter century looks likely to be dealing with crony capitalism, mainly in countries outside Western control, and dealing with the tech giants. The chapter looks at all of these issues separately. Improving the effectiveness of competition policy is likely to be crucial.

Third (Chapter 14 'Attacking the law of unintended consequences'), we need to deal with some of the results of the law of unintended consequences where government has intervened with (probably) benign intent to deal with one problem and has ended up creating other problems. The four main subjects are high consumption taxes, the impact of planning laws, the impact of rent controls and the impact of quantitative easing on asset prices. In each case government has increased inequality through its actions and suggestions for unwinding the policies are put forward.

Fourth (Chapter 15 'Making poorer people richer by cutting the cost of living') – and this is a bugbear from my time growing up in an emerging economy – I believe that we in the West and particularly in Europe have built up a high-cost lifestyle during the period when the world economy was making even relatively poor people in the West relatively rich by world standards. As pay globalises we are going to have to examine the components of the cost of living carefully. Three particular items which make up about two thirds of the cost of living of the poorest 10% in the US need to be looked at especially carefully – rents (impacted by planning policy and rent controls), food (impacted by agricultural policy) and mobile phones (impacted by licensed oligopolies). The section focusses on what can be done to bring down the cost of living in advanced economies including looking at the impact of indirect taxation.

The fifth solution (Chapter 16 'Can a universal basic income really work?') looks at the concept of a universal basic income. The economist John Kay argues strongly against such a concept, making two points – that to make it affordable would mean a very large cut in benefit levels while to protect income levels of beneficiaries would make such a scheme unaffordable.[1] Both points are clearly true at present. But looking forward to the world of a quarter of a century ahead, some of their force is likely to diminish, at least if my forecasts are roughly right.

Some may be surprised that I have not yet addressed the issue of taxation for distribution. This is addressed in Chapter 17. But although tax is part of the solution, both the UK and the US (though less so in the US since the Trump administration started to change tax rates) have fairly high top marginal rates of tax that will tend to limit the realistic possibilities of raising more income for redistribution from tax.

Chapter 18 ('Neither Trump nor Corbyn – rejecting false solutions') looks at what not to do. Populist movements on both sides of the Atlantic are queuing up to provide anti-capitalist and protectionist solutions as well as to restrict migration. There is a social case for limiting migration to a pace that a society can easily absorb but most of the economic analysis is strongly in favour of encouraging migration. To make migration more acceptable so that many of the indigenous workers don't feel that they are losing out from it, it needs to be properly supported.

I argue against this worshipping of false gods and the Canute-like belief that the tide of globalisation can be turned back. A country, even one as large as the US, that tries to cut itself off from the rest of the world will eventually risk suffering the fate of China, which lost relative power and strength from the 15th to the 20th century while it hid in isolation from the rest of the world.

The conclusion looks again at how to deal with my worst economic nightmare, which is that technology drives an underlying increase in inequality so severe that the palliative measures I have put forward pale into insignificance. My fear then is that the reaction to the increase in inequality might cause protectionist, anti-globalisation and anti-capitalist policies that would send Western economies into absolute decline and make people a lot poorer. I try to sketch out some suggestions as to what to do to prevent this happening.

## Chapter 11

# ELEPHANTS, CAMELS AND SPITTING COBRAS: WHAT HAPPENS NEXT?

F OR MY SINS, I HAVE A REPUTATION AS AN ECONOMIC FORECASTER. AND so this chapter looks at the future of inequality and of poverty over the next 25 years.

The most important feature that we are likely to see over this period is an enormous pace of change. We are at the cusp of 12 major technological changes that will revolutionise economies and turn many upside down.[1] I focus here on three of these changes because I've studied them in detail, though there is nothing in the others that suggests that they will have essentially different impacts economically.

Autonomous vehicles are about to transform transport. At this stage it looks as if the outcome will be something like the Uber model without the driver. This will remove large parts of the two main costs from car/taxi usage – the cost of car ownership and the cost of the driver. So the cost of personal transport could collapse, quite apart from the likelihood of cheaper renewable energy.

One imagines that autonomous vehicle technology will take off more quickly for freight and vans than for taxis, but eventually the changes must be dramatic. These will be especially important from 2030 onwards.[2]

The second change is robotics. This is transforming production. The combination of robotics and 3D printing means that factories can be decentralised and nearer to the customer. Adidas have already started the trend, opening new factories in Germany and the US 20 years after pulling out of both locations. Beefeater Gin is one of the world's best-selling gin brands. Only five people work on the production line in the heart of London that produces more than 25 million litres of gin a year and serves the entire worldwide market. This will ravage manufacturing jobs, especially in emerging economies.

The third is blockchain technology. This means that linked computers automatically maintain records and cross-check everything, rejecting any data which is flawed. Once participants can be assured that no suspect transaction has taken place, commerce can take place in real time and you no longer need armies of professionals in the middle following up and checking before anything can proceed.[3]

Management consultants McKinsey have said that one company in five is using a business model that will fail in the next five years. The speeding up of corporate lifespans has already been happening for some time: 'The average lifespan of a company listed in the S&P 500 index of leading US companies has decreased by more than 50 years in the last century, from 67 years in the 1920s to just 15 years today, according to Professor Richard Foster from Yale University.'[4] And from the UK fewer than 10% of the companies in the original FTSE100 list from 1984 remain in the list today (although some are parts of other companies in the present list). As the brilliant economic commentator Anthony Hilton says: 'Think about it: 90 per cent of our biggest companies have gone within a generation.'[5]

Moreover the IT changes that I have pointed out are probably just the tip of an iceberg. And as my previous book, *The Flat White Economy*, showed, many of the existing technologies currently in use are far from maturity. One would have to be both arrogant and stupid to think that one can foresee the future in detail given this.

But it would be equally stupid not to think about what might happen and at least speculate about likely future changes. The key thing is to have the humility to accept that one might easily be wrong and to keep looking out for signs that one has made a misjudgement.

The latest data shows that in most countries the peak in inequality has temporarily passed, other than the continued growth in income of the very rich. Even the number of dollar billionaires plateaued in 2016. The 'perfect storm' of inequality being caused by technology, globalisation and exploitation looks to have blown itself out a bit as bankers' pay falls and the stock market starts to rein in CEOs' pay. This phenomenon could well continue for the better part of a decade or more.

Looking at countries from 2008 to 2018 on Cebr's World Economic League Table, China is forecast to have a doubling in GDP; India's GDP is forecast to grow by roughly the same amount.

Figure 13. The camel graph 2008-18 compared with the elephant graph 1988-2008

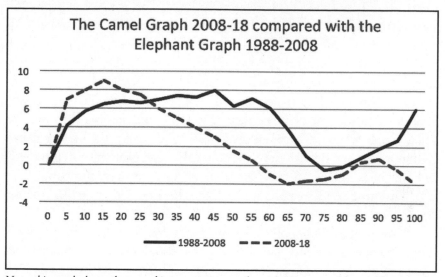

Note: *this graph shows the annual increase in income for each 5% group of the world income distribution starting from the lowest point.*

Data source: *Milanovic, op. cit., for 1988-2008 scaled into line with real income growth for the relevant period; Cebr World Economic League Table 2008-18; details of the calculation in the text.*

Because the income data for 2008-18 does not exist, I have constructed an impressionistic series based on three assumptions. I have used the country GDP forecasts and estimates to produce a first round estimate, using GDP as a proxy. The GDP growth has been adjusted to take account of the differential growth of incomes from GDP for the ten main economies and this ratio has been proxied for the other economies. For these ten main economies I have then made assessments of the distributional changes using the data available. Again I've assumed that countries in similar income categories have had similar changes. It is all very rough and ready and I would not call this particular exercise scientific, but it suggests what appears to be happening now; which is much the same as Milanovic calculated for 1988-2008 but the shape of the graph is more like a camel (technically a dromedary since it only has one hump) than an elephant. I have scaled the data to allow for the different periods involved to try to make the shapes more comparable with each other. This is a fairly messy and impressionistic exercise and I would be happy to defer to someone with the time to concentrate on replicating the work with greater accuracy!

The real difference between the two periods is that whereas inequality increased within countries until 2008 even when it was falling between countries, in the post-2008 period inequality has generally been falling within countries as well as between countries. This is because of the impact of the financial crisis on the pay of top executives and bankers, although pay of senior entrepreneurs in emerging markets has burgeoned.

The peak of the income growth is lower down the distribution as lower middle income economies like China have slowed down while poor countries like Bangladesh have accelerated. The trough of the income growth slips down as the worst-off people in Western economies (who are still the main people who suffer from globalisation) slide down the income distribution scale). And the richest two groups (although probably not the super-rich) fell back because of the collapse in bankers' pay over this period.

This produces an elephant graph that looks much more like a camel or a dromedary.

However, at some point it seems likely that this fall in inequality is likely to come to an end. This is because technology is just about to become the driving force in causing inequality. With my background as IBM Chief Economist (in the UK) I've been worrying about this for about 30 years, and one of my Gresham lectures explicitly focussed on the problem.[6] More recently the sadly deceased Sir Anthony Atkinson's last book, *Inequality: What Can be Done?*, makes the point that (quoting research driven by David Autor and his colleagues[7]): 'by allowing technological change to affect differentially not only different tasks but also the capacity of workers of different skills to undertake these tasks and the productivity of capital in these tasks, they argue that there has been a displacement of medium skill workers by machines in the conduct of routine or codifiable tasks.'[8] But that part of the increase in inequality that is driven by technology is likely to continue to grow – probably much faster than hitherto – unless the nature of technological progress changes.

So far we have seen just the tip of the impact of technology on inequality. The so-called fourth industrial revolution is likely to have effects completely different from the past three. The first three industrial revolutions were characterised by three factors:

(1) Although labour was replaced by machines, since labour was used to build the machines the net direct impact on demand for labour was partly cancelled out. Now in the fourth industrial revolution, machines will largely be built by other machines.

(2) Past changes happened incrementally. Now that the cost of robots has dropped below the tipping point of around $15K, change is hap-

pening on an almost vertical curve. Even in China it is now economic to replace human labour with robots, much more so in countries with higher wages. The result is that this change is likely to be much more violent and disruptive than previous changes.

(3) The marginal product of labour in previous industrial revolutions was well above subsistence level or the benefit level or the minimum wage if it even existed. So even if it was pressed down temporarily (e.g. the impact of the first industrial revolution in the UK), it didn't make work uneconomic.

Now, as a result of the past downward pressure in many countries, the marginal product is already quite close to the floor for wages. If the increased short-term pressure from technology pushes the marginal product to a level close to or below the minimum wage or the effective minimum wage set by the level at which benefits are paid, it is likely that, rather than simply leading to greater inequality as did past technological changes, the latest changes will lead to actual loss of jobs.

Although in the very long term jobs will probably reappear provided labour markets are flexible, because of hysteresis (the tendency for skills and abilities to atrophy when people are out of work for a sustained period) it could take a long time for this to happen.

And of course in many countries labour markets are not flexible, with minimum wages or benefit levels set too high, and this could mean that people escape from the labour market completely. If they do so, there is some evidence that it is very hard to bring them back in. 'A recent national analysis by the Oregon Office of Economic Analysis found that the long-term unemployed are around twice as likely to drop out of the labour force as to find a job'.

Because of this it is likely that unless welfare and minimum wage regulations are reformed, technology could lead to a substantial redistribution of income to the already well-off groups.

It is of course worth noting that not all the jobs disappearing as a result of technology are low skilled. Many relatively highly paid jobs in finance and professional services (perhaps even economists!) are also at risk.

The graph shown in Figure 14 for 2018-40 gives an impression of what might happen – some of the laggards in globalisation (in countries in Africa and parts of Asia especially) still catching up and helping the incomes of the poor to do better than average, the bulk of people who currently have relatively low-skill jobs in Asia, Europe and the US finding that their real incomes go down, while the richest 25% do even better as they reap the benefits of technology.

The elephant, having transformed into a feeding camel, transforms again into a striking cobra.

But of course we really do not know exactly how technology will drive inequality. And it is not certain (the purpose of making many forecasts is to prevent them coming true – if you predict that something unpleasant will happen it makes sense to try to take steps to avert the predicted result even if it means that your forecast will be disproved).

Figure 15 shows different possible cobra graphs for the changes in income for different income groups over the period to 2040. One supposes that technology has an impact on equality on about the same scale as the industrial revolution; the other that the impact is roughly twice as strong.

The policy implications of the different trends are considerable. If the underlying trend is that suggested by the more moderate change (which seems more likely but is by no means certain), it ought to be possible to contain some of the most damaging impacts of rising inequality by the policies set out in this section. But if the underlying trend is more dramatic, as suggested in the cobra graph with the faster growth in inequality, then there is likely to be a requirement for a much more radical approach. I discuss this in the final chapter of the book.

The huge reduction in extreme poverty from the 1980s and the concomitant improvement in so many other indicators such as infant mortality, deaths from malnutrition and life expectancy came largely as a result of economic development.

It is important to note that aid and charity did little to assist the reduction in poverty over this period, though both had a substantial role in causing some of the worst aspects of ill health to diminish. As pointed out before, this book's title, 'The Inequality Paradox', comes from the fact that the period of most rapid growth in inequality in the wealthy economies coincided with the period of most rapid decline in poverty in poor countries. Rises in inequality and in poverty don't go together.

The reason that aid and charity played a lesser role in reducing extreme poverty in the recent past is that in the 1980s most of the extreme poverty that existed at the time largely reflected lack of economic development. Even now there is some continuing poverty from this source and it is likely that the development of countries in Africa and Asia in the coming years will reduce this poverty to low levels. But lack of development is not the main source of extreme poverty today.

Figure 14. The cobra graph 2018-40 compared with the elephant graph 1988-2008 and the camel graph 2008-18

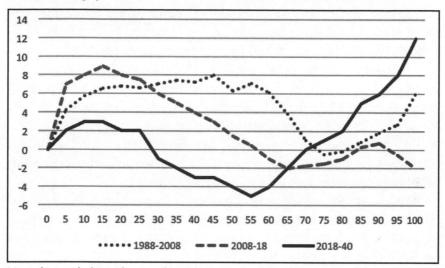

Note: *this graph shows the annual increase in income for each 5% group of the world income distribution starting from the lowest point. Data source: Cebr World Economic League Table, details of the calculation in the text.*

Figure 15. Different potential cobra graphs for 2018-40

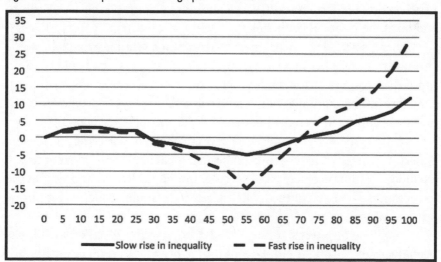

Note: *this graph shows the annual increase in income for each 5% group of the world income distribution starting from the lowest point. Data source: Cebr World Economic League Table, details of the calculation in the text.*

Every year my consultancy Cebr produces a World Economic League Table showing how GDP throughout the world is changing and is predicted to change. The 2018 edition produced in conjunction with the construction consultancy Global Construction Perspectives (GCP Global) shows which are the poorest countries in the world.[10]

Bangladesh is one of the poorest of larger economies and it is expected to be particularly fast growing in the coming years. The 2018 World Economic League Table predicts the GDP growth rate to average 7.0% from 2017-32. During that period it is predicted to rise from the world's 43rd largest economy to the 31st largest.

What the analysis shows is that there is a correlation between a current level of poverty and a forecast of rapid growth.

Of the absolute poverty that still exists, about half is in a range of 22 poor countries.[11] The good news is that most of them are now forecast in the World Economic League Table to be either already growing fast or about to start to do so.

Those countries where growth is forecast to remain low largely are predicted to be affected by problems of governmental failure or by conflict. Clearly the problems of poverty resulting from these countries is a function of a more complicated problem than simply lack of the appropriate economic structure. It would be unrealistic to expect poverty to end until the political problems are fixed.

There is a separate problem of poverty for excluded groups (in some cases self-excluded). Alleviating poverty for these groups is likely to require direct intervention to deal with the root causes of the problems. One interesting example which is attracting particular attention is the Icelandic approach to reducing drug taking amongst teenagers.[12]

In Chapter 4 we saw how social cohesion is suffering in 'middle America' where white working-class men in particular are starting to feel excluded, leading to increasing suicide, opioid addiction and falling life expectancy. The issue of inequality needs to be understood as not purely a financial problem.

This type of poverty, of excluded groups in the Western world, has been on an increasing trend. Demographic pressures could intensify this. So unless social policy and welfare policy can reverse the trend it is likely that this problem will increase.

## The impact of technology on market structure and inequality

Earlier in the book I described how one of the world's richest men, Carlos Slim, made his money from his position as the owner of the mobile phone network in Mexico.

One of the increasing problems caused by technology is its tendency – unless public policy is designed to prevent it – to monopolise its sectors. Examples such as Intel, Microsoft, Apple, Google and Amazon abound.

I first developed the underlying economics when I worked for IBM (not that the company was particularly pleased with my analysis since it was frightened that this could be used against the company in antitrust cases – I riposted by pointing out that the era of IBM being a major antitrust target was now history and that the latest IBM profits results in the late 1980s hardly pointed to monopolistic profits).

The analysis shows that one of the most crucial economic factors in the success of the digital economy is huge economies of scale – what I call 'supereconomies of scale'. The concept of economies of scale developed at the beginning of the industrial era. The concept is mentioned in Adam Smith's *Wealth of Nations*, where he points to economies of scale resulting from the division of labour. The concept has typically been associated with the intensive use of machinery, whereby long production runs of a commodity reduce the unit cost of producing that commodity.

But in the information era, where the product is not a physical one, the achievable economies of scale are much greater. The underlying economics of information were described in Nobel Prize-winner George Stigler's seminal article in 1961.[13] Typically an item of information is expensive to research and develop but can be replicated through dissemination at virtually zero cost. To give one example from my book *The Flat White Economy*, it is widely believed that the 1990s version of Microsoft Windows (3.0) cost about $550 million to develop. But to create an extra licence cost only a small administration, packaging and copying fee of a dollar or two at most.

At the time an operating system like Windows typically sold for about $70. So had Bill Gates only sold a million licences, he would have been sitting on a big loss – of nearly $500 million. But he didn't, of course: he sold about 10 million licences in the two years before Windows 3.1 was released and ended up with a substantial profit that changed the future of his company. By the time of Windows 7 and Windows 8 the typical first two years' sales of a Windows version were about 200 million licences.

So it is important that for the digital economy, sales on a huge scale are necessary to amortise research costs – even sales of as much as a million, which would be a signal of success for many products – would be unprofitable. This means that companies tend to delay the investment until they are certain of two factors working in their favour: firstly, that sales will be on a sufficient scale to enable them to make a profit; and secondly, that there will not be so much competition that they will be forced into a price war. This takes time (although sometimes the desire to keep ahead of competition will encourage companies to bring forward innovations). In my experience, supereconomies of scale have tended to mean that large changes tend to be delayed while incremental improvements tend to be accelerated to keep ahead of competition and generate product differentiation.

The other economic factor that affected the timing with which the digital economy bore fruit is its sensitivity to network effects. Network effects are a phenomenon common to communications systems. Essentially, the value of a network to an individual participant in that network increases with the number of participants in it. So a single telephone is of no use on its own – it gains some value only when there is a second phone (one often wonders who bought the first phone!) – and the value increases with the number of other phone users with whom one can be connected.

And as the value of each phone increases, the more phones tend to become available to contact on the network, until there are so many other connections that the value of an additional connection is negligible. Network effects were first developed as a concept by the President of Bell Telephones in making his case for a monopoly in 1908, but the ideas were developed and refined in the 1980s and 1990s. Robert Metcalfe, one of the co-inventors of the Ethernet, was the progenitor of Metcalfe's Law – that the value of a communications network varied with the square of the number of connections in the network. This idea was vigorously promoted by the economic guru George Gilder during the 1990s.[14]

The Nobel prize-winning economist Sir John Hicks (one of the all-time economics greats) warned in 1939 that increasing returns would lead to 'the wreckage of the greater part of economic theory'.[15] In fact it is not quite as bad as all that and modern mathematical techniques can now rescue much of economics from this fate.

Where there are network effects, investment typically doesn't take place until there is a critical mass of potential users. Network effects tend to cause investment to be held back in a similar fashion to super-economies of scale, although in the case of the latter, the tendency to delay investment is moderated by the possibility of gaining first-mover advantage. It was the combination of supereconomies of scale and network effects that meant that the economic exploitation of the digital technologies took place on a different, tardier timetable than that which had been predicted by those who understood only the technological issues.

But there is a problem with pricing under both network effects and supereconomies of scale. The problem comes from the established economic theorem that with competition the tendency is for prices to be reduced to the marginal cost of production. Now this works fine if the marginal cost is above the average cost of production, since producers can still make a profit. But with both network effects and supereconomies of scale the marginal cost is well below the average cost. So production would be at a loss in conditions of competition. That is why it is difficult to achieve competition in such industries.

One of the consequences in the real world is the persistence of monopoly in technology industries, including the examples cited above. There tends to be a battle between innovation which makes the monopolies obsolete and the market power of the incumbent which tends to reinforce monopoly.

Since many of the world's richest people have fortunes based on monopolies, it is important to prevent monopolistic excesses which reinforce inequality, and to police anti-monopoly policy carefully.

Monopolies boost inequality in a number of ways. First, wealth and income are concentrated among a small group who can gain extreme wealth from their monopolistic control of key elements of technology. Second, there is a tendency for the potential beneficiaries from this in areas where the rule of law is weak to abuse their wealth to secure political favours to support the continuation and protection of their monopolies. Third, the monopolistic power enables them to ramp up prices in such a way to affect adversely the costs of living of the poorest groups and hence their standards of living. The analysis in Chapter 15 shows that the poorest groups spend proportionately most on mobile phones (a full 7% of the income of the poorest decile in the US – more than a third as much as they spend on food!) and this is one of the areas most subject to monopolistic pressure in emerging economies.

I am assuming and proposing that going forward, there will have to be very much more emphasis on anti-monopoly policies to prevent exploitation than there has been in the past. If not then it is likely that there will be an even greater growth in inequality as a result of technology than might otherwise be predicted.

Besides technology, the other factor that is likely to come to the fore in pushing levels of inequality in the future is homogamy, the tendency for people to marry people of similar background. This reinforces the continuation of privilege through the generations as was explained in Chapter 10.

In the Western world, the proportions at university (which probably are the most important causes of homogamy) have probably matured and will only rise marginally if at all. But the effects of generations of meritocracy on entrenching both poorer cohorts across the generations and also the richer cohorts could build up over time.

Meanwhile in emerging economies it is far more likely that there will be continued growth in homogamy producing even more 'superbabies'. The stories of the 'tiger mothers' from East Asia are well documented examples.[18]

## Conclusion

Looking forward, the most likely conclusion is that the forces driving inequality will change. Overpaid bankers and globalisation will diminish in importance while technological inequality and 'superbabies' will take their place.

With technology's inherent tendency towards monopoly, it is clear that anti-monopoly policy will become increasingly important as we try to prevent the technology giants from unduly exploiting us. And we will have to try even harder to concentrate educational resources on those with the least privileged background.

## Chapter 12

# EDUCATION, EDUCATION, EDUCATION – AND EDUCATION

WHEN FIRST RUNNING TO BE PRIME MINISTER IN 1997, UK PRIME Minister Tony Blair described his top three priorities as 'Education, education and education'.[1] Rightly so.

I was once asked by a potential leadership contender for the UK Conservative Party who had justifiable hopes of becoming Prime Minister what priorities he should have and I said much the same thing – that the most important thing that government could do to make life better was to focus on education. Academic studies, particularly those by the St Louis Federal Reserve Bank, show that improving education is likely to do far more to reduce inequality than tax or other policies. 'This evidence suggests that policies aimed at human capital enhancement, e.g., free pre-school for everyone, may be as effective at combating inequality as those aimed at limiting the advantage of the wealthy, e.g., a policy of a high inheritance tax.'[2]

Earlier in this book, in Chapter 2, I showed how the spread of universal education was responsible for Scotland's leading role in inventing much of the 20th-century world. This also helped create a relatively homogeneous and increasingly equal society in urban areas in much of Scotland in the 19th and early 20th century (though rural areas remained rather less so).

The most important way in which inequality can be reduced is to improve the skills of the less well-off. There is a substantial body of economic research which demonstrates that not only inequality but overall economic prosperity and growth are both enhanced most by educational policies that improve the skills of the least well-off in societies.[3] Almost certainly in both the US and the UK the greatest scope for increasing productivity is by making the least advantaged better skilled and more productive, so this would be a win-win, both reducing inequality and also increasing productivity and the overall size of the economy.

Wikiprogress, a website set up by the OECD, puts much focus on education. The reason that education is a vital part of any social cohesion agenda is because educational outcomes affect all the many dimensions of the social cohesion triangle. When opportunities for quality education are possible across the whole of the population, schooling becomes a strong leveller of opportunities, bringing prospects for upward mobility even to disadvantaged groups. Increasing educational attainment is an important way for converging countries to reduce inequality in market incomes in the long run, particularly as returns to education change as a consequence of shifting wealth.

The OECD analysis puts much stress on publicly provided education for a mix of reasons. First, good educational opportunities mean that the prospects of social mobility are maximised. Given the concerns about 'superbabies' and the combination of genetically endowed and well parented offspring of the meritocratic elite, it is vitally important for any society that it provides the highest quality education for those least well endowed with economic or educational benefits from birth.

This in turn helps raise productivity. Many Anglo Saxon countries seem to offer little hope and encourage little advancement to their more deprived communities. More hope would boost cohesion but would also increase participation and encourage better use to be made of those opportunities that already exist. There is scope to reduce inequalities of outcome by better educating those with the worst start in life. Also, the greatest scope for raising productivity in countries like the UK and the US is from raising the attainment of those who are most likely to be left behind.

There are longer-term benefits as well. Improving the quality of education normally helps reduce malnutrition and the diseases associated with it like iron and iodine deficiencies which stunt growth and brain development and reduce brain damage from substance abuse. Also female education tends to have a multiplier effect in improving cohesion since better educated mothers tend to pass on the benefits to their children.

So by far the simplest way of reducing inequality is to invest in the education and skill development of the least well-off. Of course this will take time to show its economic benefits. But, provided that the investments in improving education and particularly that of the least well-off aren't wasted, it is by far the surest way of reducing inequality.

The potential increased importance worldwide of Type 4 Inequality from homogamy makes this even more important since schooling is the only way to counteract the unfair advantages of good parenting from the meritocrats. This could be crucial in the future.

Of course wishing the result is easier than actually devising policies to make it work.

A powerful analysis by Eduardo Porter two years ago in the *New York Times* explains the problem well and I quote from it liberally here.[4]

> The wounds of segregation were still raw in the 1970s. With only rare exceptions, African-American children had nowhere near the same educational opportunities as whites.
>
> The civil rights movement, school desegregation and the War on Poverty helped bring a measure of equity to the playing field. Today, despite some setbacks along the way, racial disparities in education have narrowed significantly. By 2012, the test-score deficit of black 9-, 13- and 17-year-olds in reading and math had been reduced as much as 50 percent compared with what it was 30 to 40 years before.
>
> Achievements like these breathe hope into our belief in the Land of Opportunity. They build trust in education as a levelling force powering economic mobility. 'We do have a track record of reducing these inequalities,' said Jane Waldfogel, a professor of social work at Columbia University.
>
> . . .
>
> For all the progress in improving educational outcomes among African-American children, the achievement gaps between more affluent and less privileged children is wider than ever, notes Sean Reardon of the Center for Education Policy Analysis at Stanford. Racial disparities are still a stain on American society, but they are no longer the main divider. Today the biggest threat to the American dream is class.

Porter goes on to explain that education is more critical than ever but the gap between the earnings of college leavers and others is larger than ever, while college is increasingly the preserve of the elite.

> The sons and daughters of college-educated parents are more than twice as likely to go to college as the children of high school graduates and seven times as likely as those of high school dropouts.
>
> Only 5 percent of Americans ages 25 to 34 whose parents didn't finish high school have a college degree. By comparison, the average across 20 rich countries in an analysis by the Organization for Economic Cooperation and Development is almost 20 percent.

Even when they start in kindergarten in the US, children from families of low socioeconomic status are already more than a year behind the children of college graduates in their grasp of both reading and math, and despite the efforts deployed by the American public education system, nine years later the achievement gap, on average, will have widened by somewhere from one-half to two-thirds. As Porter says, 'Even the best performers from disadvantaged backgrounds, who enter kindergarten reading as well as the smartest rich kids, fall behind during their schooling.'

Children from low socioeconomic groups in the US are seven times more likely to have been born to a teenage mother and only half live with both parents compared with 83% of the children of college graduates. They are more likely to suffer from bad nutrition and of course less likely to be able to benefit from expensive educational additions such as extra lessons and visits to museums and art galleries that children of better educated parents can benefit from.

When they enter the public education system, they are shortchanged again. Eleven-year-olds from the wrong side of the tracks are about one-third more likely to have a novice teacher, according to Professor Waldfogel and her colleagues, and much more likely to be held back a grade.[5]

Professor Waldfogel believes that the key to solving the problem is to reduce educational inequality before the age of 14 and claims that evidence from Australia, Canada and even the UK show it can be done.

Fifty years ago, the black-white proficiency gap was one and a half to two times as large as the gap between a child from a family at the top 90th percentile of the income distribution and a child from a family at the 10th percentile. Today, the proficiency gap between the poor and the rich is nearly twice as large as that between black and white children.[6]

A problem with class-based education in the UK reflects the private (quaintly called public) schools. These private schools cream off the children of affluent and intelligent parents and cream off the better teachers as well. I am temperamentally against banning things unless they can be proved to be creating damage on a significant scale. Just because you don't like something doesn't mean it should be banned. And I am not sure that banning private education would work because it would be relatively easy for schools to set up in different jurisdictions. The best way to remove support from private education is to make state schools so good that no one in their right mind would want to waste money educating their children less well and more expensively.[7]

Any policy to increase the quality of education in the poorest schools needs to deal with a number of problems. Teachers in more capitalist societies have traditionally lacked status. From the right they are seen as sinks for those holding intolerant left-wing views, which discourages those on the right from supporting increased investment in schools.[8] One way of building cross-party support for more investment in teaching (and also universities) would be to generate professional guidelines that would prevent the abuse of teaching positions for political propaganda purposes (my excellent Marxist supervisor at Oxford for my MPhil, Andrew Glyn, would never have dreamed of abusing his position for propaganda purposes – he was an economist first and a Marxist second, and I learned a lot from a generous and clever man).

The solution to the improvement in education for the poorest that is clearly needed will probably involve two aspects: the diversion of funds towards improved teaching (the 'pupil premium' promoted by the British Liberal Democrats and enacted by the UK's Coalition government in 2011 looks like a promising initiative[9] though the early stage assessments of its success available at present are currently mixed[10]) and the clever introduction of technology to make learning easier and more user-friendly for disadvantaged children.

It is worth noting that although disadvantaged children are typically falling back in their ability to benefit from formal education, they do not appear to be falling back as far relatively in their ability to absorb technology. The UK's 'Flat White Economy' has benefited from the widespread ability of even those who have done badly in formal education to develop tech skills and to link their innate creativity with techie solutions.

Hershbein, Kearney and Summers (the former US Treasury Secretary) have shown that some fairly radical so-called investments in education will do very little to reduce income inequality.[11]

Instead the investments have to be very carefully targeted. The first step is to return to the analysis in Chapter 4 of why inequality is bad for society and what kinds of inequality do most social damage. The analysis showed that the biggest problems caused by inequality emerged when they meant that individuals and families in society did not get their psychological needs met. In general this happens when they feel that they have little control over their lives and when work loses what Arthur Brooks called its dignity.[12]

The most frequently quoted analysis of people's needs is based on Maslow's hierarchy of needs.[13] This is a motivational theory in psychology comprising a five-tier model of human needs, often depicted as hierarchical levels within a pyramid.

Maslow stated that people are motivated to achieve certain needs and that some needs take precedence. In his analysis the most basic need is for physical survival, which is the primary motivator of behaviour. His analysis suggests that once that need is met, one tries to meet the next need up in the hierarchy. And then the next one.

This five-stage model splits between deficiency needs and growth needs. The first four levels can be treated as deficiency needs (D-needs), and the top level as growth or being needs (B-needs).

The deficiency needs in this analysis motivate people when they are not satisfied. Moreover, the need to fulfil such needs grows the longer the period over which they are denied. For example, the longer a person has no food, the more hungry he or she becomes.

The deficiency needs have to be satisfied in order before the being needs. When they are all met, one is self-actualised. Maslow noted only one in a hundred people reach that point.

Another approach is the Human Givens approach, which is very similar to the Maslow hierarchy. This points out that the major psychological needs which people have to deal with in their lives are: 'security (stable home life, privacy and a safe territory to live in); the need for attention (to give and receive it); connection to others through friendship, fun, love, intimacy; a sense of autonomy and control; being part of a wider social community, which satisfies our need to belong; the need for status; a sense of self-competence (that comes through maturity, learning and the application of skills) and a drive for meaning and purpose'.[14]

The first need of education to cope with inequality is to encourage people's inner resources to enable them to run their lives. These inner resources can include: curiosity; long-term memory; imagination (which allows us to focus our attention away from our emotions in order to solve problems more objectively); the ability to understand the world and other people and extract deeper meaning through metaphor – pattern matching; an observing self; the ability to empathise and connect with others; a rational mind both for its own sake and to cross-check emotional reactions.

The British government with its long-serving Schools Minister Nick Gibb has committed to this element of education. His speech on 'The Purpose of Education' contains the following passage:

> Adult life today is complicated, and we owe it to young people to ensure that they have the character and sense of moral purpose to succeed.
>
> There is now very clear evidence that schools can make a significant contribution to their pupils' achievement by finding opportunities to instil

key character traits, including persistence, grit, optimism and curiosity.

This is not about vague notions of 'learning how to learn' or 'therapeutic education', and we will not return to the failed approaches of the past. In 2005, the then government promoted and funded a strategy to schools named 'social and emotional aspects of learning'. This was a well-meaning attempt to ensure children received a broader education. But it failed, because it was part of a wider retreat from the importance of knowledge-based curriculums in schools. Its evaluation found that SEAL was in fact associated with declining respect for teachers and enjoyment of school.

We have recognised that a broader education – including character and values – can only succeed when it is underpinned by the highest standards of academic rigour.

The Knowledge is Power Program schools – KIPP – are one of the earliest and best groups of charter schools in the United States. Their first school opened in Houston, Texas, in 1999. They now have 162 schools educating 60,000 pupils throughout the USA, 87% of whom come from low income families.

The first pupils to graduate from KIPP schools left with academic records which no one had previously dared to expect from young people growing up in the neighbourhoods from which they came. More than 94% of KIPP middle school students have graduated high school, and more than 82% of KIPP alumni have gone on to college.

But while these students from disadvantaged backgrounds were entering colleges in greater numbers than ever before, it soon became clear that they were much more likely to drop out than their more advantaged peers.

The American academic E.D. Hirsch has made a persuasive case that an important reason for this gap is a deficit of vocabulary and knowledge. KIPP charters are middle schools – so children enter aged 11 or 12. Even the excellent education they receive after they arrive cannot overcome the disadvantage which they have already experienced. Building vocabulary and knowledge simply takes too long. Once in college, without the intensive support provided by KIPP, some are falling behind.

I have no doubt that this explanation is correct. But I am convinced that that these pupils struggled in college for another reason, too. Recent research – particularly the work of Angela Duckworth and the Nobel Laureate James Heckman – has examined the impact of character on underperformance. They have found that key attributes including resilience, self-control and social intelligence are powerful predictors of achievement in education and success in adult life.

Robert Putnam, a Harvard Professor of Public Policy, recently published 'Our Kids', an account of the decline of social mobility in the United States over the past half-century. He places part of the blame on unequal access which disadvantaged children have to extracurricular activities, compared to the greater opportunities open to children in better-off circumstances.

If we are to deliver on our commitment to social justice, breaking the cycle of disadvantage so that every child reaches their potential, we must therefore ensure that all pupils benefit from an education based on these values.

Character education is already a part of the ethos and culture of many good schools. In the United States, KIPP schools now focus on developing grit, resilience and self-confidence in their pupils, and this work is showing results. As of spring 2015, 45% of KIPP pupils have gained a college degree, compared to a national average of 34%, and just 9% from low-income families.

As pointed out above, it is easy to say what is needed and less easy to achieve it. But it is encouraging that what is needed is well understood at ministerial level in the UK at least.

The second requirement for reducing economic inequality through the education system is to ensure that those educated have monetisable skills that enable them to earn decent incomes. Even if they will not become super-rich, they need to be able to earn enough not to feel excluded from society. Not everyone has the ability to become super-rich, but very few lack the ability to earn a decent living for themselves if properly educated and trained.

The third requirement for reducing economic inequality through the educational system is giving people an understanding of the need to keep changing so that their skills can be adapted to the changing world. This means knowing how to learn and about the need to keep learning so as to keep one's abilities up to date.

## Conclusion

Education is not the only factor needed to reduce inequality, but it is the most important. Without getting education right, it is hard to imagine a society where economic inequality can be kept to levels that are not damaging.

## Chapter 13

# SAVING CAPITALISM FROM ITSELF

C APITALISM HAS PROVED ITSELF AN AMAZING SYSTEM FOR ORGANISING the provision of a wide range of goods and services of many kinds. And many of its less fortunate side-effects can often either be self-correcting or can be mitigated with remarkably little cost through regulation or some other form of limited intervention.

Perhaps capitalism's greatest virtue is its intrinsic ability to evolve, both through promoting innovation and through providing the signals that enable institutions no longer functioning to be shut down. I've always believed (partly because I was working for IBM when it happened) that it was the upping of the innovation stakes resulting from the emergence of decentralised information technology in the 1980s that proved the hammer blow that broke Soviet-style communism and led to its collapse.

But capitalism also has plenty of weaknesses which need to be managed. Often critics of capitalism imagine that a pro-capitalist is essentially anti-government. In fact the opposite is true.

Capitalism cannot operate in any real sense without strong governmental institutions. For example without strong enforcement of property rights, accumulation of capital will not take place because the capitalist has no incentive to accumulate if there is no legal title to what he owns or legal protection. One of the problems in post-Soviet Russia has been the impact of gangster capitalism discouraging business investment where the government has been unable (or possibly unwilling) to step in to protect the business from the gangster.[1] A healthy capitalist sector and a healthy government sector go hand in hand.

Another claim is that capitalism goes hand in hand with a selfishness in behaviour which is socially damaging. Here the position is more mixed. It is certainly true that the two can go together. Adam Smith pointed out that the special trick of capitalism was harnessing self-interest to the public good in this famous quote: 'It is not from the benevolence of the butcher, the brewer or the baker that we expect our dinner, but from their regard to their own interest.'[2]

However, capitalism works best when those operating it have a sense of moral purpose. In my own specialist commercial field, economic consultancy, I have always found that it is much more profitable to aim to be the best economic consultant that I possibly can be rather than simply to aim to make more money. I have also found that applying ethical principles to business in the sense of not exploiting customers or clients and ensuring that the company pays its corporate dues to society has been useful in helping the business succeed commercially.[3] Indeed, when we had a tax investigation, the conclusion was that HMRC ended up paying us money, though in between they wasted a lot of time and money and showed a greed which reminded me that governments originally evolved out of protection rackets.

When I was the Chief Economic Adviser to the Confederation of British Industry in the UK, I always argued that business ethics were merely the application of personal ethics in the business context. If you believe that you shouldn't steal, in business this means that you shouldn't take money that ought to be your shareholders', your employees' or your customers'. You shouldn't overcharge, underpay your employees or pay yourself too much of the shareholders' money. Equally you should ensure that the government's tax take is the right one. Because the fiscal authorities often try it on with little regard for common sense or the profitability of the underlying business (and seem to pick on smaller businesses which they see as soft targets), you have to use tax advice make sure that you fight your corner. But you should be careful about using tax-avoidance advice to extremes. If you think taxes are unfair or too high (which they are to a surprising extent), the right thing to do is to campaign for lower taxes rather than trying to find a loophole.

The great capitalists of the 19th and 20th centuries saw their role as making the world a better place, and making money was only incidental to this end. Many of their modern successors still largely share this goal and give most of their wealth to charity – Bill Gates and Warren Buffett are good examples. But in the modern era the pursuit of monopolistic power (although partly necessary to offset the impact of supereconomies of scale in information) and aggressive tax-avoidance policies make many modern corporations seem unnecessarily grasping. And often people from countries where wealth has emerged more quickly than behaviour has evolved and where gangsterism and business are mixed together find this ethics thing quite hard to grasp.

For capitalism to continue to exist in a form that makes it workable in a democracy requires that capitalists behave in a way that builds public support for it. Every person running a business needs to see herself or himself as an ambassador for the system that helps them flourish and therefore needs to behave accordingly. This means a corporate culture of self-restraint and ethical behaviour when doing their day jobs.

It most emphatically does not mean huge corporate social responsibility programmes – the biggest such programmes are often run by the corporates with a public reputation for the least ethical behaviour towards their employees, their customers and the tax authorities.

One of the most visible aspects of the worst kinds of capitalism is when people overpay themselves.

There are other forms of behaviour which seem unacceptable in the extreme. Equifax, the data company that was hacked while this book was being written, both has a business model that seems abusive of peoples' rights over their own data and appears to have sleazy executives. The company discovered it had been badly hacked in late July 2017 and three senior executives including the CFO between them sold $2 million in shares about three days later. This looks sleazy and criminal, though I know from my own experience that the rules on insiders selling shares can often be surprisingly and unintentionally hard to satisfy. One year when I was on the Marconi Board the directors were insiders for over nine months, which made company share ownership difficult.

I would still argue that the vast majority of capitalists behave ethically. This is because of the importance of reputation. In a competitive market a company with a reputation for cheating its customers will lose them, those with a reputation for cheating their shareholders will find it hard to raise money, and those with a reputation for cheating their employees will find it hard to get anyone to work for them. Many on the left will find this hard to believe, but I can assure them that my real-world experience in large companies and of running my own business for 25 years says that businesses are largely ethical. One example of this is that in 25 years I have only had ten bad debts, of which only three proved completely irretrievable, and I must have issued many thousands of invoices.

Where reputation really matters is when there is competition. This is why the preservation of competition is intrinsic to making capitalism work. The competition authorities need to work hard to create adequate competition because most of the benefits of capitalism come from the capitalists competing. Capitalist monopolies can be dangerous because of the way in which monopolies abuse power. Aggressive and competitive capitalist monopolies can often be more dangerous to the public interest than government monopolies, although both have their disadvantages.

Moreover, when capitalism works badly it tends (as Marx pointed out) towards monopolistic profits. This exacerbates inequality because of the high returns to the monopolist and the higher cost of living which is passed on to everyone else, as well as through inhibiting innovation and growth which will certainly exacerbate poverty if not necessarily inequality. As I will show in Chapter 15, high costs of living affect the poor most.

So part of the battle to minimise inequality is making capitalism work properly. Chapter 9 identified failures of capitalism. This chapter shows what could be done.

In one area, although the market has worked painfully slowly, it may be possible to let the market work its way through. Bankers' pay and CEO pay is now falling as investors realise that they are often over-paying. We need to keep a watching brief, but the problem at this stage is definitely making progress in solving itself.

There is a slightly different problem, which is the abuse of professional status in financial services. There should be a code of conduct for financial advice that insists that the advice is based on the interest of the client, not the adviser. It seems unclear that many of the financial service firms have been professional in that sense. I would be tempted to be rather more brutal than the financial authorities have been and shut down some of the least acceptable firms. Getting away with persistent anti-social behaviour sends the wrong message.

Cronyism is not exactly a problem of capitalism but has some features in common and can be considered under the same heading. The problem for Western economies is largely one of misbehaviour in other countries. The difficulty for the West is due process. With zero likelihood of a fair trial, measures will invariably be arbitrary. And with political power involved, it may be very difficult to be fair. It may be possible to apply sanctions to groups in one country where the political clout is less that cannot be applied to those from another country with considerable political power. Political power is a reality and pretending it doesn't exist doesn't fit with the real world. The combination of selective action and media scrutiny may be the best we can do. The measures are likely to be mainly asset freezes and travel bans. These can be surprisingly effective.

Competition policy is likely to grow in importance in the coming years. As many businesses become information based, the tendency for them to be subject to network effects and to supereconomies of scale increases. This in turn is liable to create a winner-takes-all situation and hence monopolies.

Table 1. The tech giants by market size and capitalisation

| Rank by Revenue | | | Revenue ($B) | FY | Employees | Market cap ($B) | Headquarters |
|---|---|---|---|---|---|---|---|
| 1 | United States | Apple Inc. | $215.6 | 2016 | 116,000 | $815 | Cupertino, CA, US |
| 2 | South Korea | Samsung Electronics | $173.9 | 2016 | 325,000 | $311 | Suwon, South Korea |
| 3 | United States | Amazon.com | $135.9 | 2016 | 341,400 | $478 | Seattle, WA, US |
| 4 | Taiwan | Foxconn | $135.1 | 2016 | 726,772 | $66 | New Taipei City, Taiwan |
| 5 | United States | Alphabet Inc. | $90.2 | 2016 | 72,053 | $676 | Mountain View, CA, US |
| 6 | United States | Microsoft | $85.3 | 2016 | 114,000 | $561 | Redmond, WA, US |
| 7 | Japan | Hitachi | $84.5 | 2016 | 303,887 | $32 | Tokyo, Japan |
| 8 | United States | IBM | $79.9 | 2016 | 414,400 | $145 | Armonk, NY, US |
| 9 | China | Huawei | $78.5 | 2016 | 180,000 | N/A (Private) | Shenzhen, China |
| 10 | Japan | Sony | $70.1 | 2016 | 128,400 | $51 | Tokyo, Japan |
| 11 | Japan | Panasonic | $67.7 | 2016 | 257,533 | $33 | Osaka, Japan |
| 12 | United States | Dell Technologies | $64.8 | 2016 | 138,000 | $14 | Austin, TX, US |
| 13 | United States | Intel | $59.3 | 2016 | 106,000 | $163 | Santa Clara, CA, US |
| 14 | United States | Hewlett Packard Enterprise | $50.1 | 2016 | 195,000 | $30 | Palo Alto, CA, US |
| | | Facebook | $27.6 | | | $492 | |

Source: Taken from the Fortune Global 500 2017 but adjusted to include Facebook. An even more up-to-date list is available at https://en.wikipedia.org /wiki/List_of_the_largest_information_technology_companies

Table 7 shows the top tech giants, their revenues and their market capitalisation. To declare my interests, I was once Chief Economist for IBM in the UK and when I was on the main board of Marconi we got sufficiently close to Huawei (one of the companies on this list) to consider merging, an outcome that they eventually shied away from over what they delicately called different accounting practices.

Two big issues arise from the emergence of the tech giants. The first is the emergence of excessive market power where some of them might have too much control over markets, and the second is to do with the use of customer data.

A third, but at this stage less important, issue is the use of the profits of the tech companies to lobby in their own interest. It can be seen from their quarterly disclosures that Apple, Amazon and Google alone are spending at an annual rate of $40 million a year in lobbying in the US.[4] This still puts them well below the pharmaceutical industry and many others in their US lobbying spend but the amount spent is rising fast.

Discussions about what to do with tech giants range from regulation to breaking up to letting technological change provide the regulation.

When I worked for IBM in the mid- to late 1980s I was a strong believer in leaving regulation of the IT sector to the markets and the advance of technology. One might respond, 'Well, you would say that, working for IBM.' Yet IBM at that time was moving from having made the largest corporate profit ever recorded (1985) to the largest loss ever recorded (1989). The fact that this decline from grace almost exactly mirrored the period over which I worked for the company is unfortunate, though it might be stretching the bounds of causation to suggest that someone in as lowly a position as the Chief Economist in the UK could have a significant influence on the worldwide profits of a company as big (then) as IBM. This was the period when people were starting to suggest that IBM meant 'I Blame Microsoft' rather than 'I've Been Moved'.

But IBM was a comparatively gentlemanly outfit, once described as the largest ever troop of boy scouts.[5] Modern IT companies driven by aggressive venture capitalists are much more aggressive in their pursuit of profit than IBM ever was and pose much greater public interest risks. I am now unconvinced that, even with ever-changing technology, it is safe to leave the top tech companies alone.

My conclusion is that both breaking up and regulation will be necessary. I would aim to break up any tech firm that persistently (say over three years) holds a market share of over 25%. And I would also place considerable restrictions on the uses to which tech firms can put the data that they collect on customers. There will be a significant cost from this. But the cost of the alternative, to allow a monopoly to develop and to intimidate competition and entrench itself, will almost certainly be higher.

Achieving this will ultimately require regulation of tech companies in a similar way to that in which financial institutions are regulated. For financial institutions there tend to be two types of regulation. The first type is that relating to all listed companies, which is that the stock exchange where they are listed takes the lead responsibility in ensuring corporate governance. The second relates to where they operate to ensure that their impact on the local financial system does not create problems. Every country in which financial institutions operate takes responsibility for the operating practices of these institutions in those countries. The tech companies will need to be regulated in an analogous way. This will require agreement at OECD or G-20 level on who takes responsibility for which company. At present most of the companies involved are US-based, though over the next 20 years there is likely to be an emergence of companies from elsewhere, especially China. The US (and this will probably need a more internationally sensitive President than Trump) will need to take account of corporate behaviour elsewhere as well as in the US. And the US will need a new Teddy Roosevelt to bust the trusts.

## Conclusion

The case is made here for quite an aggressive approach to those who abuse capitalism. Suggested solutions range from shutting down investment banks that persistently behave unethically to breaking up tech giants, with travel sanctions and asset freezes for crony capitalists. In addition, strict enforcement of regulations and competition policy will become increasingly important to prevent capitalism from being abused.

## Chapter 14
# ATTACKING THE LAW OF
# UNINTENDED CONSEQUENCES

I T MIGHT SURPRISE MANY PEOPLE TO DISCOVER THAT GOVERNMENT ACTIVITY very often redistributes income or assets towards the rich or at least to those who already own assets, who tend to be better off than average. This happens for two reasons. First, some lobbyists manage to bribe or coerce governments in some countries, particularly those with a tradition of corruption, to give them favours at the expense of the general population. This is the type of corruption covered in Chapter 9 of this book. But there is also a second way in which governments can exacerbate inequality. This is through the so-called 'law of unintended consequences'.

This is surprisingly often the case. And although it is rare that these effects reflect lobbying by the rich specifically to boost their income or wealth, it is undoubtedly the case that rich people who have managed to obtain a privilege of some kind apply pressure to preserve the status quo when it is in their interest.

I focus here on three examples: (1) rent controls (looking specifically at Stockholm); (2) planning or zoning controls (looking mainly at the UK and the US); and (3) quantitative easing (examples from the US, Eurozone and the UK). In addition I look at the impact of indirect taxation on the cost of living and hence on the real living standards of the poorest households.

### Rent controls
Rent controls are a great deal if you are a tenant in a rent-controlled house or flat. But the lack of market-determined rents does mean – if there is an appreciable gap between rents paid and those that would exist in the market – that there is likely to be less investment in rental property. In turn this is likely to create shortages of housing and can lead to homelessness. Meanwhile, for those who do own their properties, the resulting housing shortage is likely to push up prices and lead to an accumulation of wealth for those who already have wealth. A standard analysis of the social cost suggested that the welfare loss from the existence of Swedish

rent controls was as high as SEK 20 billion in 2012.[1]

Whereas in most other countries, where rents are controlled they are controlled at a local level, in Sweden rents are controlled at a national level.[2] Rents (these data are from 2015) are 1,050 kronor (£80) per square metre a year on average, so a single bedroom apartment of 65 sq m is about 5,700 kronor a month, or £420, according to Statistics Sweden. On average, rents cost about a quarter of people's income.

Rent regulation is a part of Folkhemmet, which reflects the old system of Swedish Social Democracy that uses high taxes to reduce income disparities and to fund a comprehensive welfare system. Rent rules were designed to protect tenants from losing their homes in times of increased demand and to reduce segregation. In Sweden, 37% of all apartments were owner-occupied in 2012, with renters occupying the rest.

The regulations, which were enacted in the 1960s and cover most rental units, have benefited millions of Swedes who currently pay an average rent of 4,980 kronor ($720) a month for a one-bedroom apartment. The average monthly cost for owner-occupied apartments in the city of Stockholm is 63% higher than for rental housing, according to preliminary data from an analysis by the Swedish Union of Tenants. The union, which negotiates rents with landlords, aims to keep payments below 25% of its members' disposable incomes.

Each year, rent rises are negotiated between the tenants' association, representing 350,000 tenants, and the Stockholm property agency, representing 5,000 private rental companies. Over the past decade, rents have risen by 19% – not far ahead of inflation, which was about 12%. The 2014 rent rise for the city was 1.12%

However, the system has been experiencing acute pressures. Building of rental homes almost dried up after a financial crisis in the early 1990s, and there is a dire shortage of properties. Demand is such that it is almost impossible to get a direct contract.

With nearly half of all Stockholmers – about 500,000 people – in the queue, it can take 20 or 30 years to get to the top of the pile. Rents in new build apartments are higher because the companies have been exempted from rent controls, although quality is said by some to be higher. Low rents in the municipal sector mean many properties require renovation and repair.

The result is a thriving rental property black market, with bribes of as much as SEK 100,000 per room to obtain a direct contract. Many people sublet space in their rental apartments. A tenant who advertised a tiny closet for rent found there were many potential takers.

Stockholm City Council now has an official housing queue, where 1 day waiting = 1 point. To get an apartment you need both money for the rent and enough points to be the first in line. Recently an apartment in inner Stockholm became available. In just five days, 2,000 people had applied for the apartment. The person who got the apartment had been waiting in the official housing queue since 1989.[3] To quote a 2016 BBC report, 'The city's queue for rent-controlled housing is so long that it is being considered by the Guinness Book of Records. On average, it takes nine years to be granted a rent-controlled property – and that jumps to two decades in some of the most popular neighbourhoods.'[4]

Swedes tend to stay put in their apartments and discourage builders from constructing properties for lease. This has exacerbated a housing shortage that has sent prices and private debt to record levels in Sweden.

A growing number of builders, landlords and analysts are calling for the government to scrap rent regulations to alleviate the housing shortfall. Home prices have more than doubled since 2000 and Swedish households with mortgages owe their creditors an average of almost four times their disposable income. The central bank and the International Monetary Fund have warned that soaring debt levels make the economy vulnerable to a severe shock if unemployment rises or prices collapse. The IMF in its 2016 annual consultation with the Swedish government has called for Sweden to phase out the system of rent controls in order to encourage more efficient use of housing.[5]

The Swedish Financial Supervisory Authority capped mortgages at 85% of property values in 2010, raised capital requirements for banks, and is considering forced amortization, requiring borrowers to make principal repayments, to try to stem debt growth. The regulator is also considering lowering the mortgage cap, introducing loan-to-income limits, and restricting the use of floating mortgage rates.

'If you want to further address the issue of household indebtedness then you probably have to look at all types of measures that are directly aimed at households,' said Uldis Cerps, executive director for banking at the FSA in Stockholm. 'It's a broad set of issues we're presently examining.'

While the growth in household borrowing slowed to a 20-year low of 4.5% in the middle of 2012 following the mortgage cap, it has since accelerated as housing prices have continued to gain, though increasingly strict mortgage rules have caused house prices to fall back slightly in late 2017.[6]

The combination of low rents and a lack of vacant units means that

Swedes with apartments in attractive areas have little incentive to move. Some have more space than they need, which adds to the housing shortage. This inefficient use of housing has led to a shortage of 40,000 units, the Swedish National Board of Housing, Building and Planning estimates.

So the Swedish system of rent control leads to immense shortages of housing, a disconnect between those who have won the lottery and obtained a rent-controlled flat and others who have to pay the market price, sharply rising house prices and an increase in asset values for the rich who own property.

What is clear is that only a relatively small part of the population, about a third, gain from this. The rest all end up having to pay extra in the marketplace.

The real winners are the companies and the private individuals who own property, whose property goes up much more rapidly in value than any other investment. It is difficult to think of a measure better designed to enrich those who are already rich at the expense of the poor and less privileged. And yet it is an extreme example of the law of unintended consequences – the rent controls which have done so much to increase inequality were intended to reduce it!

### Planning to create a shortage and raise prices

Tight planning controls have much the same economic impact as rent controls. They create an artificial shortage of property – typically housing – and hence force the cost of housing upwards.

Few would be so silly as to impose such controls for no good reason. And there are genuine reasons for controlling land use – particularly in a country such as the UK with a relatively high population density and some stunning vistas that could easily be spoiled by developments.

To quote the travel writer Bill Bryson:[7]

> ... stand on the eastern slopes of Noar Hill in Hampshire and you have a view that is pretty well unimprovable. Orchards, fields and dark woods sit handsomely upon the landscape. Here and there village rooftops and church spires poke through the trees. It is lovely and timeless and tranquilly spacious, as English views so often are. It seems miles from anywhere, yet not far off, over the Surrey Hills is London. Get in a car and in an hour, you can be in Piccadilly Circus or Trafalgar Square. To me that is a miracle, that a city as vast and demanding as London can have prospects like this on its very doorstep, on every side.

Bryson goes on to attribute this to the green belt, which is a planning policy preserving a belt of landscape, partly agricultural and partly woods and trees, around London and some other towns and cities in the UK (Bryson says England but the legislation is wider). Bryson attributes this to the 1947 Town and Country Planning Act, which he praises.

Technically Bryson is wrong – the green belt policy for London long predated the Town and Country Planning Act because it was first put forward as policy by the Greater London Planning Committee in 1935 in response to the ribbon development satirised as Metroland.[8]

But Bryson is eloquent in his desire to preserve the green belt in an unchanged form, regardless of any economic argument for the other side:

> The Economist magazine, for one, has for years argued that the green belts should be cast aside as a hindrance to growth. As an Economist writer editorializes from a dementia facility somewhere in the Home Counties: 'The green belts that stop development around big cities should go, or at least be greatly weakened. They increase journey times without adding to human happiness.'
>
> Well, they add a great deal to my happiness, you pompous, over-educated twit. Perhaps I see this differently from others because I come from the Land of Shocking Sprawl. From time to time these days I drive with my wife from Denver International Airport to Vail, high in the Colorado Rockies, to visit our son Sam. It is a two-hour drive and the first hour is taken up with just getting out of Denver. It is a permanent astonishment to me how much support an American lifestyle needs – shopping malls, distribution centres, storage depots, gas stations, zillion-screen multiplex cinemas, gyms, teeth-whitening clinics, business parks, propane storage facilities, compounds holding fleets of trailers, FedEx trucks or school buses, car dealerships, outlets of a million types, and endless miles of suburban houses all straining to get a view of distant mountains.
>
> Travel twenty-five or thirty miles out from London and you get Windsor Great Park or Epping Forest or Box Hill. Travel for thirty miles out from Denver and you just get more ...

Bryson gets very upset about The Economist's views on the green belt, but one senses that he sees any organ with economist in its title as already damned and so he reserves his main bile for articles making a similar point in The Guardian: 'If it was only The Economist calling for the destruction of the green belt, my despair would be manageable, but lately *The Guardian* has decided to come down on the side of dismemberment.' He also castigates planning expert Paul Cheshire from the London School of Economics who argues (also in the *Guardian*, to Bryson's evident despair), 'What green belt really seems to be is a very British form of discriminatory zoning, keeping the urban unwashed out of the Home Counties.' Bryson's response is at least self-deprecating: 'Well, let me say at once that I have uttered huge amounts of tosh in my time, but I take my hat off to Prof Cheshire.'

Bryson clearly feels strongly, but most balanced policymakers would consider both sides of the argument rather than just one.

Every independent review of the factors driving the high cost of housing in the UK from the report which I personally wrote on behalf of the CBI and the RICS in 1992,[9] to the official housing review written by my successor as CBI Chief Economic Adviser, Kate Barker,[10] to the Future Homes Commission Report chaired by my former boss Sir John Banham,[11] has confirmed that the UK's unusually restrictive planning laws are one of the key factors leading to extremely high housing costs.

One of the UK's specific problems is that to a considerable extent the planning process is under the control of local people. These, especially in the more sparsely populated rural areas, are those for whom the scarcity value of their own property would be reduced if development took place – it is not surprising that they vote to minimise such development and hence boost the scarcity value of their own property.

The high cost of property very substantially adds to inequality. In the US the lowest income groups spend 42% of their income on housing (it is very approximately 20% for the highest income groups). In the UK the figures are much more stark. The lowest income groups spend 60% on rent if they rent privately.[12] This massive cost reflects the lack of housing supply. As I pointed out in *The Flat White Economy*, 'A report by Cebr and London First in October 2015 has shown that lack of housing is costing the London economy at least £1 billion per annum. In September 2015 the accountancy firm Deloitte reported that 5% of its 2014 intake of trainee accountants had to share bedrooms because of the cost of housing while in January 2015 the Guardian reported a 74% increase in the number of young people looking to share a bedroom (for economic reasons...).'

Housing shortages caused by planning restrictions have a double impact on inequality. First, they push up rents which are a much higher proportion of budgets for lower income groups. Second, they push up the value of owned property. Since property is disproportionately owned by the wealthier groups (the survey of multi-millionaires for the first edition of *Prospect* magazine showed that about 50% of all of City bonuses and equivalent windfalls were invested in the housing market), an increase in the value of housing boosts the wealth of the rich.[13] So inequality is increased twice by this measure.

It is quite clear that a balance has to be struck between reducing the impact of inequality of planning and the preservation of attractive views. Both are important and their relative importance can vary. Arguably in the coming years, the relative importance of reducing inequality will increase.

The conflict between the desire to preserve attractive views and the desire to mitigate the impact of planning on inequality is clearly greatest in a small relatively densely populated island like the UK. Yet an interesting analysis has emerged which shows that even in the US, where the population density is much lower, planning policy is having an impact on inequality.

What the study shows is that for most of the past 100 years, per capita incomes in poorer US states have grown more rapidly than incomes in richer states, narrowing the gap between them. Over the past three decades, though, the rate of convergence has slowed sharply. It has become more difficult for poorer states to catch up with richer states. In a paper presented at the Municipal Finance Conference, Peter Ganong of the University of Chicago and Daniel Shoag of Harvard attribute this slowdown in convergence to increasingly tight land use regulations in wealthy areas.[14]

Their argument is that historically much of the convergence in income across states was driven by the migration of labour from poorer states to wealthier states. This migration held down wage growth in richer states and boosted wage growth in poorer states. This historical pattern was disrupted by increasingly strict land use regulations. Regulation boosted housing costs in richer states so that migration was no longer an attractive option for low-skill, low-wage workers. But migration remained attractive for high-skilled workers, and they continued to move to wealthy places

Ganong and Shoag link this changing migration pattern to local housing regulation, using an innovative measure of land use regulation drawn from state appeals court records. They show that in higher income places where land use regulations were not tightened, convergence continued at its historical rate.

The authors also contend that the divergence in the migration patterns of skilled and unskilled households contributed additionally to rising income inequality. Specifically, they calculate that the increase in hourly wage inequality from 1980 to 2010 would have been approximately 10% smaller if convergence in economic growth across states had maintained the pace observed from 1940 to 1980.

This research highlights the important role played by land use regulation in explaining regional migration patterns, slowing convergence, and increasing inequality. So, even in a country like the US which is much less densely populated than the UK, planning policy is increasing inequality.

My impression is that planning restrictions are not normally pushed by those who are deliberately trying to push up their property values directly. But I'm sure that when there is pressure to alleviate housing shortages by adjusting planning regulations to permit the building of more houses, one of the interests brought to bear to prevent these adjustments is the desire of those who have already climbed up the ladder to prevent others from doing so. So in this way inequality is aided and abetted by those preventing development. And some play a cunning trick of masquerading as campaigning for environmental protection when in reality all they are doing is trying to keep up the value of their houses.

## Inequality from quantitative easing

It may surprise some people to discover that a monetary technicality such as quantitative easing has an impact on the distribution of income, but this is widely believed to be the case.

The origins of quantitative easing are in the perceived lack of demand that results from the international situation. Global imbalances are the major explanation for this, with the high Chinese savings ratio and the German fiscal surplus as major driving forces. I covered this in one of my Gresham Professorial Lectures[15] and it has been the underlying explanation of the Federal Reserve Bank's economic policy (see articles and books by Alan Greenspan and Ben Bernanke). There is a counter-view which puts the blame on monetary policy in the developed economies, but there seems to be less evidence to support that view.[16]

Quantitative easing has been widespread in Japan, the Eurozone, the UK and the US. It could only be pursued in a country or economy that could command sufficient reputation for its currency to survive the policy (it is in effect the same policy adopted in Zimbabwe with disastrous results, since the Zimbabwean currency did not survive), and it needs to be implemented in essentially non-inflationary times.

The story goes like this – if someone in the world saves too much, for balance someone else has to dissave an equivalent amount. The Chinese (and some others including the Germans) save much more than they invest domestically, so others have to borrow too much. Many governments have ratios of debt to GDP that ring alarm bells (though whether these are really high is an interesting conundrum, especially if debt can be written off). So the private sector has been encouraged to spend more and save less by the combination of ultra low interest rates and bond repurchases though central banks.

Initially these have encouraged dissaving and more spending, but after a time the private sector has come up against even more restrictive prudential limits on borrowing than governments. However, one element that has continued to make it possible for ultra low rates and quantitative easing to work even after a long period has been asset price inflation. With many assets (especially property), provided their prices can be boosted sufficiently, increased borrowing can be encouraged.

The problem with this is that boosting asset prices makes the rich richer, makes property less affordable to poorer groups, and hence boosts inequality of wealth. By contrast, the main alternative of boosting infrastructural spending if anything reduces inequality[17] but is subject to the constraint of governmental debt credibility.

So the policy of using ultra loose monetary policy to boost growth at a time when government investment is constrained has negative distributional consequences. On the whole, in many circumstances I would argue that the boost to growth justifies the increase in inequality of wealth but it is unfortunate that the circumstances are such that this is necessary. The problem now is how to get out of the ultra loose monetary policy that was introduced a decade ago for what were thought to be cyclical reasons. It is not clear that this will be easy or painless.

**Impact of government spending on indirect taxes affecting the cost of living**
One other way in which the public sector impacts on the living standards of the poorest groups is through the high cost of public services.

Discussion of whether the public sector is less efficient than the private sector is full of academic studies purporting to show private sector inefficiency. One suspects political bias. My practical knowledge of private sector contractors providing services to the public sector is that they can be efficient but this depends on having strong and consistent public sector clients. Private contractors will generally put in a low initial price in the hope of making profits on contract variations.

However, there *is* data on trends in efficiency, which is a different question from that concerning the absolute levels. While there might be reasons why it is difficult to compare absolute levels of efficiency between the public and private sectors, these should not preclude analysis of trends in such efficiency.

Cebr has done an analysis of relative public and private sector productivity for the UK. For the UK as a whole, total productivity for the whole economy (including in the public sector) rose by 20.7% between 1997 and 2013 despite the much publicised weakness after 2008.[18] Meanwhile public sector productivity rose by only a measly 1.2% in total over the same period.[19]

Had productivity in the public sector risen at the national average rate since 1997, the level of public services provided in 2015 could have been provided while spending only 36.5% of GDP in 2015 instead of the 43.6% that we actually spent. And this is not a silly calculation. When I was giving my Gresham Professorial lectures a few years ago I showed that the public sector in the UK cost more than twice as much in relation to GDP as those in Singapore and Hong Kong, which achieved higher life expectancy, better education and better public infrastructure than we did in the UK.

In cash terms, the cost from lack of public sector productivity performance is over £150 billion, which could have contributed to lower taxes or to improved services or most likely a mixture of both. The £150 billion could have more than eliminated VAT (which generated net receipts of £121.3 bn in 2016/17) had it been applied to that purpose. There is general acceptance that indirect taxes are regressive and so worsen inequality (see the discussion of tax progressivity in Chapter 5).

With a high cost of government adding to the tax burden and hence squeezing the cost of living, it is clear that poverty at least and quite possibly inequality is being added to by the cost of the public sector in the UK. Might this also be true elsewhere?

## Conclusion

This chapter has shown how the public sector can exacerbate inequality through the law of unintended consequences. This is especially likely to be the case if interventions are made without thinking through the likely market effects on behaviour.

*Chapter 15*

# MAKING POORER PEOPLE RICHER
# BY CUTTING THE COST OF LIVING

ECAUSE I WAS BROUGHT UP IN AN EMERGING ECONOMY I'VE ALWAYS seen the West as an aberration with underdevelopment and poverty the norm. That point of view has some defects, but as a tool of economic analysis it is often a helpful way to analyse Western economies to think of them as unusual rather than the norm.

During the period when only a small part (roughly 15%) of the world's population had benefited from industrialisation, the West had an effective monopoly of the supply of sophisticated products. With a culture roughly shared between North America and Europe (and with Japan, the only non-Western economy to have broken the monopoly at that time, subject to pressure to adjust its exchange rate to keep it uncompetitive), these countries built up a cost base and a system of social protection that reflected the lack of competition from low cost economies.

With globalisation and the emergence of competition from lower cost economies putting a ceiling on pay levels for less skilled jobs in the West, the high cost of living that has developed over time is now becoming a factor that is reducing living standards for the poorest people in the West. Both poverty and inequality can be reduced by driving down the cost of living, especially for basics such as food and housing. Somewhat unexpectedly, the high cost of mobile telephony in the West is also a factor driving increased inequality.[1]

**Keeping down the costs of basics**
In Western economies many basic costs have been allowed to balloon up while the economies were generally prosperous and had standards of living many times higher than those in the emerging or less developed economies.

Now, when the level of prosperity in Western economies for poorer people is often lower, ratcheting these costs back down again would do much to improve the situation of the least well-off. Within the Western world these high prices are especially prominent in Europe and less so in

Figure 16. IMF comparison of the cost of living by country

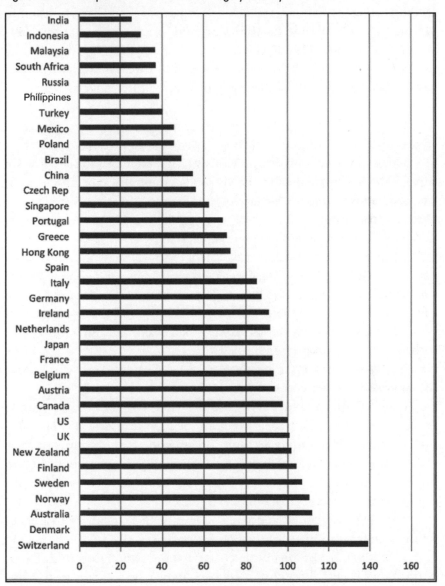

*Source: IMF.*

the US. This reflects three factors: first, the high levels of public expenditure in many European countries which are being reflected in consumption taxes such as VAT as well as in high social charges which put up the cost of labour and hence feed through into prices; second, the tendency in Europe to favour producer interests that lead to higher prices; and third, the particular tendency in the EU to support agricultural interests leading to expensive food (and also the impact of the EU's opposition to genetic modification and its effects on food prices), although the US is by no means innocent in this area.

Costs are high in Europe also as a result of weaknesses in competition policy and a result of planning and agricultural policies that push up the costs of housing and food.

Figure 16 shows how high the cost of living is in the West generally. It gives IMF data using cost of living baskets for different countries.

One example of how the previously richer countries in the West are much more expensive than the newly richer countries in the East is given by the data for Singapore. Singapore is rather more prosperous than most Western economies, yet its cost of living is only 62.4% of that in the US and 61.8% of the cost of living in the UK.

Table 8 shows more recent data from the AOL cost of living comparison for June 2016 looking at selected food items. And although there are clearly some questions to be asked about the cost comparisons (some of the data looks implausible) it does give a clear impression that the cost of living is noticeably higher in the West than elsewhere and that it is also rather higher in Europe than in the US.

It is worth looking in much more detail at two items which enter differentially into the cost of living of the poor and the rich.

Using US data and excluding cash contributions, the poorest quintile in the US spend 18.1% of their expenditure on food and 44.8% on housing. These two items alone account for just short of two thirds of their total expenditure. By comparison the richest quintile spend only 12.5% on food and 20.2% on housing.[2] These proportions are likely to be similar for other advanced economies.

Thus expensive food and housing are likely particularly to impact on the standards of living of the poorest groups.

Tables 8 and 9 compare the costs of some basic foods in different parts of the US with those costs elsewhere in the world. Of the items identified only chicken is cheaper in the US than in the emerging economies. Bread, milk, eggs and vegetables are many times more expensive in the US. But the situation in Europe looks to be even worse, with food costs roughly twice those in the US, let alone the emerging economies.

The high basic costs of living make a major contribution to inequality, penalising the poor disproportionately.

Table 8. Comparison of the cost of selected foods in the West and elsewhere

| *Chicken* | *Bread* | *Coffee* |
|---|---|---|
| **Sample of U.S. Prices:** | **Sample of U.S. Prices:** | **Sample of U.S. Prices:** |
| Portland, Ore.: $1.59 | Portland, Ore.: $1.79 | Portland, Ore.: $8.99 |
| Little Rock, Ark.: $0.88 | Little Rock, Ark.: $1.97 | Little Rock, Ark.: $5.99 |
| Los Angeles, Calif.: $1.59 | Los Angeles, Calif.: $2.29 | Los Angeles, Calif.: $11.19 |
| **Sample of World Prices:** | **Sample of World Prices:** | **Sample of World Prices:** |
| Kuwait: $2.01 | India: $0.28 | Kuwait: $0.27 |
| Spain: $2.03 | London: $0.74 | Brazil: $2.10 |
| Hong Kong: $2.50 | Moscow: $0.77 | Belgium: $4.13 |
| Taiwan: $2.92 | Brazil: $1.17 | Hong Kong: $5.00 |
| Brazil: $3.79 | South Africa: $1.27 | Paris: $7.00 |
| South Africa: $3.85 | Germany: $2.50 | Spain: $7.11 |
| Germany: $6.00 | Australia: $4.22 | South Africa: $14.34 |
| Paris: $6.37 | Spain: $6.23 | London: $18.26 |

*Source: AOL online June 2016.*

Table 9. Comparison of the cost of selected foods in the West and elsewhere

| *Milk* | *Eggs* | *Lettuce* |
|---|---|---|
| **Sample of U.S. Prices:** | **Sample of U.S. Prices:** | **Sample of U.S. Prices:** |
| Portland, Ore.: $1.99 | Portland, Ore.: $2.29 | Portland, Ore.: $1.39 |
| Little Rock, Ark.: $2.33 | Little Rock, Ark.: $1.00 | Little Rock, Ark.: $1.34 |
| Los Angeles, Calif.: $2.49 | Los Angeles, Calif.: $5.99 | Los Angeles, Calif.: $1.79 |
| **Sample of World Prices:** | **Sample of World Prices:** | **Sample of World Prices:** |
| India: $0.70 | India: $0.39 | Brazil: $0.43 |
| Brazil: $1.02 | Brazil: $0.84 | Canada: $1.47 |
| South Africa: $1.03 | Hong Kong: $1.80 | Germany: $1.56 |
| Paris: $1.79 | Kuwait: $2.33 | London: $1.58 |
| Hong Kong: $2.00 | Moscow: $3.39 | Moscow: $1.88 |
| Moscow: $3.89 | Belgium: $4.09 | Australia: $1.97 |
| Canada: $3.92 | Australia: $4.80 | Paris: $3.07 |
| Taiwan: $4.60 | London: $5.28 | Kuwait: $4.52 |

*Source: AOL online June 2016.*

Table 10 looks at the costs of a monthly rental for a one bedroom apartment outside a city centre. Obviously it is likely that there are some weaknesses with the data, but three points are clear. First, costs are noticeably higher in the West than in the emerging economies (though Berlin and Rome are exceptions). Second, Singapore and Hong Kong, both of which have very limited land availability but also have tight zoning regulations, have relatively high costs, as has Dubai. Third, the UK and the US are noticeably expensive. Again these are countries with tight zoning regulations.

Table 10. Comparative costs of monthly rental for one-bedroom apartment outside city centre (costs in euro)

| | | |
|---|---|---|
| Germany | Berlin | 482.96 |
| Italy | Rome | 350 |
| France | Paris | 752.73 |
| UK | London | 1300.13 |
| US | New York | 1627.56 |
| US | Los Angeles | 1232.04 |
| US | Atlanta | 778.22 |
| Singapore | | 1271.29 |
| Hong Kong | | 1249.29 |
| South Africa | Johannesburg | 317.87 |
| Dubai | | 1266.19 |
| China | Beijing | 524.92 |
| India | Mumbai | 246.6 |
| Korea | Seoul | 584.51 |
| Mexico | Mexico City | 277.36 |
| Brazil | Rio de Janiero | 397.38 |
| Japan | Tokyo | 676.72 |
| Nigeria | Lagos | 40.7 |

*Source: Numbeo Property Prices comparison https://www.numbeo.com/property-investment /compare_cities.jsp?country1=Nigeria&country2=Italy&city1=Lagos&city2=Anzio+%28Rome %29&tracking=getDispatchComparison.*

The previous chapter shows that a key factor driving up the cost of living in any locality is likely to be its zoning restrictions. When these artificially drive up the cost of property they contribute to inequality. Our calculations suggest that much of the potential benefits to poorer groups from economic growth in cities like Singapore, Hong Kong, London and New York is eroded by the rising cost of housing. Removing or amending the restrictions that push up the price of housing would make a major contribution to improving the standard of living of poorer people in these cities particularly.

Therefore, as with food, to the extent that supply and demand conditions can be adjusted to bring down the cost of housing, it is likely that there will be a significant amelioration in economic inequality.

There is one other basic expenditure which enters into the cost of living of all but the very most impoverished people – the cost of running a mobile phone. Poor people (the bottom quintile of expenditure) spend 6.7% of their total expenditure on mobile telephony in the US. The top quintile spend only 2.1%.[3] It is likely that this ratio is roughly similar in other economies.

Table 11 shows the amazing variation in the monthly cost of running a mobile phone around the world. Given that this is a natural monopoly that is highly regulated in different countries, it is likely that there is scope to bring some of the costs in the more expensive countries down closer to the lower cost levels. And as the calculations above show, cutting the costs of mobile telephony benefits the poor three times as much as it benefits the rich.[4]

Table 11. Monthly cost of running a mobile phone by country at market exchange rates ($ per month)

| US | 35.62 |
|---|---|
| France | 40.27 |
| Germany | 18.02 |
| UK | 16.45 |
| Italy | 15.92 |
| Spain | 37.8 |
| Singapore | 8.63 |
| Hong Kong | 5.96 |
| China | 4.07 |
| India | 2.8 |
| Korea | 19.32 |
| Japan | 33.64 |
| Russia | 6.09 |
| South Africa | 10.23 |
| Emirates | 9.89 |
| Mexico | 11.12 |

*Source: International Telecommunications Union (Table 4.2 in the ITU's Measuring the Information Society 2015).*

## Conclusion

What all this shows is that there is considerable scope to bring down the cost of living for basics that would substantially reduce inequality in real terms in the Western world as well as sharply reducing poverty.

In the West these items were allowed to become expensive at times when the cost of living was of less concern because of the prosperity in the West that came with a monopoly in the supply of sophisticated goods. Now, after globalisation, Western economies need to bring down these costs again. This particular problem is more acute in Europe than in the US. There is some hope for the UK in this regard, because some of the problems, particularly those resulting from expensive food, may be alleviated as the UK leaves the EU.

## Chapter 16

# CAN A UNIVERSAL BASIC INCOME
# REALLY WORK?

I F INEQUALITY, PARTICULARLY TYPE 3 INEQUALITY CAUSED BY TECHNOLOGY, continues to grow, it is likely that policymakers will need to look carefully at providing a universal basic income (UBI).

Conventionally in Western economies (but not, on the whole, elsewhere) social security is paid to the retired, the sick and to those out of work. In the US this is time limited, in Europe rather less so. There are also in-work benefits in some countries.

A UBI is paid to everyone whether they work or not. The advantage of the system is that there is no disincentive to work other than that caused by taxation because the UBI is not withdrawn when the recipient works or increases his or her earnings. The disadvantage is that a UBI is very costly.

Those in favour of a UBI argue that such a scheme is transparent, administratively efficient and encourages people to do more work and invest more in their own skills than the welfare systems in operation at present. There have been some experiments on this which are inconclusive. However the Finnish government announced that it will for two years from 2017 perform a test on a randomly selected 2,000 unemployment benefit recipients. They will be paid €560 a month but will still have access to the non-cash benefits to which they would otherwise be entitled. Their behaviour will be monitored compared with another group who will receive the current mix of benefits. This experiment will end at the end of 2018, though it appears that the cause is more the different ideological views of the latest ministers rather than any evidence gleaned from the experiment itself. The new (May 2018) Italian government has also committed to introducing a form of UBI, though since it has given little evidence that it can pay for it, it should not be presumed that this will actually happen.

The cost of a UBI depends on the amount paid. I have done some calculations based on the Federal Poverty Guidelines in the US. Table 12 sets these out.

Table 12. Federal Poverty Guidelines 2015: 48 contiguous states & DC

| Persons in household | 100% Federal Poverty Level | Medicaid eligibility threshold 138% FPL |
|---|---|---|
| 1 | $11,770 | $16,243 |
| 2 | 15,930 | 21,984 |
| 3 | 20,090 | 27,725 |
| 4 | 24,250 | 33,465 |

Source: Obamacare facts http://obamacarefacts.com/federal-poverty-level.

The gross cost of paying a basic income in the US at the Federal Poverty Level is estimated to be $2.98 billion, nearly 17% of GDP of $18 billion. But there would be some offsetting savings. The US currently spends about 5% of GDP on existing social security expenditures,[1] which would presumably be replaced by the UBI. Proponents of a UBI believe that other expenditures could be reduced as well leading to a net cost of only 7% of GDP.

Nevertheless, to impose a UBI today even in the US would mean an increase in taxation of about a quarter. This is unlikely to be politically acceptable.

But perhaps in 20 years' time the maths will work better. First, by then it is likely that the social security cost of not implementing a UBI will be rising because of the impact of the current welfare system and minimum wages on unemployment. Second, to the extent that technology continues to drive inequality, it is likely that tax receipts could be relatively buoyant as a result of the progressiveness of the tax system (although this may require governments to close loopholes that enable such companies to pursue aggressive tax-avoidance strategies and will also require such companies to pursue ethical policies that eschew such strategies).

Provided that governments squeeze other items of spending and don't spend the additional tax revenues elsewhere, my rough and ready calculation is that by some time between 2030 and 2035 a UBI at a level worth $12,000 a year per adult in today's money would be affordable with at most a 10% surcharge on taxes.

The magazine *Business Insider* has done some illustrative calculations about what could be done to introduce a UBI in the UK:[2]

So, we decided to do some back-of-the-envelope math to calculate what this might look like in the UK. We wanted to know how much each Brit would get if the current welfare budget was axed completely and the total pot was divided equally among everyone in the country?

We decided to use numbers for the 2013-14 financial year because those are the most complete numbers provided by the Office for National Statistics and the Office for Budget Responsibility:

- UK WELFARE BUDGET FOR 2013-14
- Total welfare spending: £251 billion
- Population: 64.5 million
- Of which, children: 15 million

If that budget was recast as a universal basic income, this is what you would get:

- UK BASIC INCOME BUDGET FOR 2013-14
- Basic income per head for all residents, annually: £3,891
- Basic income per head for all residents, monthly: £324
- Basic income per head for adults only, annually: £5,081
- Basic income per head for adults only, monthly: £423

One of the criticisms of basic income is that it would kill off the desire to work. Few studies have been done of this, but those that have indicate that people only reduce their work hours by a small amount on average.

The fact that a fiscally neutral basic income scheme would pay out only £423 per month (€585 or $644) to adults means almost everyone receiving it would still need a job. £423 a month is simply not enough to survive – or even pay rent – in most areas of Britain.

It might disincentivise some work, however. Young people living for free with their parents might suddenly feel rather rich. And that would mean employers currently offering unpleasant jobs with low pay might need to increase their pay rates or go out of business.

That might not be a bad thing: A basic income pre-supposes that most people want to work anyway, because productive activity is how we create meaning and identity. Basic income would give workers the freedom to not be forced into the jobs that no one wants – think about rubbish collectors – or to let people grow richer by taking on those onerous tasks. It might force society to revalue unpleasant but necessary tasks, and reward them more justly.

It would alter the labour market in favour of labour, in other words.

My own calculations suggest that, first of all, the UBI rate for the UK would have to be much higher than suggested in the *Business Insider* calculations. I would be looking for rates of weekly UBI payments of at least £700 per month with supplements for children. Even these would be on the low side for those who were unable to work at all. It might just be possible to finance this with inheritance taxes and voluntary taxes, which I suggest in the next chapter, but it would be foolish to rely on these assumptions.

In about a quarter of a century's time, however, it is much more likely that this could be affordable, though this would rely on public provision of other services not expanding to take account of economic growth in the meantime.

One of the more detailed studies of a universal basic income has been in the Republic of Ireland. The manifesto of the political party Fianna Fail for the 2016 general election proposed a Basic Income Commission to investigate this.[3] The initial considerations calculated that it would be possible but would require an income tax rate of 45%.[4]

On 5 June 2016 Switzerland had a referendum on providing a universal basic income after 130,000 people had signed a petition calling for one. The proposal was defeated by 1,897,528 votes to 568,660. Nevertheless, to achieve 23.1% of the vote was considered a success by the proponents. Although the referendum did not state a figure, the proponents of the UBI proposed a level of 2,500 Swiss francs for adults (about $1,650 at PPP in 2014) and 625 francs for children per month.

As mentioned at the start of this chapter, Finland started a pilot experiment to pay a randomly selected group of 2,000 unemployed people aged 25 to 58 a monthly €560 (£475) on 1 January 2017. The pilot will be discontinued when it ends on 1 January 2019. This appears to be because the (changed) government has a different scheme which uses more compulsion to try to force people into work. But interviews with some on the scheme seem to suggest that it had had the effect of increasing the number working, especially in gig-economy-type part-time jobs.

Of course it is important to understand that one of the advantages of bringing in a universal basic income is that it would allow workers to carry out low productivity jobs if they wished to. Often these might be artistic, craft or charitable (or even writing books!).

There is some experience of the behaviour induced by cash handouts in a range of countries around the world, recorded in the report 'Basic Income Around the World – The Unexpected Benefits of Unconditional

Cash Transfers' by Otto Lehto for the UK's Adam Smith Institute.[5] The report covers cash transfers in Alaska and Iran as well as smaller-scale experiments elsewhere and conditional experiments in Brazil and Mexico. The main conclusion appears to be that giving poor people in the countries covered additional cash does not encourage 'bad' spending. This is encouraging, although it seems unlikely that money given to those poor people who suffer from addiction problems would be spent as well.

It is worth rehearsing the reasons why Type 3 Inequality is likely to require a UBI. First some history of the technological changes:

- We are entering what is generally known as the fourth industrial revolution.
- The first industrial revolution used water and steam and was associated with the beginnings of mechanisation in industries such as textiles (this lasted from about 1760 to the First World War).
- The second industrial revolution was associated with electricity and mass production of automobiles, radios and less sophisticated consumer products (this started in the late 19th century and was largely completed in the West by the late 1960s).
- The third industrial revolution started in the latter part of the 20th century and involved the beginnings of the digital age (this started in the West in the 1960s and is still happening).
- The fourth industrial revolution is essentially the mass exploitation of digital technology into robotics, artificial intelligence, autonomous vehicles, 3D printing and bioengineering (this is expected to have its main effects within the next 25 years).

The key point to note is that the speed of spread of the fourth industrial revolution is expected to be much faster than its predecessors. This is consistent with my analysis of advancing technology when I was working for IBM where I observed that major technological changes tended to be implemented about ten years later than the technical experts predicted but tended to be taken up about 20 times faster than they had predicted.

The 2016 Economic Report to the President by the Bureau of Economic Advisers has put the probability at 83% that a worker making less than $20 an hour in 2010 will eventually lose their job to a machine.[6] Even workers making as much as $40 an hour face odds of 31%. This implies a major potential social security cost from higher technological unemployment if a UBI is not introduced.

But it is sensible to ask why, when all the previous industrial revolutions led to more jobs, not fewer, there are fears that the fourth industrial revolution will destroy jobs.

There appear to be three reasons why many people think it may be different this time.

First, previous industrial revolutions were absorbed slowly over time. Even in the UK, which by most measures led the first industrial revolution, after 150 years only a fifth of the workers in industry were in mechanised sectors.[7] As pointed out above, the fourth industrial revolution is likely to take place with virtually all its changes being fully absorbed over as short a period as 25 years. So this revolution is likely to be many orders of magnitude quicker than its predecessors.

Secondly, in previous industrial revolutions, even if men were replaced by machines, men were still needed to make the machines. Now machines make machines. So the loss of jobs in the industries where men are replaced by machines is unlikely to be made up by an increase in the number of jobs in the industries where the replacement machines are made.

Thirdly, although in theory the technology of the industrial revolution might still have been associated with a net gain in jobs if the wage level were able to be flexible downwards, it is likely that the conflict between the wage level for unskilled labour and statutory minimum wages or levels of social security benefit will make it impossible for wages to be sufficiently flexible for the gains in jobs at the lower end of the income scale to be realised (unless there is a complete reformation of labour markets – see below). Technology is likely to drive a widening of the divergence of marginal productivity levels and hence potential wages such that without a reform such as the UBI (and the consequent abolition of minimum wages) it will not be possible.

Just to give an example, there were 297,600 taxi drivers in the UK in 2015 (and 62,754 licenced taxis in London alone).[8] All of these jobs are likely eventually to be at risk when self-driving vehicles become a reality, which is expected to happen within the next 20 years. Taxi driving is a basic source of income for people with few qualifications other than a determination to better themselves. Within a generation these jobs will disappear. Meanwhile official data suggests there are only 230,000 taxi and limo drivers in the US, which is a bit surprising since the population is roughly five times larger than that of the UK – one suspects the real figure is higher! But there are 3.5 million truck drivers in the US, according to the American Trucker Association,[9] and their jobs will be at risk from autonomous vehicles.

Without both eliminating minimum wage laws and replacing social security with payments that are not reduced when people start to work, it is highly likely that the replacement of unskilled labour by machines in the fourth industrial revolution will cause unemployment to rise and the cost of social security to jump sharply, probably to unsustainable levels. So reform will be necessary to enable people with low marginal productivity to continue to work.

Based on the calculations for the US, it is likely that the potential timing when a UBI might be affordable might be earlier in Europe than in the US. This is for two reasons – current levels of social security spending are already higher in Europe than in the US and so the potential scope for savings when this spending is replaced by a UBI is greater, and secondly Europe seems to be tolerant of higher levels of taxation than the US. Against this is the high basic cost of living in Europe. Provided that action could be taken to reduce the cost of living, however, it might well be affordable to introduce UBIs in many European countries during the 2030s or 2040s, about ten years earlier than might make sense for the US.

A final benefit of UBI is that countries can have the right to limit access to it for immigrant workers. UBI is about reallocating the income and wealth of a country between its inhabitants. There is a moral case for offering some support to migrants in difficult circumstances, but the case for insisting that migrants have to have been in a country for quite a long period before they are eligible is a way of limiting the extent to which migrants might be seen to be having a slightly unfair advantage over the indigenous inhabitants.

## Conclusion

The main virtue of a UBI is that it is paid whether people work or not and so does not produce what in effect is a high marginal rate of tax of the kind that occurs when in-work benefits are withdrawn. And compared with unemployment-related benefits it has the advantage that it does not create an incentive against getting a job.

If it is the case that technology drives down the likely productivity of many in less skilled occupations, then it may be that these advantages will outweigh the disadvantages of a UBI – that it is very expensive or that it has to be paid at a very low level. It is important to note that the case for bringing in a UBI depends on abolishing minimum wage regulations at the same time. The idea is that the UBI enables people to do jobs that can only yield low rates of pay but makes it possible for these to be combined with higher levels of total income than would otherwise exist.

What is clear is that in current circumstances UBI is too expensive and cannot be afforded in any country except at a very low level where it would not provide a level of welfare that would conventionally be considered acceptable. My prediction is that it might be affordable in 20-40 years. But whether it will make sense will depend on whether the forecast that technology will wipe out many current jobs without creating so many opportunities for those displaced turns out to be a correct prediction. If it is, a UBI may turn out to be not an unaffordable luxury but an expensive necessity.

## Chapter 17

# USING TAXATION FOR REDISTRIBUTION

## Introduction

**T**HIS CHAPTER LOOKS AT THE USE OF THE TAX SYSTEM FOR REDISTRIB-ution. It points out that most developed economies already do a lot to redistribute using taxes and benefits (sometimes with negative long-term effects on motivation), and the scope for doing much more may be limited.

But smart use of the tax system might both raise more revenue and make it have more positive effects in reducing inequality and especially poverty while at the same time improving incentives.

The chapter looks first at the extent of current redistribution through the tax and benefits system in a range of countries. It then looks at the limits of this process. Then it looks at particular tax issues:

(1) The optimal top rates of tax.
(2) Voluntary taxes.
(3) Taxing wealth not income.

## Redistribution

There is already substantial redistribution through the tax and benefit system in most countries; indeed it is possible that in more than a few the attempt to redistribute through the tax and benefit system has been extended beyond the point of maximum effectiveness.

The key OECD study on this argues that tax and transfers reduce income inequality, although this analysis presumes that pre-tax and transfer incomes are unaffected by the redistribution. It argues that three quarters of the reduction in inequality reflects transfers and a quarter reflects taxes on incomes and capital. In most countries indirect taxes play a relatively small role one way or the other.[1]

It is claimed that in the UK indirect taxes in fact play a significantly regressive role in the redistribution of income,[2] but more detailed analysis disputes this. The IFS says that total tax payments in the UK are 'concentrated' which implies a net progressivity.[3]

However, the Brookings study in the US quoted elsewhere suggests that the scope for further redistribution through the tax and benefit system might be limited even in the US. And clearly if – even in an economy like the US with limited mobility out of the country – there is little scope for redistribution through the tax system, there will be even less scope in countries in Europe, for example, with higher marginal rates of tax and much higher international labour mobility.

### The optimal top rate of tax

Table 13 shows the top rates of tax in a range of countries.

### Table 13. Top marginal tax rate

|  |  |
|---|---|
| Denmark | 60.2% |
| Sweden | 56.6% |
| Belgium | 53.7% |
| Spain | 52.0% |
| Netherlands | 52.0% |
| France | 50.7% |
| Austria | 50.0% |
| Japan | 50.0% |
| Greece | 49.0% |
| Finland | 49.0% |
| Portugal | 49.0% |
| Italy | 48.6% |
| Canada | 48.0% |
| Ireland | 48.0% |
| Israel | 48.0% |
| Australia | 47.5% |
| Iceland | 46.2% |
| United Kingdom | 45.0% |
| United States | 41.9% |
| South Korea | 41.8% |
| Switzerland | 41.7% |
| Luxembourg | 41.3% |
| Slovenia | 41.0% |
| Chile | 40.0% |
| Norway | 40.0% |
| Turkey | 35.7% |
| New Zealand | 33.0% |
| Poland | 32.0% |
| Mexico | 30.0% |
| Singapore | 22.0% |
| Estonia | 21.0% |
| Slovakia | 19.0% |
| Hungary | 16.0% |
| Czech Republic | 15.0% |
| Hong Kong | 15.0% |

*Sources: various, based on an article by George Eaton, 'Which Countries Have the Highest Top Rate Taxes?', New Statesman, 27 January 2014. http://www.newstatesman.com/politics /2014/01-countries-have-highest-top-tax-rates. This data is slightly out of date though top tax rates do not change dramatically over time.*

In most Western economies the scope for raising more income from higher rates of tax on wealthy people is limited. Studies around the world suggest the top revenue-raising marginal rate of tax is 35-40%.[4] Yet virtually all major economies have top marginal rates at or above this, as Table 18 above shows. While higher rates may initially reduce inequality by making the rich poorer, they risk, by reducing government revenue, making the poor poorer as well.

What Table 13 suggests is that in some countries there is scope for higher rates of tax to reduce income inequality. Studies (see the discussion of the Scully curve in Chapter 7) show that reducing top rates of tax much below 30% do not seem to boost economic activity. But it also sug-gests that in many others the cost in lost economic growth resulting from the high compulsory marginal rates of taxes almost certainly creates more damage than is gained from the income redistributed.

## Voluntary taxes

The difficulty with redistributing through the income tax system comes from the damage to incentives. And this is exacerbated, particularly in a small country, if taxes are much higher than elsewhere, because rich people move to lower tax environments. And even if they don't move, it is easy for effort to be reduced if the benefits from work are low.

I once had a call on a Friday evening for an important piece of analy-sis for one of my clients which had to be presented to the then Mayor of London, Boris Johnson, on the Monday afternoon. I worked hard all weekend with countless phone calls to the US and elsewhere. And yet, after paying employers' national insurance contributions, employees' na-tional insurance contributions and income tax, my take home was roughly a third of my gross earnings, working out at £100 per hour worked over the weekend. Had I not been highly committed to customer service I would hardly have considered it worthwhile. I certainly didn't do it for the money. Meanwhile the tax man, who hadn't done a stroke of work over the weekend while I was up early and to bed late each day and worked all day, got twice as much as me.

Having said that, although compulsory taxation reduces incentives and also often creates a sense of unfairness, a case can be made for voluntary taxation for redistribution. Most people don't work actually for themselves. They work to earn income for many other people – both their direct family and many others as well. Moreover, if you are well-off, you tend to spend over your lifetime a remarkably small proportion of what you earn.

There is a case therefore for setting up a system of voluntary income tax supplements. The suggestion is that the maximum compulsory rate is say 35% but that income earners are encouraged to pay an additional voluntary amount of up to 20%. They might be given some limited say in how the money is used based on how much they have contributed. All this would have to be very public and any choices would have to be made very openly to prevent the danger of corruption.

There is a history of such behaviour from a century ago: Stanley Baldwin, the future Prime Minister, was appointed to the junior ministerial post of Financial Secretary to the Treasury in 1917, where he sought to encourage voluntary donations by the rich to repay the United Kingdom's war debt. He relinquished to the Treasury one-fifth of his own fortune, a total of £120,000, and wrote to *The Times* about this, signing himself with the initials associated with his position, FST.[5]

In June 2017 Norway announced a system whereby people could pay additional taxes voluntarily. At time of writing this has produced little revenue, but this may not be surprising since Norway already has high rates of compulsory tax. In the UK Westminster Council has proposed a voluntary 'mansion tax' on properties worth more than £10 million, though this has also not yet attracted much enthusiasm except from those who would not be expected to pay it.[6]

Looking back further, the respected former MP and Cabinet Minister Peter Lilley suggested a voluntary income tax, particularly for those who are especially concerned about inequality. The ideas set out here have some resemblance to his.

Where the present is different from the past is that many wealthy people now feel guilty about their excess wealth and income and are keen to show that they are not socially uncaring. The fashion has gone against the 'loadsamoney' style. It has also gone against conspicuous consumption (see the discussion of the two restaurants Pidgin and Sketch in Chapter 4). The rich now give substantially to charity despite the evidence that quite a lot of their donations do not go to charitable causes. The latest data for the UK show that 60% of larger charities' incomes does go to the intended recipients, but some charities account for their incomes net of fund-raising costs which make this an exaggerated figure.[7] In these cases far better to give to government where, even if there is some inefficiency, it is much clearer that the money is likely to go to those who need most.

Normally when rich people make large charitable contributions they like some sense that their contributions are appreciated by being made visible, or having something named after them, or possibly linking these taxes to the honours system. It shouldn't be beyond the wit of the many working in government to find some way of doing it. In London the Royal Parks, which until recently has been a government arm but is becoming a charity, has raised additional funding by getting the relatively wealthy people who live by the main London parks to sponsor a tree. Quite a few residents including my wife (who happens to be the Chairman of the Friends of Regents Park and Primrose Hill) and I have sponsored a series of cherry trees in Regents Park for a few thousand pounds each.

My theory is that the money raised from voluntary taxes could go to a fund for redistribution. I am not entirely convinced by the case for predistribution promoted by organisations like the Resolution Foundation in the UK which involve giving significant lump cash sums to people when they reach the age of 25, since giving large cash sums to people who are not used to the money might be a recipe for disaster (there is some evidence from football pools and lottery winners!).[8] My instinct would be to use this fund instead to support education for the least well-off, which ought to yield a better return in reduced inequality. But it might make sense to conduct some pilot experiments to see what works best.

### Taxing wealth not income

Taxing income can ossify the economic system by limiting growth and preventing new money from entering the system. But taxing wealth and using this to fund a degree of redistribution doesn't face the same drawbacks through negative effects on incentives.

The most obvious way of redistributing which minimises the impact on incentives is to tax inheritance. There are practical problems, but one suspects that the degree of political resistance to a substantial inheritance tax on all inheritances other than those to partners would·be much less than people imagine.

An inheritance tax of 50% (other than on inheritance to spouses and partners) does face the objection that this is tax on money on which tax has already been paid when it was earned in income or inherited from the past. So it could only be introduced with substantial consultation. It should be noted that in many countries inheritance taxes are already high. In such countries, the issue is more to do with the moral legitimacy of the tax, particularly when it is combined with already high rates of income tax. Without legitimacy, people will strive to reduce their tax bill through transfers and complicated international arrangements.

The key is for taxes to be seen to be well spent and for the tax authorities not to be greedy. And for governments to applaud the payment of tax and treat high income tax payments as a cause for congratulation rather than as another excuse for assaulting the rich.

One way of boosting inheritance tax yields might be to combine a top inheritance tax rate of 50% with a reduction in top rates of compulsory income tax to a maximum rate of 35%, possibly combined with a system for additional voluntary taxation income and wealth taxation. The yields from inheritance tax should be used for redistribution while those from other taxes can be used to fund other government services and investments.

## Conclusion

The trick with taxation is not to be greedy and to encourage compliance. It is important that the tax is seen to be legitimate and well spent and that the methods used by the fiscal authorities are not such as to encourage a dangerously adversarial attitude. It is also important that money used by the public sector is not obviously wasted or abused for political purposes.

In general it is better to tax wealth than income. Meanwhile there are plenty of ways in which voluntary taxes could be encouraged, provided compulsory tax rates are not excessive and certainly not above the points of optimal income raising of around 35%.

## Chapter 18

# NEITHER TRUMP NOR CORBYN –
# REJECTING FALSE SOLUTIONS

THE MOST IMPORTANT REASON FOR WRITING THIS BOOK IS, HAVING explained what is happening and why many people are facing squeezed living standards, to warn against accepting the simple solutions from the extremists on both sides; the Corbyn/Sanders anti-capitalists on the one hand, who claim capitalism has failed and should be replaced, and the Trumpites on the other, who believe that stopping free trade or stopping migration will somehow insulate the economy from some of the tougher impacts of globalisation.

I try to show in this book that both are wrong.

As I have argued in previous chapters, the recent growth in inequality is a complicated and changing phenomenon that is not susceptible to simplistic solutions. A significant but still small part of it reflects exploitation (this is less important in the more advanced economies), and while globalisation has caused the bulk of the recent growth in inequality in the West, cutting economies off from the benefits of globalisation through abandoning free trade or through limiting migration will actually make this problem worse.

The proposed solutions put forward by both the Corbyn/Sandersites and the Trumpites will actually inhibit the economy from dealing with Type 3 Inequality caused by technology, which is ultimately likely to be the most important challenge in the coming years.

Let me deal with the Corbyn/Sanders critique first. This treats inequality as essentially Type 1 Inequality caused by exploitation. It therefore tries to hamstring those who are wealthy or who have high incomes through a combination of higher taxes and regulations, including a proposal for a maximum wage and a high minimum wage, on the assumption that the solution to the problem is to make the rich poorer.

Corbyn set out his views in the Labour Party manifesto for the 2017 UK General Election, but that manifesto covers a wide range of issues that go well beyond the subject of this book.

In 2016, after he had been elected leader of the Labour Party in the UK, he prepared a manifesto that concentrates on economic issues. This is it in full:[1]

### 1) Full employment and an economy that works for all:

We will create a million good quality jobs across our regions and nations and guarantee a decent job for all. By investing £500 billion in infrastructure, manufacturing and new industries backed up by a publicly-owned National Investment Bank and regional banks we will build a high skilled, high tech, low carbon economy that ends austerity and leaves no one and nowhere left behind. We will invest in the high speed broadband, energy, transport and homes that our country needs and allow good businesses to thrive, and support a new generation of co-operative enterprises.

### 2) A secure homes guarantee:

We will build a million new homes in five years, with at least half a million council homes, through our public investment strategy. We will end insecurity for private renters by introducing rent controls, secure tenancies and a charter of private tenants' rights, and increase access to affordable home ownership.

### 3) Security at work:

We will give people stronger employment rights from day one in a job, end exploitative zero hours contracts and create new sectoral collective bargaining rights, including mandatory collective bargaining for companies with 250 or more employees. We will create new employment and trade union rights to bring security to the workplace and win better pay and conditions for everyone. We will strengthen working people's representation at work and the ability of trade unions to organise so that working people have a real voice at work. And we will put the defence of social and employment rights, as well as action against undercutting of pay and conditions through the exploitation of migrant labour, at the centre of the Brexit negotiations agenda for a new relationship with Europe.

### 4) Secure our NHS and social care:

We will end health service privatisation and bring services into a secure, publicly-provided NHS. We will integrate the NHS and social care for older and disabled people, funding dignity across the board and ensure parity for mental health services.

**5) A national education service, open to all:**

We will build a new National Education Service, open to all throughout their lives. We will create universal public childcare to give all children a good start in life, allowing greater sharing of caring responsibilities and removing barriers to women participating in the labour market. We will bring about the progressive restoration of free education for all; and guarantee quality apprenticeships and adult skills training.

**6) Action to secure our environment:**

We will act to protect the future of our planet, with social justice at the heart of our environment policies, and take our fair share of action to meet the Paris climate agreement – starting by getting on track with our Climate Change Act goals. We will accelerate the transition to a low-carbon economy, and drive the expansion of the green industries and jobs of the future, using our National Investment Bank to invest in public and community-owned renewable energy. We will deliver clean energy and curb energy bill rises for households – energy for the 60 million, not the big six energy companies. We will defend and extend the environmental protections gained from the EU.

**7) Put the public back into our economy and services:**

We will rebuild public services and expand democratic participation, put the public back into our economy, give people a real say in their local communities, and increase local and regional democracy. We will rebuild our economy with public investment to deliver wealth for all, across our regions and nations in a genuinely mixed economy. We will act to 'insource' our public and local council services, increase access to leisure, arts and sports across the country and expand our publicly-controlled bus network. We will bring our railways into public ownership and build democratic social control over our energy.

**8) Cut income and wealth inequality:**

We will build a progressive tax system so that wealth and the highest earners are fairly taxed, act against executive pay excess and shrink the gap between the highest and lowest paid – FTSE 100 CEOs are now paid 183 times the wage of the average UK worker, and Britain's wages are the most unequal in Europe. We will act to create a more equal society, boost the incomes of the poorest and close the gender pay gap.

**9) Action to secure an equal society:**

We will ensure that the human rights of all citizens are respected and all are protected from discrimination and prejudice. We will take action to tackle violence against women and girls, racism and discrimination on the basis of faith, and secure real equality for LGBT and disabled people. We will defend the Human Rights Act and we will guarantee full rights for EU citizens living and working in Britain – and not allow them to be used as pawns in Brexit negotiations.

10) **Peace and justice at the heart of foreign policy:**

We will put conflict resolution and human rights at the heart of foreign policy, commit to working through the United Nations, end support for aggressive wars of intervention and back effective action to alleviate the refugee crisis. British foreign policy has long failed to be either truly independent or internationally co-operative, making the country less safe and reducing our diplomatic and moral authority. We will build human rights and social justice into trade policy, honour our international treaty obligations on nuclear disarmament and encourage others to do the same.

Clearly not all the Corbyn measures would necessarily be damaging. But my assessment is that those that discourage high skills from settling in the UK, that reduce the flexibility of the labour market and that force rates of pay above the marginal product of labour are unlikely to benefit the economy.

Meanwhile, although Keynesian economics has its place, there are questions about the credibility of a £500 billion fiscal boost in a UK economy where debt is already nearly 90% of GDP. In a world of global demand deficiency it is arguable that there *is* in fact a magic money tree which can be used to finance spending. But probably not on this scale.

The difficulty with this manifesto is that it seems to reveal no understanding of what is driving the pressures on incomes of working people. There is merely a promise to provide better benefits and working conditions and implicitly higher wages. This would be fine if the only cause of the downward pressure was Type 1 Inequality and the conditions of the poor could be improved simply by taking money from the rich and redistributing it. But as we have shown, technology and globalisation have been much more important causes. Giving people higher salaries and raising their costs to employers when the pressures on them result from a falling marginal productivity of labour will make more jobs uneconomic and as a result they will disappear. This is essentially what happened in Venezuela, leading to economic collapse and then to food shortages and malnutrition.

There is also little sense that the rich and wealthy generally contribute to society by creating wealth and spending. Yet evidence seems to suggest that on the whole the rich at least in the more developed democracies contribute far more to society than they take out (see Chapter 8). Taxation on a scale that seems to be abusive is likely to drive the rich away and hence cause the loss of these benefits.

The Sanders manifesto[2] said the following:

Demanding that the wealthy and large corporations pay their fair share in taxes. As president, Sen. Sanders will stop corporations from shifting their profits and jobs overseas to avoid paying U.S. income taxes. He will create a progressive estate tax on the top 0.3 percent of Americans who inherit more than $3.5 million. He will also enact a tax on Wall Street speculators who caused millions of Americans to lose their jobs, homes, and life savings.

Increasing the federal minimum wage from $7.25 to $15 an hour by 2020. In the year 2015, no one who works 40 hours a week should be living in poverty.

Putting at least 13 million Americans to work by investing $1 trillion over five years towards rebuilding our crumbling roads, bridges, railways, airports, public transit systems, ports, dams, wastewater plants, and other infrastructure needs.

Reversing trade policies like NAFTA, CAFTA, and PNTR with China that have driven down wages and caused the loss of millions of jobs. If corporate America wants us to buy their products they need to manufacture those products in this country, not in China or other low-wage countries.

Creating 1 million jobs for disadvantaged young Americans by investing $5.5 billion in a youth jobs program. Today, the youth unemployment rate is off the charts. We have got to end this tragedy by making sure teenagers and young adults have the jobs they need to move up the economic ladder.

Fighting for pay equity by signing the Paycheck Fairness Act into law. It is an outrage that women earn just 78 cents for every dollar a man earns.

Making tuition free at public colleges and universities throughout America. Everyone in this country who studies hard should be able to go to college regardless of income.

Expanding Social Security by lifting the cap on taxable income above $250,000. At a time when the senior poverty rate is going up, we have got to make sure that every American can retire with dignity and respect.

Guaranteeing healthcare as a right of citizenship by enacting a Medicare for all single-payer healthcare system. It's time for the U.S. to join every major industrialised country on earth and provide universal healthcare to all.

Requiring employers to provide at least 12 weeks of paid family and medical leave; two weeks of paid vacation; and seven days of paid sick days. Real family values are about making sure that parents have the time they need to bond with their babies and take care of their children and relatives when they get ill.

Enacting a universal childcare and prekindergarten program. Every psychologist understands that the most formative years for a human being is from the ages 0-3. We have got to make sure every family in America has the opportunity to send their kids to a high quality childcare and pre-K program.

Making it easier for workers to join unions by fighting for the Employee Free Choice Act. One of the most significant reasons for the forty-year decline in the middle class is that the rights of workers to collectively bargain for better wages and benefits have been severely undermined.

Breaking up huge financial institutions so that they are no longer too big to fail. Seven years ago, the taxpayers of this country bailed out Wall Street because they were too big to fail. Yet, 3 out of the 4 largest financial institutions are 80 percent bigger today than before we bailed them out. Sen. Sanders has introduced legislation to break these banks up. As president, he will fight to sign this legislation into law.

Like the Corbyn plans, not everything in the Sanders economic manifesto is unworkable. But there seems little to encourage the adaptation of the economy to the newest technology or to deal with the challenges that new technology is likely to set. Instead there is a focus on tax and spend. The track record of such policies is that while they can be beneficial in dealing with cyclical problems, they are less successful in dealing with structural ones and also less successful if taken to extremes. There seem to be diminishing returns to scale for public sector intervention.

The most pernicious of the Corbyn/Sanders ideas are those that are likely to push up the cost of labour above its marginal benefits to employers. Employers (except those in the public sector – and even they eventually have a budget constraint) cannot afford persistently to employ those who don't earn enough to pay their salaries and overheads and allow their employers to turn a profit. So pushing the cost of labour up on its own is likely to lead to rising unemployment. This is especially the case when restrictions on firing mean that hiring is a long-term commitment. It is ironic that in general (and there are occasional exceptions) comparing like countries with like, those countries with the highest levels of employment and lowest levels of unemployment tend to be those countries like the US and the UK where it is easiest to dismiss staff who are not performing, not those countries with restrictions on sacking people.

But it is important not to look at the Corbyn/Sanders proposals from a static perspective. In the longer term, it may well be that the biggest damage that they do is through ossifying the economic structure and preventing it from adapting to economic change. Roles for trade unions, restrictions on firing, or reducing purchases of labour in other ways all are likely to ossify the structure of employment in a form increasingly unfit for purpose. This isn't just theory – a casual glance at Western Europe shows how this starts to damage economies.

Italy has had no economic growth at all in the 21st century. Its rate of unemployment in September 2016 was 11.7%, its rate of youth unemployment was 39.2% in July 2016. Despite labour law reform in July 2015 affecting new hires, most employees are protected from being sacked. And the effect of the labour law is to prevent less competent employees from changing jobs because if they do so they will lose their protection from being sacked. Meanwhile productivity is stagnant and profitability depressed. The longer it goes on, the weaker and less well adapted the economy becomes.

What happened in Venezuela? Because the Venezuelan argument is important, it is worth looking in some detail at what happened there to see what failed.

Hugo Chavez took over as leader of Venezuela in 1998, having tried to gain power in an attempted coup six years earlier. He and his handpicked successor Victor Maduro (Chavez died in 2013) have run the country since.

A key point about Venezuela is its dependence on oil. When the price of oil was $100 a barrel, 60% of government revenues and 95% of export revenues were from oil. One of the problems this caused was that over time the country became afflicted by a bad case of 'Dutch Disease' where the real exchange rate made the country uncompetitive in the non-oil economy.

Chavez posed as a social reformer and indeed initially made good use of the country's good fortune with oil to reduce poverty and improve health. Before he came to power Venezuela had traditionally kept public finances that were in balance in as many years as they were in deficit. Chavez and Maduro grew public spending from 28.8% of GDP when they entered power in 1998 to 47.2% in 2014. Meanwhile they also instituted programmes of land reform and nationalisation.

Even when the price of oil was high, rising public expenditure and weakening non-oil production were causing the budget to go into deficit and debt to accumulate. By 2012 the government's budget deficit had reached 15.6% of GDP after being in surplus as recently as 2005.

In turn the monetisation of the debt led to inflation. Venezuela had traditionally had an inflation problem, but the annual rate of inflation had generally remained between 15% and 30%. But as the impact of the monetisation developed, inflation started to climb – to 56% in 2013, 69% in 2014, and 181% in 2015. Then inflation really accelerated to 274% in 2016, 2,616% in 2017 and had reached 13,379% in April 2018.

The collapse in output has been exacerbated by exchange controls and fluctuating Forex policies. Because of an uncompetitive exchange rate resulting from the dependence on oil, most staples have been traditionally imported. Foreign exchange policy has been changed with bewildering frequency which has led to a shortage of imported goods, including foods and medicines. This in turn has led to the malnutrition and health problems that have been widely reported.

GDP started to collapse in 2014 and fell by 18% in real terms in 2016. This year GDP is estimated by the IMF to be 31.5% lower than in 2013. At present the latest IMF forecasts, released in April 2018, predict that the economy will continue to decline in real terms till 2021 at least, reaching a level more than 40% lower than in 2013.

Although the land reform and the nationalisation policies have played a role in Venezuela's economic collapse, just as relevant has been the overspending, the reliance on growing government deficits and the subsequent monetisation of the resulting debts.

It is also worth noting that it took nearly 20 years before the consequences of the policies led to economic collapse, though many of the economically risky policies did not get applied until after Chavez had been in power for more than five years.

Where Sanders and Corbyn seem to wish to adopt similar policies to Chavez is in their approaches to government spending and to uneconomic wage levels. On the other hand both the UK and US are much stronger economies than Venezuela and presumably would take longer to ruin.

## The Trump manifesto

Donald Trump, to most commentators' surprise, won the 2016 US Presidential election (and his party less surprisingly won both houses of Congress). This brings Trump manifesto moves into focus. While, having taken office, he has changed his positions with bewildering rapidity, the manifesto on which he was elected is still partly relevant.

What may seem at first sight extraordinary is how much of the Sanders/Corbyn analysis is repeated in the Trump manifesto set out below:

### The Trump Economy:
### 25 Million New Jobs Created In The Next Decade[3]

President Trump proposed sweeping reforms in tax, trade, energy and regulatory policies. The Trump campaign's economist estimates that the plan would conservatively boost growth to 3.5% per year on average, well above the 2% currently projected by government forecasters, with the potential to reach a 4% growth rate.

Growth averaged at least three and a half percent per year in the 55 years between World War II and the year 2000. With the faster growth from the Trump Plan, the economy will create 25 million new jobs over the next decade. For each 1 percent in added GDP growth, the economy adds 1.2 million jobs. Increasing growth by 1.5% would result in 18 million jobs (1.5 times 1.2 million times 10 years) above the projected current law job figures of 7 million, producing a total of 25 million new jobs for the American economy.

Every income group receives a tax cut under the Trump plan, with a million more being removed from the income tax rolls and low-income Americans paying no income tax at all.

The greatest percentage reduction in tax bill goes to working and middle class taxpayers:

A married couple earning $50,000 per year with two children and $8,000 in child care expenses will save 35% from their current tax bill.

A married couple earning $75,000 per year with two children and $10,000 in child care expenses will receive a 30% reduction in their tax bill.

A married couple earning $5 million per year with two children and $12,000 in child care expenses will get only a 3% reduction in their tax bill.

The plan lowers the business tax rate to 15%. The current business rate 35% rate is one of the highest in the world, making domestic investment unattractive. It includes a 10% tax on repatriation, instantly bringing trillions of dollars back into the U.S. economy now parked overseas.

The plan also allows U.S.-based manufacturers to elect full expensing of plant and equipment, an invitation to massive investment. If they elect this approach, they will give up the ability to deduct interest expense.

Tax brackets in the individual income tax will be reduced from 7 to 3. Tax rates will be 12%, 25% or 33%, with thresholds very similar to the House GOP plan.

The plan will close special interest tax breaks and cap deductions at $100,000 for single filers and $200,000 for married filers, eliminating many costly tax loopholes while stimulating growth.

The standard deduction will be $30,000 dollars for married couples and $15,000 dollars for single individuals. Most taxpayers will have no need to itemize, simplifying their tax returns and making it easier to file.

The plan provides a child care deduction for children up to 13 years of age for average child care expense. There's an income cap, so the new deductions don't apply to the rich.

Finally, the plan eliminates the carried interest loophole for Wall Street and the death tax, which falls especially hard on small businesses and farmers.

One of the keys to unlocking growth is scaling-back years of disastrous regulations unilaterally imposed by our out-of-control bureaucracy.

In 2015 alone, federal agencies issued over 3,300 final rules and regulations, up from 2,400 the prior year. Every year, overregulation costs our economy $2 trillion dollars a year and reduces household wealth by almost $15,000 dollars.

Mr. Trump has proposed a moratorium on new federal regulations that are not compelled by Congress or public safety, and will ask agency and department heads to identify all needless job-killing regulations and they will be removed.

This includes eliminating some of our most intrusive regulations, like the Waters of the U.S. Rule. It also means scrapping the EPA's so-called Clean Power Plan which the government itself estimates will cost $7.2 billion a year. This Obama-Clinton directive will shut down most, if not all, coal-powered electricity plants in America.

A complete regulatory overhaul will level the playing field for American workers and add trillions in new wealth to our economy – keeping companies here, expanding hiring and investment, and bringing thousands of new companies to our shores.

Trade will be an important driver of economic growth along with other key structural reforms. Donald Trump will ensure that every single one of our trade agreements increases our GDP growth rate, reduces our trade deficit, and strengthens our manufacturing base.

There will be no Trans-Pacific Partnership, even if the President and Congress are reckless enough to pass it in a lame duck session against the will of the American people.

Donald Trump will appoint the toughest and smartest trade negotiators to fight on behalf of American workers and direct the Secretary of Commerce to identify every violation of trade agreements a foreign country is currently using to harm our workers.

NAFTA will be renegotiated to get a better deal for American workers. If our partners do not agree to a renegotiation, America will withdraw from the deal.

China will be labeled a currency manipulator. Any country that devalues their currency in order to take unfair advantage of the United States will be met with sharply, and that includes tariffs and taxes.

The U.S. Trade Representative will bring trade cases against China. China's unfair subsidy behavior is prohibited by the terms of its entrance to the WTO. If China does not stop its illegal activities, including its theft of American trade secrets, Donald Trump will use every lawful presidential power to remedy trade disputes, including the application of tariffs.

The Trump energy policy will make us energy independent, create millions of new jobs, and protect clean air and clean water. We have one of the world's most diverse resource bases – from abundant coal, oil, and natural gas to geothermal, solar, and wind. We are also the world's leader in energy technologies like nuclear power.

The United States will become the world's dominant leader in energy production. The first step will be to undo the damage of the last

8 years. By 2030, the Obama-Clinton energy restrictions will eliminate another half a million manufacturing jobs, reduce economic output by $2.5 trillion, and reduce incomes by $7,000 per person.

The Trump Administration will unleash an energy revolution that will bring vast new wealth to our country. We will support coal production. We will support safe hydraulic fracturing. We will allow energy production on federal lands in appropriate areas. We will also open up vast areas of our offshore energy resources for safe production.

Lifting unnecessary restrictions on all sources of American energy (such as coal and onshore and offshore oil and gas) will (a) increase GDP by more than $100 billion annually, add over 500,000 new jobs annually, and increase annual wages by more than $30 billion over the next 7 years; (b) increase federal, state, and local tax revenues by almost $6 trillion over 4 decades; and (c) increase total economic activity by more than $20 trillion over the next forty years.

The Trump Administration will ensure a reliable, streamlined regulatory and permitting process for energy infrastructure projects, and will work with their sponsors to find workable solutions so that worthy energy infrastructure projects can be completed on time and on budget.

Finally, a Trump Administration will support continued research into advanced energy technologies, but we will not be in the business of government picking winners and losers. We need to allow the free market and the innovative spirit of the American people to produce the new energy technologies of tomorrow, without undue government interference.

The "Penny Plan" would reduce non-defense, non-safety net spending by one percent of the previous year's total each year. Over ten years, the plan will reduce spending (outlays) by almost $1 trillion without touching defense or entitlement spending.

Like the Corbyn and Sanders plans, the Trump plan is also not entirely silly. Indeed the tax, regulation and energy components are likely to be net economically beneficial, while the infrastructural spending plans make sense on their own, although they will face problems in funding.

But the trade plans if implemented will do much more damage than the good that is done from these other components and indeed risk causing the world to deteriorate into trade wars, with the potential for mutually assured economic destruction. Even if there is no retaliation (which would require superhuman patience on the part of the other countries) the static losses from these policies would be substantial. Meanwhile the immigration proposals are likely equally to cost the economy. My own note on Trump's election suggested that world GDP growth would be noticeably slower as a result of Trump's victory.[4]

## The new chauvinism

Those against globalisation in both the UK and the US seem to think that they can somehow escape the impact of globalisation by imposing trade restrictions. Sadly it ain't so.

If one country were 50% of world GDP, it could isolate itself from the rest of the world at relatively limited cost for quite a long time. It would lose the static gains from trade and rather more importantly lose the incentives to innovate that come from trade (China's 500-year stagnation reflected this precise point). But the short-term cost would be relatively low – perhaps 5% of incomes for the first ten years or so.

But the US is only 16% of world GDP at PPP values and 22% in nominal terms. Were it to, say, halve its imports from China, it would lose the benefits of cheap inputs and the dollar would rise. It would be likely that exports would fall by at least as much as imports. Exports would be more expensive because they would lose the value of cheap components as well as facing a more adverse exchange rate. Living standards could be as much as 10% lower. Some jobs would be gained in the import substituting sectors. But probably at least as many would be lost in the exporting sectors.

But that would be just the first-round effect. After that, there would be the loss of the stimulus to adapt to modern trading patterns as the US trade patterns settled into a mercantilist pattern.

The history of protectionism is that it saves very few jobs at a very high consumer cost.

## How does trade affect the US economy?

The Congressional Budget Office in the US has produced a major report on how international trade agreements affect the US.[5] Its key conclusions are overwhelmingly positive, though it points out that there can be some short-term and some sectoral disbenefits.

International trade yields several benefits for the US economy. Trade increases competition between foreign and domestic producers. That increase in competition causes the least productive US businesses and industries to shrink; it also enables the most productive businesses and industries in the US to expand to take advantage of profitable new opportunities to sell abroad and obtain cost savings from greater economies of scale.

As a result, trade encourages a more efficient allocation of resources in the economy and raises the average productivity of businesses and industries in the US.

Through that increase in productivity, trade can boost economic output and workers' average real (inflation-adjusted) wage. In addition, US consumers and businesses benefit because trade lowers prices for some goods and services and increases the variety of products available for purchase.

Not everyone benefits from trade expansion, however. Although increases in trade probably do not significantly affect total employment, trade can affect different workers in different ways. Workers in occupations, businesses and industries that expand because of trade may make more money, whereas workers in occupations, businesses and industries that shrink may make less money or experience longer than average unemployment. Such losses can be temporary or permanent.

Nevertheless, economic theory and historical evidence suggest that the diffuse and long-term benefits of international trade have outweighed the concentrated short-term costs. That conclusion has consistently received strong support from the economics profession.[6]

Meanwhile, not part of the economic manifesto is the Donald Trump immigration plan.[7]

### Donald J. Trump's 10 Point Plan to Put America First

1. Begin working on an impenetrable physical wall on the southern border, on day one. Mexico will pay for the wall.

2. End catch-and-release. Under a Trump administration, anyone who illegally crosses the border will be detained until they are removed out of our country.

3. Move criminal aliens out day one, in joint operations with local, state, and federal law enforcement. We will terminate the Obama administration's deadly, non-enforcement policies that allow thousands of criminal aliens to freely roam our streets.

4. End sanctuary cities.

5. Immediately terminate President Obama's two illegal executive amnesties. All immigration laws will be enforced – we will triple the number of ICE agents. Anyone who enters the U.S. illegally is subject to deportation. That is what it means to have laws and to have a country.

6. Suspend the issuance of visas to any place where adequate screening cannot occur, until proven and effective vetting mechanisms can be put into place.

7. Ensure that other countries take their people back when we order them deported.

8. Ensure that a biometric entry-exit visa tracking system is fully implemented at all land, air, and sea ports.

9. Turn off the jobs and benefits magnet. Many immigrants come to the U.S. illegally in search of jobs, even though federal law prohibits the employment of illegal immigrants.

10. Reform legal immigration to serve the best interests of America and its workers, keeping immigration levels within historic norms.

This plan is aimed at substantially reducing immigration into the US. Yet analysis carried out by Cebr shows how modern economies benefit from immigration, not only through the greater amounts of taxes paid by migrants than are taken out in benefits but in three much more important ways:[8]

(1) Modern economies are based on creativity. One of the strongest stimulators of creativity is diversity.

(2) Immigration reduces skills bottlenecks. Even economies with underemployed resources tend to have skills bottlenecks which constrain growth. A survey quoted in *The Guardian* in the UK suggests that skills shortages even in an economy with substantial migration cost the economy at least £2 billion a year.[9] Just imagine what the cost would be without migration to fill these jobs. Immigration reduces the extent and cost of skills bottlenecks.

(3) Immigration, although on balance doing not much to net wages, tends to reduce the wage share of GDP and boost the profits share of GDP. Because GDP is higher, the lower share works out as just as high as the higher share of the smaller cake in the low immigration case. Indeed, over time, it is likely that immigration initially reduces wages slightly but ultimately boosts them substantially. This is because high levels of profitability for companies, provided they are not obtained through restriction of competition, tend to boost growth through encouraging higher levels of investment and innovation. This is especially so when creativity is being boosted for the reasons set out above.

So it is likely that the Trump economic proposals if actually implemented, far from making America great again, would actually impoverish the US economy. He claims that he will boost growth to over 3.5% per annum. In reality the policy, due to the lost benefits from trade and from migrants, would be likely to cause growth to fall to below 2% after an initial spurt of higher growth.

The biggest cost of the Trump economic proposals could be a further loss of faith in democratic politics and in Western values. Although the West has often been guilty of gross hypocrisy, Western values are nearer to providing a basis for different peoples to live in reasonable harmony than any alternatives yet put forward. If Trump's policies fail and the US retreats into a self-absorbed chauvinism, the alternatives on offer from Russia, China and the Islamic world are unattractive while the superficially more attractive lifestyles on offer from Europe have the disadvantage that they do not appear to be sustainable economically.

This chapter also looks in some detail at the costs of implementing the election manifesto commitment of the Conservative Party in the UK General Election 2017 to reduce net migration to 'tens of thousands'. The precise text from the Conservative manifesto is set out here:

Britain is an open economy and a welcoming society and we will always ensure that our British businesses can recruit the brightest and best from around the world and Britain's world-class universities can attract international students. We also believe that immigration should be controlled and reduced, because when immigration is too fast and too high, it is difficult to build a cohesive society.

Thanks to Conservatives in government, there is now more control in the system. The nature of the immigration we have – more skilled workers and university students, less abuse and fewer unskilled migrants – better suits the national interest. But with annual net migration standing at 273,000, immigration to Britain is still too high. It is our objective to reduce immigration to sustainable levels, by which we mean annual net migration in the tens of thousands, rather than the hundreds of thousands we have seen over the last two decades.

We will, therefore, continue to bear down on immigration from outside the European Union. We will increase the earnings thresholds for people wishing to sponsor migrants for family visas. We will toughen the visa requirements for students, to make sure that we maintain high standards. We will expect students to leave the country at the end of their course, unless they meet new, higher requirements that allow them to work in Britain after their studies have concluded. Overseas students will remain in the immigration 55 statistics – in line with international definitions – and within scope of the government's policy to reduce annual net migration.

Leaving the European Union means, for the first time in decades, that we will be able to control immigration from the European Union too. We will therefore establish an immigration policy that allows us to reduce and control the number of people who come to Britain from the European Union, while still allowing us to attract the skilled workers our economy needs.[10]

The role of migrants is especially important in the UK for the Flat White Economy, the new digitally based economy heavily based in the East End of London that is described in my eponymous book.[11] This economy has emerged from the mix of the creative economy that was already prevalent in East London and the tech economy that has emerged in recent years. Key elements are online retail (where the UK leads the world by some distance) and online marketing.

The book describes the emergence of the Flat White Economy as the fortuitous accident of three phenomena – the UK's strong lead in online retail and marketing, the maturing of online technology and the availability of very large amounts of digitally skilled relatively cheap labour as a result of Southern Europe's economic weakness. As I put it: 'They can't get jobs in their own countries so they come to London, partly for fun and partly in hope of a job. Once there, they realise how expensive it is to stay in London and so are very keen to find work even if they have to live a backpacker's existence in London.' This very elastic supply of labour is a key element in the success of the Flat White Economy.

Chapter 7 of *The Flat White Economy* ('Immigration, Britain's Secret Economic Weapon') argues:

To understand the full impact of immigration on economic growth, one needs to treat it as a dynamic process that not only has a direct effect, but a substantial enabling effect to boost other economic processes that are taking place at the same time.

My analysis of the economic impact of immigration suggests a threefold effect:

* First: migration alleviates skill bottlenecks and hence removes barriers to faster growth.

* Second: migration boosts diversity and also boosts creativity which enhances productivity with both direct and indirect effects on economic growth.

* Third: migration makes business more profitable, enhancing investment and hence growth. Even if the initial impact is to place downward pressure on wages through the enhanced supply of labour relative to demand, the secondary effect is to boost wages through faster growth.[12]

Because my analysis takes account of these dynamic effects of immigration, which are well supported by academic analysis, it suggests the effects of cutting immigration are greater than those estimated by conventional analysis.

The latest UK data from the ONS Index of Services (using components 58-60, 62 and 63) show that the sector grew by 9.8% to reach 9.7% of GDP in 2016, a strong acceleration from even the buoyant figures for the previous four years. Since 2011, this sector's share of GDP has increased by a fifth and it is now, other than construction, the largest single sector of the whole UK economy.

As the economy adjusts to take account of its increasing dependence on this digital economy, there are implications.

Had it not grown in 2016 and everything else had been unchanged, GDP growth would have been 0.9% rather than the 1.8% recorded.

The conventional analysis of the economic impact of limiting migration in the UK is best described in an excellent paper by Jonathan Portes and Giuseppe Forte in Vox.[13] Their 'scenarios imply that net EU migration to the UK could fall by up to 91,000 on the central scenario, and up to 150,000 on a more extreme scenario. This is comparable to other estimates that employ different methodologies (Vargas-Silva 2016,[14] Migration Watch 2016[15]).'

The conventional analysis assumes that a reduction in migrants would be associated with higher productivity for the remaining population. 'Boubtane et al.[16] find that migration in general boosts productivity in advanced economies, but by varying amounts; for the UK, the estimated impact is that a 1 percentage point in the migrant share of the working-age population leads to a 0.4-0.5% increase in productivity.'

They argue that the central estimate of impact of Brexit in leading to reduced migration on GDP 2020 is 0.63% to 1.19%. Their analysis suggests that the central impact for 2030 is 0.92% to 3.38% for GDP per capita.

The OBR in its fiscal sustainability reports has also drawn attention to the positive impact of migration on the economy and hence the fiscal position.

To quote the Migration Observatory:[17]

> The Office for Budget Responsibility (OBR, 2016) forecasted fiscal aggregates – such as net government borrowing and debt as a percentage of GDP – under alternative scenarios of net migration. In their central forecast they use the ONS principal population projection, which assumes net migration of 329,000 in 2015 and 256,000 in 2016, declining to 185,000 in 2021. In the 'high migration' scenario, net migration falls to 265,000 by 2021. In the 'low migration' scenario, net migration falls to 105,000 by 2021.
>
> The OBR estimates suggest that the government budget surplus in 2020-2021 would be higher under the high migration scenario and lower in the low migration scenario: it projected a £16.9bn surplus in 2010-2021 under the high migration scenario, compared to £5.2bn in the low migration scenario. Debt as a share of GDP would also be lower under the high migration scenario (73.3% vs. 76.1% by 2020-2021).

Cebr's analysis of the impact of reducing migration was carried out on two assumptions. Both reduce net migration (operating only on inward migration) by 200,000 from the 273,000 figure. This is done either quickly over a two-year period or slowly over an eight-year period. The period starts in 2019. Thus on the slow reduction scenario, migration only reaches its target level in 2027. On the fast reduction scenario it reaches its target in 2021.

The final level of migration at 73,000 per annum was assumed to be consistent with the pledge to reduce migration to 'tens of thousands'.

Cebr built a small model to analyse the economic impact based on Cebr's UK Economic Forecasting Model UKMOD9. One of its weaknesses is that it is linear, whereas in the real world this is clearly unlikely to be the case for the relationships. But it gives a rough and ready set of estimates that probably get as close to reality as is easily feasible without excessive expenditure.

The key assumption is the impact on productivity. Comments from leading Conservatives indicate that they would expect some creaming off with the bulk of the restrictions on migrants being restrictions on low-skilled migrants, which would imply an intention to use migration restrictions to boost productivity. However, certainly for the Flat White Economy, the migrants tend to come into the UK without a job and then get one. It would be difficult to cherry-pick these migrants.

When *The Flat White Economy* was updated in 2016, it was calculated that just under 40% of the increase in employment in the sector since 2008 had reflected EU migrants compared with 28% for the City of London, the other main high-skill occupation associated with the employment of migrants.

This is backed up by the data from the Migration Observatory at Oxford University. For occupations, the category 'IT and telecoms professionals', accounting for 3.1% of employed migrants, is the occupation 9th most dependent on migrants.[18] For sectors, computer programming and consultancy, with 26% of its workforce being migrants, is the 7th most migrant intensive sector.[19] The proportions in London would be substantially higher – 36% of all migrant employees and 45% of all migrant self-employed worked in London in 2015.[20]

The Cebr analysis suggests that, far from productivity rising if migration is reduced for knowledge-intensive sectors, it might instead fall because of the loss of creativity from lower diversity in the workforce, and for the other reasons listed above.

Balancing the potential impact of some cherry-picking of the most skilled migrants against the impact on productivity in the digital economy which will be negative, the Cebr calculations only allow for a minor net increase in productivity from a reduction in migration of 0.05% per 1% increase in the share of migrants in the labour force.

The results show that both GDP and GDP per capita in the UK would be significantly reduced by reduced migration.

By 2025, GDP is reduced by 1.5% on the slow reduction scenario and by 3.1% on the faster reduction scenario.

By 2030 GDP is reduced by 4.1% on the slow reduction scenario and by 5.7% on the faster reduction scenario.

By 2040, although one should be very cautious about numbers from an extrapolation that goes so far, GDP is reduced by 8.9% on the slow reduction scenario and by 10.4% on the faster reduction scenario.

Similarly, for GDP per capita, by 2025, GDP/capita is reduced by 0.9% on the slow reduction scenario and by 1.5% on the faster reduction scenario.

By 2030 GDP/capita is reduced by 1.9% on the slow reduction scenario and by 2.7% on the faster reduction scenario.

By 2040, although again one should be very cautious about numbers from an extrapolation that goes so far, GDP/capita is reduced by 4.1% on the slow reduction scenario and by 4.9% on the faster reduction scenario.

Of course reductions in GDP on this scale have a knock-on effect on tax collection. The analysis of the slow reduction scenario shows tax receipts down by £15.6 billion in 2025; £43.0 billion in 2030 and £93.3 billion in 2040. However these numbers exaggerate the impact on the deficit since with fewer people in the country the need for public services would be reduced. Assuming public spending would be scaled to the population, the net impact on the deficit is £9.5 billion in 2025; £25.9 billion in 2030 and £57.7 billion in 2040.

The analysis of the fast reduction scenario shows tax receipts down by £32.7 billion in 2025; £60.2 billion in 2030 and £109.3 billion in 2040. Allowing for the reduced need for public services the net impact on the deficit is £20.0 billion in 2025; £36.3 billion in 2030 and £64.5 billion in 2040.

The numbers here are quite shocking – they display the extent to which the UK economy has become based on migration and show the scale of the potential negative consequences if migration slows to a very small amount.

The numbers themselves should be seen as illustrative. It is highly unlikely that changes in migration on this scale would take place without major adjustments elsewhere which would of course change the numbers.

What they do show, however, is that if the UK cuts off migration without making adjustments to boost productivity, especially productivity in the public sector, the scale of the economic damage could be dramatic.

One way of reducing migration is to make your country unattractive to migration. This can be done without curtailing freedom of movement and is therefore attractive to some people. But it is actually the silliest way of dealing with migration. Every country should aim to make itself as great a place to live in as possible. If this leads to too much migration, this is a problem of success. It can be dealt with by restricting access to the universal basic income when it is introduced and if necessary by restricting migration. Migration should also be accompanied by sufficient boosts to infrastructure and public services (easily financed by the boost to taxation, as the calculations above which assume such spending show) so that the indigenous inhabitants don't feel they are losing out in a zero-sum game in competing for housing, education or other resources.

## Conclusion

This chapter shows that populist anti-capitalist solutions are unlikely to work. While in most cases the decline may not be as severe as in Venezuela recently, the long-term negative effects are about as certain as anything in economics. There are simply no examples other than economic disaster for extreme socialism. Even the lighter brews of socialism, as in Scandinavia, have had to be amended and watered down further to continue to work over time, especially in the internationally competitive economic environment of the 21st century. And my suspicion is that the modern world has accelerated the economic punishment of those who get their policies wrong.

Again, there are few examples of protectionism working other than the infant industry example. Even in emerging economies, the two countries in the world that have transformed themselves fastest from poverty to prosperity have been Hong Kong and Singapore, both of which did so completely without protection, so it is hard to say that protection is necessary or even helpful to infant industries. At best one can say that infant industry protection doesn't cause growth to collapse and may hold back economies less than more general protectionism. For developed economies, even the infant industry argument rarely holds and the main effect of protectionism is to ossify economic structure and prevent the adaptation that developed economies need to keep on making in order to face off economic challenges from the emerging economies.

It is important here to distinguish between limiting migration and limiting trade in goods. The economic effects are different even though the inspiration behind both – a desire to insulate oneself from the changes going on elsewhere in the world – might be the same. Limiting migration damages growth and creativity very quickly, but provided that a country continues to trade, the long-term economic damage might be to lower GDP per capita by a quarter or at most a third compared with what might otherwise have taken place.

But limiting trade could over 100 years cause a country's GDP to decline relatively by as much as three-quarters or even more. This is because of the ossification effect and the damage to innovation. China fell all the way down the league table from being the richest country in the world to one of the poorest over 500 years as a result of shutting itself off from the outside world.

*Chapter 19*
# CONCLUSION

THIS BOOK ARGUES THAT INEQUALITY, FAR FROM BEING MAINLY A FORM of exploitation, is largely an economic phenomenon which requires economic responses. It also points out that the damage done by inequality is caused less by material differences in levels of wealth or income but more by the psychological effects caused by the feelings of rejection by society of those whose relative position is deteriorating.

Responding to this damage is a complex process involving the development of more inclusive communities and finding ways of returning control over their lives to the people affected as well as improving education (including helping to form realistic expectations) and helping where possible to improve the material standard of living.

The book argues that utopian solutions to the problem of inequality are unlikely to work and are the enemy of more marginal improvements that could do so. It provides a wide range of ideas for reducing inequality.

The book also shows that extremism of either the anti-capitalist type or of the protectionist or anti-immigrant type will actually make the economic problems to which people are reacting worse. Corbyn/Sanders' or Trump's (and to a much watered-down extent Teresa May's) solutions are not the answer to a political problem that has its roots in a set of new economic challenges that have not been shared before.

The problem of overpay for bankers and CEOs is gradually resolving itself through a protracted market process. If this does not happen quickly enough there is ammunition in the lockers to help resolve the issue more quickly.

Cronyism is more difficult to solve but can be attacked in those parts of the world that are institutionally hostile to corruption. While they may have limited influence in emerging economies, travel bans could stop crooks and their associates from visiting the world's more desirable places in the West.

But serious solutions to the excesses of inequality need to start with education. Again, it may be that simply improving the education of the poor is insufficient and some limits on private education may be necessary. Equally it will be important for the system to reward success sufficiently to provide an incentive for people to get themselves educated. So it will always be both impossible and undesirable to eliminate inequality completely.

Many of the economic solutions for reducing inequality are more microeconomic than macro. Anti-monopoly policy reduces excess costs of living, improving the position of the poor. It also limits the possibilities of excess gains by monopoly capitalists. A healthy competition policy also makes business behave more ethically to keep shareholders, customers and employees.

Welfare reform allows people to work at low productivity jobs while having an income level that is not quite on the breadline.

Western governments need to focus much more on keeping the cost of living down, through the right planning policies, avoiding agricultural protection and aggressive anti-monopoly policies. These not only make welfare cheaper but improve the standards of living of everyone and by an amount that rises proportionately the poorer one is.

Taxation for redistribution has to be handled carefully. Excessive income taxes in many cases reduce revenues and make the poor worse off, not better. Inheritance taxes could be raised in some countries, though there is a case for international agreement on this. And if the taxman is prepared to exercise self-restraint and bring top tax levels down to the revenue maximising levels of around 35-40%, it is likely that many rich people would be prepared to pay voluntary tax supplements. This would particularly be the case if they had some say in how the additional revenue was spent (obviously within limits). Ultimately the combination of inheritance taxes and voluntary taxes should generate sufficient funds to make welfare reform possible. And if they generate more, there is plenty of scope for redistribution of wealth.

I am conscious that technological progress and homogamy may mean that these policies will not succeed in preventing inequality from increasing further. There are two answers to this. First, the degree of intensity with which the authorities follow the policies listed above can be increased; second, reducing inequality is not the only goal of economic policy. Allowing growth (properly measured) and reducing poverty are also important.

Sometimes economic forces mean that a high level of inequality can only be avoided by risking Venezuela-style economic collapse leading to poverty and malnutrition. If there is a choice between high inequality and no poverty and low inequality and rising malnutrition, one would have to have been blinded by ideology to condemn the poor to malnutrition.

All this works if the forecast for the underlying change in inequality is that set out in the less extreme of the two cobra graphs in Chapter 11. But if the impact of technology is more extreme – which it could be – and we are in the world of the more extreme cobra graph where the cobra is rearing up and spitting, then the proposed solutions will have to be put through in a much more aggressive form.

One might need to abolish private education completely, though I don't like this because when the public sector is worse than the private sector at providing something, I don't like simply to abolish the group that does things better. Far superior is to make the public sector better.

Anti-monopoly policy might have to be intensified. Restrictions on the use of data may have to be on a much more serious scale. Taxation of inheritance might have to be 50% or more. The key point is to realise that the problems are essentially economic, not a Marxist conspiracy theory of the rich exploiting the poor. Solutions, therefore, if they are to work, need to work with the grain of economics. It remains important to remember that inequality and poverty don't automatically go together and to avoid policies that might reduce inequality but worsen poverty.

It may not be possible to make the world a perfect place. But it is possible to make it a better place than it might otherwise be.

# NOTES

### Foreword

1. There are some examples where it did work. Probably the best example was Russia during the Second World War, when Stalin managed to create a successful wartime industrial economy. But making it work required wartime focus (not too much choice of what needed to be made – just arms and more arms!); popular mobilisation resulting from the necessity of winning the war and defending the homeland from the Nazi invader; and of course utter brutality in forcing compliance.

2. See, for example, Milton Friedman, 'The Hong Kong Experiment', *The Hoover Digest*, 1998, no. 3.

3. https://www.tralac.org/discussions/article/6574-the-rise-of-developing-countries-in-the-world-economy-and-environmental-considerations-of-development.html Blog posted 6 November 2014.

4. Cebr's World Economic League Table 2018, available from Cebr website.

5. https://www.forbes.com/sites/kristinstoller/2017/05/24/the-worlds-largest-tech-companies-2017-apple-and-samsung-lead-facebook-rises/#400fed3dd140.

6. I was also a main board director of the telecom equipment company Marconi, helping rescue the company from the near bankruptcy that the previous management had driven it towards.

### Prologue

1. This data for 2013 was marginally updated in April 2018. The latest estimates suggest that the 2013 poverty level on this definition has fallen to 10.9% rather than 10.7% and the number to 783 million rather than 769 million. See http://blogs.worldbank.org/developmenttalk/april-2018-global-poverty-update-world-bank for more detail and explanations.

2. 'New Insights on Poverty', https://www.ted.com.

3. http://www.xinhuanet.com/english/2018-03/05/c_137018278.htm.

4. https://www.statista.com/statistics/381356/london-homelessness-rough-sleepers-timeline/.

5. http://abc7news.com/news/data-shows-sf-has-2nd-highest-homeless-population-in-us/1407123/.

6. Thomas Piketty, *Capital in the Twenty-First Century*, Harvard University Press, 2014.

7. Three different sources: Matthew 26:10, Mark 14:7 and John 12:8. Also an earlier quotation from Deuteronomy 15:11.

8. They are called public schools because when they came into existence the alternative was private tuition.

9. My own former school, Stonyhurst, was started in St Omer in France when penal laws prevented Catholic education in England. The school moved to Bruges and then Liege before being allowed into England in 1794.

10. Arthur Brooks, President of the American Enterprise Institute based in Washington, DC, makes the important point that it is necessary to reinstate the 'dignity of labour'. His analysis, which is essentially similar to that in this book but uses different words, is that the psychological problems of many previously hard-working blue-collar males emerge from the decline in what he calls the dignity of labour. Arthur C. Brooks @arthurbrooks February 13, 2017 | *Foreign Affairs* The dignity deficit: Reclaiming Americans' sense of purpose.

### Chapter 1

1. http://www.independent.co.uk/sport/football/premier-league/wayne-rooney-salary-four-times-greater-than-entire-manchester-united-squad-in-1969-accounts-reveal-a6838386.html.

2. While I was writing this Wayne Rooney scored his 250th goal for Manchester United, also overtaking Sir Bobby Charlton's record number of goals for his club.

3. There had been a maximum wage in the English Football League of £8 per week during the season for the period from 1921 until the Second World War started in 1939. Post-war this wage was set at £12 in 1947 rising to £20 in 1958. The cap was abolished in 1961.

4. This section is based on my Gresham Professorial Lecture on Inequality given on 18 September 2013 http:// http://www.nationalarchives.gov.uk/education/politics /g3/www.gresham.ac.uk/lectures-and-events/how-does-globalisation-affect-inequality -globally.

5. Jonah Goldberg, *Suicide of the West: How the Rebirth of Tribalism, Populism, Nationalism, and Identity Politics is Destroying American Democracy*, Crown Forum, 2018.

### Chapter 2

1. Thomas Piketty, *Capital in the Twenty-First Century*, Harvard University Press, 2014.

2. See for example, Steven N. Kaplan and Joshua D. Rauh, 'Family, Education, and Sources of Wealth among the Richest Americans, 1982-2012', *American Economic Review*, vol. 103, no. 3, May 2013, pp. 158-62, who argue that the data is much more consistent with economic factors than Piketty's sociological explanations.

3. D. Autor, D. Dorn, L.F. Katz, C. Patterson and J.V Reenen, 'Concentrating on the Fall of the Labor Share', *American Economic Review* Papers and Proceedings [Internet] 2017; 107 (5), pp. 180-85.

4. https://www.theatlantic.com/business/archive/2016/06/the-problem-with-inequality-according-to-adam-smith/486071/ by Dennis Rasmussen.

5. https://obamawhitehouse.archives.gov/the-press-office/2013/12/04/remarks-president-economic-mobility.

6. Adam Smith, *The Theory of Moral Sentiments*, 1759.

7. Adam Smith, *The Wealth of Nations*, 1776.

8. See the next note.

9. *A Theory of Justice* is a work of political philosophy and ethics by John Rawls, in which the author attempts to solve the problem of distributive justice (the socially

just distribution of goods in a society) by utilising a variant of the familiar device of the social contract. The resultant theory is known as 'Justice as Fairness', from which Rawls derives his two principles of justice. Together, they dictate that society should be structured so that the greatest possible amount of liberty is given to its members, limited only by the notion that the liberty of any one member shall not infringe upon that of any other member. Secondly, inequalities either social or economic are only to be allowed if the worst-off will be better off than they might be under an equal distribution. Finally, if there is such a beneficial inequality, this inequality should not make it harder for those without resources to occupy positions of power, for instance public office.

10. http://blog.acton.org/archives/71399-hayek-inequality-poverty-alleviation.html.

11. http://blog.bearing-consulting.com/wp-content/uploads/2012/09/Economic.Growth.and_.Income.Inequality.pdf.

12. Piketty, op. cit., p. 15.

13. Anthony B. Atkinson, *Inequality, What Can be Done?*, Harvard University Press, 2015, p. 45.

14. https://macaulay.cuny.edu/eportfolios/thorne15/files/2015/03/Cole-Milton-Friedman-on-Income-Inequaity.pdf.

15. Milton and Rose D. Friedman, *Free to Choose*, Harcourt Brace Jovanovich, 1980, p. 148.

16. 'The Methodology of Positive Economics', in *Essays in Positive Economics*, University of Chicago Press, 1953.

17. Ibid., Section 5.

18. *Economics and Equality*, edited by the Rt Hon Aubrey Jones, Papers presented to Section F (Economics) of the 1975 Annual Meeting of the British Association for the Advancement of Science, Philip Allan Publishers Ltd 1976

19. Anthony Atkinson, *The Economics of Inequality*, Oxford University Press, 1975.

20. Anthony B. Atkinson, Thomas Piketty and Emmanuel Saez, 'Top Incomes in the Long Run of History', *Journal of Economic Literature*, 2011, 49: 1, 3-71.

21. Op. cit.

22. Claudia Goldin and Lawrence F. Katz, *The Race between Education and Technology*, NBER Working Paper No. 12984, issued March 2007.

23. D. Autor, D. Dorn, L.F. Katz, C. Patterson and J.V. Reenen, 'Concentrating on the Fall of the Labor Share', *American Economic Review* Papers and Proceedings [Internet]. 2017; 107 (5): 180-5.

24. Mai Dao, Mitali Das, Zsoka Koczan and Weicheng Lian, 'Routinisation, Globalisation, and the Fall in Labour's Share of Income', *Vox*, 8 September 2017.

25. Daron Acemoğlu and James Robinson, *Why Nations Fail: The Origins of Power, Prosperity, and Poverty*, Crown Business, 2012.

26. Friedman tried to explain the idea in very simple terms (*Capitalism and Freedom*, pp. 191-4; *Free to Choose*, pp. 120-3), though his discussion is actually rather hard to follow on a first reading.

27. http://www.dklevine.com/general/aandrreview.pdf.

28. Martin Jacques, *When China Rules the World: The End of the Western World and the Birth of a New Global Order*, Penguin, 2009.

29. Larry Bartels, *Unequal Democracy: The Political Economy of the New Gilded Age*, Princeton University Press, 2010.

30. Oddly there is at least one place where businesses do have the vote, less than a mile from my office. The City of London Corporation is the world's oldest continuously surviving 'democratic' institution, dating from Anglo-Saxon times. Democracy as it evolved meant that the City's rulers first consulted and then allowed to vote on legislation the commoners, who were the freemen who had served their apprenticeships and who had become 'free' to set up their own businesses. Today, because of the preponderance of people who work in the City over those who live there (a daytime population of over 600,000 compared with 9,000 residents) it is deemed acceptable in this unique case for there to be a business vote based on property ownership. Currently there are 24,000 business voters. I must declare a family interest since my father, Sir Francis McWilliams, was elected as a Common Councilman, then Alderman and eventually became the Lord Mayor of the City of London with this electorate, though his ward, Aldergate, was dominated by Barbican residents.

31. Jeffrey Sachs, *The Price of Civilization: Economics and Ethics After the Fall*, Random House, 2012.

32. Joseph Stiglitz, *The Price of Inequality: How Today's Divided Society Endangers Our Future*, Penguin Books, 2016.

33. See this review in *The Guardian*: https://www.theguardian.com/books/2012/jul/13/price-inequality-joseph-stiglitz-review.

34. 'An Ordinary Joe', *The Economist*, 23 June 2012.

35. Paul Krugman, *The Return of Depression Economics*, Allen Lane, 2008.

36. Paul Krugman, *End This Depression Now!*, W.W Norton Ltd., May 2012.

37. Paul Krugman, 'Challenging the Oligarchy', *New York Review of Books*, 17 December 2015 http://www.nybooks.com/articles/2015/12/17/robert-reich-challenging-oligarchy/.

38. 'Changes in Relative Wages, 1963–1987: Supply and Demand Factors', *Quarterly Journal of Economics* 107, no. 1, February 1992.

39. L.F. Katz and D.H. Autor, 'Changes in the Wage Structure and Earnings Inequality', in *Handbook of Labor Economics*, ed. O. Ashenfelter and D. Card, vol. 3A, 1999, pp. 1463-1555.

40. Robert Reich, *The Work of Nations: Preparing Ourselves for 21st Century Capitalism*, Alfred A. Knopf, 1992.

41. Lawrence Mishel, Heidi Shierholz and John Schmitt, 'Don't Blame the Robots: Assessing the Job Polarization Explanation of Growing Wage Inequality', EPI–CEPR working paper, November 2013.

42. Simon Johnson and James Kwak, *13 Bankers: The Wall Street Takeover and the Next Financial Meltdown*, Pantheon, 2010.

43. Angus Deaton, *The Great Escape: Health, Wealth and the Origins of Inequality*, Princeton University Press, 2015.

44. Branko Milanovic, *Global Inequality: A New Approach for the Age of Globalisation*, Harvard University Press, 2016.

45. Martin Wolf, *Why Globalisation Works*, Yale University Press, 2005.

46. https://www.ft.com/content/5557f806-5a75-11e7-9bc8-8055f264aa8b.

47 https://blogs.imf.org/2017/09/20/growth-that-reaches-everyone-facts-factors -tools/.

48. Kohler et al., 'Greater Post-Neolithic Wealth Disparities in Eurasia than North America and in Mesoamerica', *Nature* 351, 30 November 2017.

49. https://capx.co/why-inequality-can-make-us-all-richer/?omhide=true&utm _source=CapX+Newsletter&utm_campaign=a425ee4ab4-EMAIL_CAMPAIGN _2017_07_17&utm_medium=email&utm_term=0_dcdc78d804-a425ee4ab4 -179153845.

50. http://www.economicsuk.com/blog/002193.html.

51. http://www.economicsuk.com/blog/002223.html.

52. https://www.gc.cuny.edu/CUNY_GC/media/CUNY-Graduate-Center/PDF /Centers/LIS/imperialism_forcirculation_3.pdf.

53. https://promarket.org/inequality-imperialism-first-world-war/.

54. John A. Hobson, *Imperialism: A Study*, James Pott & Co., 1902; reprinted in 1975 by Gordon Press New York.

55. https://www.google.co.uk/search?q=inequality+and+disappearing+large+firm +premium&rlz=1C1GGRV_enGB751GB751&oq=inequality+and+disappearing+large +firm+premium&aqs=chrome..69i57.10744j1j8&sourceid=chrome&ie=UTF-8.

56. Presented at the meeting of the American Social Sciences Association in conjunction with the American Economics Association Conference in Philadelphia, 5-7 January 2018.

57. https://www.oxfam.org/en/pressroom/pressreleases/2018-01-22/richest-1 -percent-bagged-82-percent-wealth-created-last-year.

58. https://www.credit-suisse.com/corporate/en/research/research-institute/global -wealth-report.html.

59. https://www.oxfam.org.uk/media-centre/press-releases/2017/01/eight-people -own-same-wealth-as-half-the-world.

60. https://www.oxfam.org/en/pressroom/pressreleases/2018-01-22/richest-1 -percent-bagged-82-percent-wealth-created-last-year.

61. http://www.100people.org/statistics_100stats.php?section=statistics.

## Chapter 3

1. I am grateful to Daron Acemoglu, Elizabeth and James Killian, Professor of Economics at the Massachusetts Institute of Technology and co-author *of Why Nations Fail*, for this distinction.

2. Milton Friedman and Rose D. Friedman, *Free to Choose: A Personal Statement*, Harcourt, 1980.

3. The term is taken from Samuel P. Huntington, *Clash of Civilizations and the Remaking of World Order*, Simon and Schuster, 1996.

4. For more details read the relevant section of the OECD glossary of statistical terms https://stats.oecd.org/glossary/detail.asp?ID=5528.

5. This is the theory presented by the interesting but amateur historian Gavin Menzies in his best-selling book *1421: The Year China Discovered the World*, Bantam, 2003.

6. http://www.chengho.org/museum/web/history.html.

7. For example, David Landes, one of the most respected economic historians, asked why China failed to turn its lead in technology in the 15th century into a sustained advance in technology in 'Why Europe and the West? Why Not China?', *Journal of Economic Perspectives*, vol. 20, no. 2, Spring 2006, pp. 3-22.

8. Peter Jay, *The Wealth of Man*, Public Affairs, 2000.

9. https://www.washingtonpost.com/archive/lifestyle/1979/05/30/peter-jay-racing-home-to-england/0506621d-801d-48a2-b525-1b8fdd04746d/.

10. This is essentially the view of Max Weber in his path-breaking book, *The Protestant Ethic and the Spirit of Capitalism*, Andesite Press, 2015; originally published in German as *Die protestantische Ethik und der Geist des Kapitalismus*, J.C.B. Mohr, Tübingen, 1905.

11. See my last book, *The Flat White Economy*, Duckworth, 2016.

12. Molly B. Kroker, 'The "Great Divergence" Redefined: the Rise and Fall of the West and the Recovery of China', *Inquiries Journal* 6, 2014, no. 9. https://www.inquiriesjournal.com/articles/917/3/the-great-divergence-redefined-the-rise-and-fall-of-the-west-and-the-recovery-of-china.

13. For a fuller explanation see the American historian Arthur Herman's book, *How the Scots Invented the Modern World*, Crown Publications, 2002.

14. See the new biography of Telford by Julian Glover: *Man of Iron: Thomas Telford and the Building of Britain*, Bloomsbury, 2017.

15. There are two main series for this: C. Feinstein, 'Changes in Nominal Wages, the Cost of Living, and Real Wages in the United Kingdom over Two Centuries, 1780-1990', in P. Scholliers and V. Zamagni (eds), *Labour's Reward*, Edward Elgar, 1995, pp. 3-36, 258-66, and P.H. Lindert and J.G. Williamson, 'English Workers' Living Standards During the Industrial Revolution: A New Look', *Economic History Review* 36 (1983), 1-25. Both are described well in Robert C. Allen, 'The Great Divergence in European Wages and Prices from the Middle Ages to the First World War', *Explorations in Economic History* 38, 2001, 411-47, available online at http://www.ideal-ibrary.com.

16. Groningen Growth and Development Centre, Faculty of Economics and Business, Groningen University http://www.rug.nl/ggdc/historicaldevelopment/ (in 1990 Geary-Khamis dollars). Geary-Khamis dollars are hypothetical units of currency with the same purchasing power as one US dollar in the relevant base year, in this case 1990.

17. The only study I can find in the academic literature that even considers this issue is Keunho Park and Hiroko Kawasakiya Clayton, 'The Vietnam War and the "Miracle of East Asia"', *Inter-Asia Cultural Studies* 4, issue 3, 2003, 372-98, which points out that it is traditional for economic development studies 'to search for general theories of economic development ... accidental factors, including the Vietnam War, should be abstracted from economic development ...'.

18. Stephen Daggett, Specialist in Defense Policy and Budgets, 'Costs of Major U.S. Wars', 29 June 2010, Congressional Research Service 7-5700 www.crs.gov RS22926.

19. D.F. McWilliams, 'Offshore Manufacturing in a Developing Country: A Malaysian Case Study', Lincoln College Oxford, unpublished M.Phil thesis.

20. All the numbers for the world economic history used here are from the Maddison Data Archive at the Groningen Growth and Development Center at Groningen University in the Netherlands. Angus Maddison was a major scholar whose life work was producing historically comparable data. His series cover world GDP, population and GDP per capita and go back to the year 1. The figures are calculated in Geary-Khamis dollars at 1990 prices. This is essentially a purchasing power parity measure. This is appropriate for the historical data for periods when market exchange rates often did not exist or were unrepresentative.

21. Now the principal of Gresham College.

22. https://www.gresham.ac.uk/series/the-rise-and-fall-of-european-empires-from -the-16th-to-the-20th-century/ gives Sir Richard Evans' views on the subject.

23. Claudia Goldin and Lawrence F. Katz, *The Race between Education and Technology*, Harvard University Press, 2010; Lawrence F. Katz and Kevin M. Murphy, 'Changes in Relative Wages, 1963-1987: Supply and Demand Factors', *Quarterly Journal of Economics* 107, no. 1, February 1992; Laurence F. Katz and David H. Autor, 'Changes in Wage Structure and Earning Inequality' https://eml.berkeley .edu//~saez/course131/Katz-Autor99.pdf; Robert Reich, *The Work of Nations: Preparing Ourselves for 21st Century Capitalism*, Alfred A. Knopf, 1992; Lawrence Mishel, Heidi Shierholz and John Schmitt, 'Don't Blame the Robots: Assessing the Job Polarization Explanation of Growing Wage Inequality', EPI-CEPR working paper, November 2013.

24. Mai Dao, Mitali Das, Zsoka Koczan and Weicheng Lian, 'Routinisation, Globalisation, and the Fall in Labour's Share of Income', *Vox*, 8 September 2017.

25. https://www.pwc.co.uk/services/economics-policy/insights/the-impact-of-automation-on-jobs.html.

26. Ernest W. Burgess and Paul Wallin, 'Homogamy in Social Characteristics', *American Journal of Sociology*, vol. 49, no. 2, September 1943, pp. 109-24.

27. https://www.forbes.com/sites/eriksherman/2017/08/20/genetic-engineering -will-make-income-inequality-much-worse/#4a66e7f03d75.

### Chapter 4

1. https://www.kingsfund.org.uk/publications/inequalities-life-expectancy?gclid =CjwKEAiAoaXFBRCNhautiPvnqzoSJABzHd6hYsCcymR-HfLV9lGlZPZZB0 ttHKVUlVf2TokAwwNUF-BoCksTw_wcB://www.rcpch.ac.uk/news/rcpch-launches -landmark-state-child-health-report.

2. Fred Hirsch, *The Social Limits to Growth*, Routledge & Kegan Paul, 1977.

3. Impact of the Shortage of Housing on Young People - Parliamentresearchbriefings .files.parliament.uk/documents/LLN-2016.../LLN-2016-0056.pdf.

4. Office for National Statistics, 'UK Perspectives 2016: Housing and Home Ownership in the UK', 25 May 2016.

5. Cambridge Centre for Housing and Planning Research, 'Estimating the Scale of Youth Homelessness in the UK', p. 3.

6. PricewaterhouseCoopers, *UK Economic Outlook,* July 2016, p. 17.

7. C. Larsen, *The Rise and Fall of Social Cohesion*, Oxford University Press, 2013.

8. E. Durkheim, *The Division of Labor in Society*, trans. G. Simpson, The Free Press, 1960 [1893].

9. Both passages from 'On England', speech to the Annual Dinner of the Royal Society of St George at the Hotel Cecil, 6 May 1924, in Stanley Baldwin, *On England and Other Addresses*, Philip Alan, 1933, p. 341.

10. https://www.theguardian.com/society/2006/jan/21/health.politics.

11. http://www.gcph.co.uk/latest/blogs/555_life_expectancy_in_calton-no_longer_54.

12. I am grateful to Dr Amanda Diotaiuti for drawing this to my attention.

13. https://www.brookings.edu/bpea-articles/mortality-and-morbidity-in-the-21st-century/.

14. http://www.pnas.org/content/112/49/15078.

15. Sir Francis McWilliams GBE, *'Pray Silence for Jock Whittington': From Building Sewers to Suing Builders*, Malu Publications.

16. https://www.nytimes.com/2016/06/24/us/politics/partisanship-republicans-democrats-pew-research.html?_r=0.

17. Ibid.

18. https://www.washingtonpost.com/news/in-theory/wp/2016/03/11/three-reasons-political-polarization-is-here-to-stay/?utm_term=.157049936bbf.

19. There is a good description of the history of the Swedish tax system in Mikael Stenkula, Dan Johansson and Gunnar Du Rietz, 'Marginal Taxation on Labour Income in Sweden from 1862 to 2010', *Scandinavian Economic History Review*, 62:2, 2014, pp. 163-87,

### Chapter 5

1. Anthony Atkinson, 'On the Measurement of Inequality', *Journal of Economic Theory*, vol. 2, issue 3, 1970, pp. 244-63.

2. Gerald Auten (Office of Tax Analysis, U.S. Treasury Department) and David Splinter (Joint Committee on Taxation), 'Income Inequality in the United States: Using Tax Data to Measure Long-term Trends', 12 November 2017 [draft version subject to change], U.S. Congress Working Paper available at: http://davidsplinter.com/AutenSplinter-Tax_Data_and_Inequality.pdf.

3. This is a standard result for this type of analysis. See the references to a range of studies on p. 17 of Bruce D. Meyer and James X. Sullivan, 'Measuring the Well-Being of the Poor Using Income and Consumption', NBER Working Paper No. 9760, June 2003.

4. Auten and Splinter, op. cit.

5. Source: World Income Database (mainly compiled by Thomas Piketty and Emmanuel Saez) http://wid.world/.

6. This is earlier data and is no longer contained in the latest version of the database, so should be considered less robust than the other data.

7. Please note that for the UK the series changes slightly during the period and starts in 1981, not 1980. But this doesn't seriously affect the trend.

8. There are good summaries of the Giles critiques in the *New York Times* and *The Economist*: https://www.nytimes.com/2014/05/31/upshot/everything-you-need-to-know-about-thomas-piketty-vs-the-financial-times.html?_r=0; http://www.economist.com

/news/finance-and-economics/21603022-latest-controversy-around-thomas-pikettys-blockbuster-book-concerns-its.

9. Ibid.

10. http://publications.credit-suisse.com/tasks/render/file/index.cfm?fileid=AD783798-ED07-E8C2-4405996B5B02A32Ehttps://www.ons.gov.uk/peoplepopulationand community/birthsdeathsandmarriages/families/methodologies/theginicoefficient.

11. 18 September 2013 https://www.gresham.ac.uk/lectures-and-events/how-does-globalisation-affect-inequality-globally.

12. https://www.oecd.org/els/soc/49499779.pdf.

13. Istvan Gyorgy Toth, 'Time Series and Cross-country Variation of Income Inequalities in Europe on the Medium Run: Are Inequality Structures Converging in the Past Three decades?' Gini Policy Institute http://www.gini-research.org/system/uploads/566/original/GINI_Policy_Paper_3.pdf?1384954508

14. Original income includes sources of earned income such as wages, salaries and pensions, and unearned income, i.e. income from investments. However, income from benefits such as state pensions, family credit and income support is not included. Gross income comprises all sources of income, that is original income plus income from benefits. Disposable income is gross income less income tax and national insurance contributions.

15. 'London's Contribution to the UK Economy 1992' and a succession of subsequent Cebr reports.

16. Tim Worstall, The Truth about Income Inequality CapX, 25 May 2017.

17. Milanovic tweet, 13 August 2017: Two centuries of global income inequality reflecting world's economic history (recalculated using the new Maddison project data). https://twitter.com/BrankoMilan/status/896687954587942912.

18. https://www.ons.gov.uk/peoplepopulationandcommunity/personalandhousehold finances/incomeandwealth/compendium/wealthingreatbritainwave4/2012to2014/chapter 2 totalwealthwealthingreatbritain2012to2014#distribution-of-aggregate-total-wealth.

19. Christopher A. Sarlo, 'Understanding Wealth Inequality in Canada', Frazer Institute, April 2017.

20. http://www.resolutionfoundation.org/app/uploads/2016/09/Examining-an-elephant.pdf.

21. This discussion is heavily based on the helpful analysis by the Canadian Conference Board in http://www.conferenceboard.ca/hcp/hot-topics/worldinequality.aspx #ftn3-ref.

22. Richard Freeman, Speech at the OECD Policy Forum on Tackling Inequality, Paris, 2 May 2011.

23. https://www.cebr.com/reports/world-economic-league-table-2017/.

24. BBC News Report 3 May 2018 based on Musicians Union survey downloaded from https://www.bbc.co.uk/news/entertainment-arts-43976334.

25. Max Roser and Esteban Ortiz-Ospina, 2017, 'Income Inequality', published online at https://ourworldindata.org/income-inequality/.

26. Effects of taxes and benefits on UK household income: financial year ending 2016, ONS https://www.ons.gov.uk/peoplepopulationandcommunity/personaland-

householdfinances/incomeandwealth/bulletins/theeffectsoftaxesandbenefitsonhouse-holdincome/financialyearending2016.

27. For a slightly unedifying discussion of this see the Twitter link between the author and @jdportes.

28. Nanak C. Kakwani, 'Measurement of Tax Progressivity: An International Comparison', *Economic Journal* 87 (345), March 1977, pp. 71-80.

29. Barry Bracewell-Milnes, 'Measurement of Tax Progressivity: A Comment', *Economic Journal* 89 (355), September 1979, pp. 648-1.

30. Effects of taxes and benefits on UK household income: financial year ending 2016, ONS https://www.ons.gov.uk/peoplepopulationandcommunity/personaland-householdfinances/incomeandwealth/bulletins/theeffectsoftaxesandbenefitsonhouse-holdincome/financialyearending2016.

31. David Willetts, *The Pinch: How the Baby Boomers Took Their Children's Future – And Why They Should Give it Back*, Atlantic Books, 2010. An interesting review is shown here: https://www.theguardian.com/books/2010/feb/20/pinch-baby -boomers-willetts-millar.

### Chapter 6

1. http://blogs.worldbank.org/developmenttalk/2017-global-poverty-update -world-bank.

2. 'The State of the US Economy', a report by Douglas McWilliams on his five-week sabbatical in the US, September 2013, Cebr.

3. See Chapter 5 for more details.

4. José Cuesta, Mario Negre and Christoph Lakner, 'Know Your Facts: Poverty Numbers', 7 November 2016 http://voxeu.org/article/know-your-facts-poverty-numbers.

5. In my Gresham lecture on inequality (18 September 2013) I referred to this quote from the BBC GCSE Bite Size page for geography: 'Globalisation operates mostly in the interests of the richest countries, which continue to dominate world trade at the expense of developing countries. The role of LEDCs in the world market is mostly to provide the North and West with cheap labour and raw materials.' The BBC quoted in support of this 'environmentalists, anti-poverty campaigners and trade unionists'. http://www .bbc.co.uk /schools/gcsebitesize/geography/globalisation/globalisation _rev5.shtml.

6. Max Roser and Esteban Ortiz-Ospina, 'Global Extreme Poverty', published online at https://ourworldindata.org/extreme-poverty/.

7. François Bourguignon and Christian Morrisson, 'Inequality among World Citizens: 1820-1992', *American Economic Review*, vol. 92, no. 4, 2002, pp. 727-44.

8. http://www.bbc.co.uk/news/resources/idt-841ebc3a-1be9-493b-8800-2c04890 e8fc9. The BBC data is from 2016 and the population estimates have been updated since.

9. https://www.quora.com/What-percentage-of-the-worlds-population-lives-in-a-war-zone-and-how-does-this-figure-compare-to-that-of-previous-generations.

10. https://www.pri.org/stories/2012-03-22/why-world-bank-has-no-real-intentions -reducing-poverty.

11. http://www.fao.org/state-of-food-security-nutrition/en/.

12. See https://www.cnbc.com/2017/07/06/global-food-prices-set-two-year-high -in-june-as-meat-dairy-wheat-climb.html for a chart showing this.

13. http://www.who.int/nutgrowthdb/jme_brochure2016.pdf.

14. https://www.pri.org/stories/2012-03-22/why-world-bank-has-no-real-intentions-reducing-poverty.

15. All this data is from the Maddison-Project, http://www.ggdc.net/maddison/maddison-project/home.htm, 2013 version. For more details see J. Bolt and J.L. van Zanden, 'The Maddison Project: Collaborative Research on Historical National Accounts', *Economic History Review* 67 (3), 2014, 627-51.

16. Martin Ravallion, *The Economics of Poverty: History, Measurement, Policy*, Oxford University Press, 2015.

17. https://www.gov.uk/government/uploads/system/uploads/attachment_data/file /503015/Rough_Sleeping_Autumn_2015_statistical_release.pdf.

18. http://www.europarl.europa.eu/RegData/etudes/BRIE/2016/578991/IPOL_BRI(2016)578991_EN.pdf.

19. http://www.endhomelessness.org/library/entry/SOH2016.

20. https://www.economist.com/news/international/21719790-going-will-be-much-harder-now-world-has-made-great-progress.

21. https://www.brookings.edu/wp-content/uploads/2017/02/global_20170228_global-middle-class.pdf.

22. https://www.firstthings.com/web-exclusives/2013/11/whats-behind-the-stunning-decrease-in-global-poverty http://www.cityam.com/article/1379464840/anti-globalisation-campaigners-got-it-wrong-trade-defeating-poverty. Article by Douglas McWilliams.

23. Max Roser, 'Life Expectancy', published online at https://ourworldindata.org/life-expectancy/.

24. These are estimates from the Global Burden of Disease 2013 Institute for Health Metrics and Evaluation, Washington. This study has just been updated (May 2018) but the latest report does not change any key conclusions.

25. https://ourworldindata.org/literacy/.

26. http://www.xinhuanet.com/english/2018-03/05/c_137018278.htm.

27. https://ourworldindata.org/extreme-poverty.

28. http://news.bbc.co.uk/today/hi/today/newsid_8714000/8714127.stm.

29. I asked, only partly in jest, if they would allow me to use the description in my advertising. I don't think they saw the joke.

30. http://www.reuters.com/article/us-eurozone-greece-poverty-idUSKBN15Z1NM

31. http://www.middleeasteye.net/news/poverty-iraq-promised-reforms-1887217637

## Chapter 7

1. Arthur Okun, *Equality and Efficiency: The Big Tradeoff*, Brookings Press, 1975; republished with a foreword by L. Summers, 2015.

2. Era Dabla-Norris, Kalpana Kochhar, Nujin Suphaphiphat, Frantisek Ricka, Evridiki Tsounta, 'Causes and Consequences of Income Inequality: A Global Perspective', IMF, Washington, June 2015.

3. Bert Bakker, *Onbegrepen Europa nieuw licht op een eeuwenoude tweedeling*, Atlas Contact, 2017.

4. *Financial Times* (London) Saturday 28 April 2018. I am grateful to Mr Martin Piers for drawing this letter to my attention.

5. This section is heavily based on a good review article: Markus Brückner and Daniel Lederman, 'Effects of Income Inequality on Economic Growth', *Vox*, 7 July 2015.

6. O. Galor, 'Inequality, Human Capital Formation, and the Process of Development', Brown University Working Papers, 2011-17.

7. J.D. Ostry, A. Berg and G.D. Tsangarides, 'Redistribution, Inequality, and Growth', IMF Staff Discussion Note no. SDN/14/02, February 2014.

8. M. Brueckner and D. Lederman, 'Effects of Income Inequality on Aggregate Output', World Bank Policy Discussion Paper 7317, 2015.

9. O. Galor and J. Zeira, 'Income Distribution and Macroeconomics', *Review of Economic Studies* 60, 1993, pp. 35-52.

10. Robert J. Barro, 'Economic Growth in a Cross Section of Countries', *Quarterly Journal of Economics* 106, issue 2, 1991, pp. 407-43.

11. Gerald W. Scully, 'What is the Optimal Size of Government in the United States', National Centre for Policy Analysis report no. 188, Dallas, Texas, November 1994.

12. https://www.fraserinstitute.org/sites/default/files/measuring-government-in-the-21st-century.pdf.

13. This is mainly taken from Table 16 in Patrick Minford, 'Tax and Growth: Theories and Evidence', *Taxation, Government Spending and Economic Growth*, Institute for Economic Affairs, London, November 2016, pp. 105-21.

14. Robert J. Barro, 'Economic Growth in a Cross Section of Countries', *Quarterly Journal of Economics* 106, issue 2, 1991, pp. 407-43.

15. R. Koester and R. Kormendi, 'Taxation, Aggregate Activity and Economic Growth: Cross-country Evidence on Some Supply-side Hypotheses', *Economic Inquiry* 27, 1989, pp. 367-86.

16. P. Hansson and M. Henrekson, 'A New Framework for Testing the Effect of Government Spending on Growth and Productivity', *Public Choice* 81, 1994, pp. 381-401.

17. P. Cashin, 'Government Spending, Taxes and Economic Growth', IMF Staff Papers 42(2), 1995, pp. 237-69.

18. E.M. Engen and J. Skinner, 'Taxation and Economic Growth', *National Tax Journal* 49, 1996, pp. 617-42.

19. W. Leibfritz, J. Thornton and A. Bibbee, 'Taxation and Economic Performance', OECD Working Paper 176, 1997.

20. A. Alesina, S. Ardagna, R. Perotti and F. Schiantarelli, 'Fiscal Policy, Profits, and Investment', *American Economic Review* 92, 2002, pp. 571-89 (this covers essentially the same ground as the paper by the same authors below).

21. M. Bleaney, N. Gemmell and R. Kneller, 'Testing the Endogenous Growth Model: Public Expenditure, Taxation and Growth over the Long Run', *Canadian Journal of Economics* 34(1), 2000, pp. 36-57.

22. S. Folster and M. Henrekson, 'Growth Effects of Government Expenditure and Taxation in Rich Countries', Stockholm School of Economics Working Paper 391, 2000.

23. A. Bassanini and S. Scarpettta, 'Does Human Capital Matter for Growth in

OECD Countries? Evidence from PMG Estimates', OECD Economics Department Working Paper 282, 2001.

24. Patrick Minford, 'Tax and Growth: Theories and Evidence', *Taxation, Government Spending and Economic Growth*, Institute for Economic Affairs, London, November 2016, pp. 105-21.

25. I. Ball and G. Pflugrath, 'Government Accounting: Making Enron Look Good', *World Economics* 13(1), January-March 2012.

26. G. Leach, *The Negative Impact of Taxation on Economic Growth*, Reform, 2003.

27. Alberto Alesina, Silvia Ardagna, Roberto Perotti and Fabio Schiantarelli, 'Fiscal Policy, Profits and Investment', March 1999, revised September 2000 http://citeseerx.ist.psu.edu/viewdoc/download?doi=10.1.1.203.5980&rep=rep1&type=pdf.

28. http://www.heritage.org/Research/Reports/2010/06/Confronting-the-Unsustainable-Growth-of-Welfare-Entitlements-Principles-of-Reform-and-the-Next-Steps.

29. A. Niskanen, 'Welfare and the Culture of Poverty', *Cato Journal* 16, no. 1, 1996.

30. Charles Murray, *Losing Ground: American Social Policy 1950-1980,* Basic Books, 1984, pp. 58, 125, 115.

## Chapter 8

1. I am grateful for the article on this in 'Quote and Counterquote' for its explanation http://www.quotecounterquote.com/2009/11/rich-are-different-famous-quote.html.

2. In the 1938 anthology of Hemingway stories, *The Fifth Column and the First Forty-Nine Stories*, New York, Charles Scribner and Sons.

3. Douglas McWilliams and Mark Pragnell, 'The Rich – Are they Different?', *Prospect*, 20 October 1995.

4. Property is always going to be important in areas where for either geographical or planning reasons there is a shortage of land. Many of the key companies in Hong Kong and Singapore are property-based as a result. And the property industry is also a critical one for London today – by and large London has been well served by its developers, but with property so intrinsic to economic cycles, it has been a roller-coaster ride.

5. https://www.uk.capgemini.com/experts/thought-leadership/world-wealth-report-2016.

6. Knight Frank, The Wealth Report http://content.knightfrank.com/research/83/documents/en/the-wealth-report-2017-4482.pdf.

7. Zoe Dare Hall, 'Who Are London's Super Rich Property Buyers', *Daily Telegraph*, 18 May 2017.

8. Caroline Freund and Sarah Oliver, 'The Origins of the Superrich: The Billionaire Characteristics Database', *Petersen Institute Working Papers* 16, 1 February 2016.

9. Ibid.

10. Steven N. Kaplan and Joshua Rauh, 'It's the Market: The Broad-Based Rise in the Return to Top Talent', *Journal of Economic Perspectives* 27, no. 3, Summer 2013, pp. 35-56.

## Chapter 9

1. One of the most notable discussions of the deserving and undeserving poor, and also incidentally Type 1 Inequality, was in Robert Tressel's *The Ragged Trousered Philanthropists*, published posthumously in 1914: 'Poverty is not caused by men and women getting married; it's not caused by machinery; it's not caused by "over-pro-duction"; it's not caused by drink or laziness; and it's not caused by "over-popula-tion". It's caused by Private Monopoly.' The concept dates from well before Victorian times, though it is associated with that era. In Elizabethan times, the Queen's adviser William Cecil (later Lord Burghley) introduced Poor Law reforms leading to legisla-tion starting in 1563 to help the 'deserving poor'.

2. http://www.wsj.com/specialcoverage/malaysia-controversy.

3. Jeffrey Sachs blog, 'What I did in Russia'. http://jeffsachs.org/2012/03/what-i-did-in-russia/.

4. Bernard Black, Reinier Kraakman and Anna Tarassova, 'Russian Privatization and Corporate Governance: What Went Wrong?', 52 *Stanford Law Review* (2000), pp. 1731-1808.

5. https://www.cebr.com/reports/world-economic-league-table-2018/.

6. http://www.bloomberg.com/news/articles/2014-12-18/bp-s-dudley-relives-russian-nightmare-alongside-rosneft-boss. Indeed, the latest reports on this suggest that blood tests subsequently revealed an attempt to poison him (*Daily Telegraph*, 30 April 2018) although they do not reveal who had done this.

7. http://www.thisismoney.co.uk/money/news/article-1507704/Marconi-men-share-16387m-windfall.html.

8. https://www.quora.com/Would-companies-be-better-off-hiring-cheaper-CEOs.

9. This section is heavily based on http://www.bloomberg.com/news/articles/2013-06-06/costco-ceo-craig-jelinek-leads-the-cheapest-happiest-company-in-the-world.

10. http://www.bloomberg.com/news/articles/2013-06-06/costco-ceo-craig-je-linek-leads-the-cheapest-happiest-company-in-the-world.

11. http://money.cnn.com/gallery/investing/2015/12/23/best-ceos-2015/.

12. http://www.nytimes.com/roomfordebate/2013/11/10/prosecuting-executives-not-companies-for-wall-street-crime/bankers-have-done-more-damage-than-mobsters.

13. https://www.russellsage.org/sites/all/files/Rethinking-Finance/Philippon_v3.pdf.

14. http://www.bis.org/publ/rpfx16.htm.

15. https://blogs.cfainstitute.org/investor/2012/06/28/investment-management-fees-are-much-higher-than-you-think/.

16. Burton G. Malkiel, 'Asset Management Fees and the Growth of Finance', *Journal of Economic Perspectives* 27, no. 2, Spring 2013, pp. 97-108.

17. The classic book on this is Fred Schwed Jr, *Where are the Customers' Yachts? or A Good Hard Look at Wall Street*, first published in 1940. The most recently pub-lished edition with illustrations by Peter Arno and an introduction by Jason Zweig was published in 2005 by Wiley. The title comes from a question to a broker looking out over the harbour in New York. 'Whose are these yachts?' 'Oh, those are the bro-kers' yachts.' 'So where are the customers' yachts?'

18. This article can be accessed in various guises. I have quoted from the text

made available by Vanguard. But the most accessible version is John C. Bogle, 'The Road Not Taken', *Journal of Portfolio Management*, Fall 2017, 44 (1) 83-90; DOI: https://doi.org/10.3905/jpm.2017.44.1.083

19. http://www.investopedia.com/articles/investing/030916/buffetts-bet-hedge-funds-year-eight-brka-brkb.asp.

20. http://www.ibtimes.co.uk/pay-structure-uks-finance-industry-too-high-admits-standard-life-chairman-1560626#.

21. Gavyn was a contemporary of mine in my M.Phil course at Oxford and is (I assume now was) a fellow cricketer. I'm normally quite a good judge of character and I would be very surprised if he turned out to be a crook or even someone who had behaved unprofessionally, despite working for Goldman. But he has certainly made more money than anyone else in our M.Phil class, mainly through finding arbitrage opportunities from his economic understanding (he ended up running a hedge fund). I don't agree with his left-wing politics but I do not find it difficult to respect people with views that are different from mine! I suspect there are many others working for Goldman who are perfectly honest.

22. http://www.corp-research.org/goldman-sachs.

23. http://www.businessinsider.com/the-secret-goldman-sachs-greece-deal-thats-described-as-a-very-sexy-story-between-two-sinners-2012-3?IR=T.

24. https://www.thenation.com/article/Goldman-greek-gambit/.

25. https://en.wikipedia.org/wiki/Carlos_Slim.

26. http://www.forbes.com/sites/doliaestevez/2014/07/09/in-a-surprising-move-mexican-billionaire-carlos-slim-to-sell-telecom-assets-in-compliance-with-new-anti-trust-rules/#3bf93d252624.

27. http://www.nytimes.com/2016/08/10/world/americas/mexicos-carlos-slim-helu.html?_r=0.

## Chapter 10

1. http://www.ukbusinessforums.co.uk/threads/clogs-to-clogs-in-three-generations-and-variants.224877/.

2. One is reminded of the comment of the famous footballer George Best about what had happened to his wealth: 'I spent a lot of money on booze, birds and fast cars. The rest I squandered ...' http://www.the42.ie/17-most-memorable-george-best-quotes-1094674-Nov2015/.

3. http://familylinevideo.com/family-documenting-three-generations/.

4. http://www.encyclopedia.com/humanities/dictionaries-thesauruses-pictures-and-press-releases/shirtsleeves-shirtsleeves-three.

5. https://www.ft.com/content/25a029f6-64f7-11e4-bb43-00144feabdc0.

6. Guglielmo Barone and Sauro Mocetti, 'Intergenerational mobility in the very long run: Florence 1427-2011', June 2015 http://www.eui.eu/Documents/DepartmentsCentres/Economics/Seminarsevents/Mocetti.pdf

7. I've always been tempted to buy a property on one of the Italian lakes but once, when I got near to doing so, I checked the likely transactions charges. They amounted to nearly 20% of the property value. If you lose a fifth of your investment every time you have a property transaction you are unlikely to transact very fre-

quently. It is not surprising that I backed off from the potential purchase quickly. For more detail see http://www.homesinitaly.co.uk/smx/home/fees/.

8. George-Levi Gayle and Andrés Hincapié, 'Which Persists More from Generation to Generation—Income or Wealth?' *Regional Economist*, Federal Reserve Bank of St Louis, July 2016.

9. http://scienceblogs.com/gregladen/2011/03/01/how-long-is-a-generation/.

10. **Energy:** oil, gas, coal, any consumable fuels.

> **Materials:** chemicals, metals & alloys, mining, packaging.
>
> **Industrials:** construction, engineering, distribution, transport, HR & office services.
>
> **Consumer products**
>
> **Discretionary** (more sensitive to economic cycles): automobiles, home building & appliances, leisure, textiles & clothing, hotels, restaurants, advertising, entertainment, publishing, retailing.
>
> **Staples** (less sensitive to economic cycles): food & drugs, brewing & spirits, supermarkets, tobacco, non-durable household goods & personal products.
>
> **Healthcare:** pharmaceuticals, biotechnology, health services & equipment.
>
> **Financials:** banking, investments, hedge funds, insurance, property & real estate.
>
> **IT & telecoms:** software, internet, technological hardware (computers, phones etc.), electronic equipment, semi conductors, network carriers.
>
> **Direct inheritance:** land, divorce settlement (inheritance of entire net worth).

11. I am grateful to my old friend David Collas for suggesting this point to me.

12. http://www.independent.co.uk/student/news/number-of-students-who-marry-after-studying-the-same-subject-at-university-on-the-rise-new-data-10380976.html.

13. https://www.theatlantic.com/sexes/archive/2013/04/college-graduates-marry-other-college-graduates-most-of-the-time/274654/.

14. A good study by the Joseph Rowntree Foundation looks in depth at the relationship between poverty and parenting: https://www.jrf.org.uk/sites/default/files/jrf/migrated/files/parenting-poverty.pdf.

15. Jay Belsky, 'The Determinants of Parenting: A Process Model', *Child Development*, 1984, 55, pp. 83-96.

16. Daniel S. Shaw, 'Parenting Programs and Their Impact on the Social and Emotional Development of Young Children', PhD thesis, University of Pittsburgh, USA December 2014.

17. Memorial eulogy by Sir Francis McWilliams at the funeral for his sister Helen Harris, 19 January 2017.

18. Susanne Huber and Martin Fieder, 'Worldwide Census Data Reveal Prevalence of Educational Homogamy and its Effect on Childlessness', Department of Anthropology, University of Vienna, Vienna, Austria http://journal.frontiersin.org/article/10.3389/fsoc.2016.00010/full.

19. Sebastian Aguiar, 'Intelligence: The History of Psychometrics', Institute for Ethics and Emerging Technologies, 31 October 2014. http://ieet.org. Retrieved 9 November 2015.

20. My mother used to run kindergartens in Malaysia and ended up in the mid-1970s with about 600 children being educated in three sites. Most of the children

(largely of Chinese or South Asian background) were fluently trilingual (Chinese or a South Asian dialect; English and Bahasa Kebangsaan – Malay) by the age of six. And even people in menial jobs such as domestic service would spend as much as a third of their income to send their children to kindergarten to improve their chances in life.

## Part IV
1. https://www.johnkay.com/2017/04/05/basics-basic-income/

## Chapter 11
1. A good description of these is given in 'Disruptive Technologies: Advances That Will Transform Life, Business, and the Global Economy' by the McKinsey Global Institute, May 2013 http://www.mckinsey.com/business-functions/digital-mckinsey/our-insights/disruptive-technologies

2. Let me be clear. Autonomous vehicles will create huge opportunities and if managed properly should make traffic safer, quicker, less stressful and cheaper. See my paper on this: https://cebr.com/wp/wp-content/uploads/2017/07/Abolishing-traffic-jams-v3.0.docx.

3. Anthony Hilton, 'Which Party is Even Remotely Ready for the Tech Revolution?', *Evening Standard*, Thursday 18 May 2017.

4. http://www.bbc.co.uk/news/business-16611040.

5. Anthony Hilton, op. cit.

6. https://www.gresham.ac.uk/lectures-and-events/how-does-globalisation-affect-inequality-globally

7. David H. Autor, Frank Levy and Richard J. Murnane, 'The Skill Content of Recent Technological Change: An Empirical Exploration', *Quarterly Journal of Economics* 118, 2003, pp. 1279-1333.

8. Anthony B. Atkinson, *Inequality: What Can be Done?*, Harvard University Press, 2015, p. 88

9. http://calbudgetcenter.org/blog/bringing-down-the-unemployment-rate-depends-on-getting-the-long-term-unemployed-back-to-work/.

10. Cebr World Economic League Table 2018, released 26 December 2017.

11. See World Economic League Table 2018 for details.

12. https://www.theatlantic.com/health/archive/2017/01/teens-drugs-iceland/513668/.

13. George J. Stigler, 'The Economics of Information', *Journal of Political Economy* 69, issue 3, June 1961, pp. 213-22.

14. Best described in George Gilder, *Microcosm: The Quantum Revolution in Economics and Technology*, Touchstone, 1990.

15. J.R. Hicks, *Value and Capital*, Oxford University Press, 1939.

16. A. Chua, *Battle Hymn of the Tiger Mother*, Penguin, 2011.

## Chapter 12
1. http://www.britishpoliticalspeech.org/speech-archive.htm?speech=202.

2. George-Levi Gayle and Andrés Hincapié, 'Which Persists More from Generation to Generation – Income or Wealth?', *Regional Economist*, Federal Reserve Bank of St Louis, July 2016.

3. See for example the European Expert Network on Economics of Education (EENEE) EENEE Analytical Report No. 21 prepared for the European Commission by Jo Blanden and Sandra McNally, February 2015. This provides a useful summary.

4. Eduardo Porter, 'Education Gap between Rich and Poor is getting Wider', *New York Times*, 22 September 2015. https://www.nytimes.com/2015/09/23/business /economy/education-gap-between-rich-and-poor-is-growing-wider.html

5. Bruce Bradbury, Miles Corak, Jane Waldfogel and Elizabeth Washbrook, 'Too Many Children Left Behind: The U.S. Achievement Gap in Comparative Perspective', for the Russell Sage Foundation https://www.russellsage.org/publications/too-many -children-left-behind.

6. To understand this better see https://cepa.stanford.edu/content/widening-aca demic-achievement-gap-between-rich-and-poor-new-evidence-and-possible.

7. I am grateful to Roland Johnson, House Master at Stowe School, for discussing this point with me.

8. See https://www.spectator.co.uk/2016/02/to-survive-as-a-tory-teacher-you-have-to-keep-quiet/ for an interesting description of life as a teacher by someone whose views did not fit with the prevailing left-wing orthodoxy.

9. https://www.gov.uk/government/publications/pupil-premium-conditions-of -grant-2016-to-2017.

10. http://www.suttontrust.com/wp-content/uploads/2015/06/Pupil-Premium -Summit-Report-FINAL-EDIT.pdf.

11. Brad Hershbein, Melissa S. Kearney and Lawrence H. Summers, 'Increasing Education: What it Will and Will Not Do for Earnings and Earnings Inequality', Brookings Upfront, Tuesday 31 March 2015.

12. Arthur C. Brooks @arthurbrooks February 13, 2017 | Foreign Affairs The dignity deficit: Reclaiming Americans' sense of purpose.

13. https://www.simplypsychology.org/maslow.html gives a simple description of Maslow's hierarchy of needs.

14. This is the classic Human Givens approach to psychological balance. I don't fully subscribe to the approach which I believe to be too absolute and too unwilling to cope with the diversity of human experience, but I think it gives useful guidance for understanding common psychological issues. http://www.hgfoundation.com/what _are_the_human_givens.html

## Chapter 13

1. The novelist John Le Carré's description of his visit to his Russian publisher in his autobiography *The Pigeon Tunnel* is probably the most dramatic description of gangster capitalism I've ever read or observed.

2. Adam Smith, *The Wealth of Nations*, p. 14.

3. Cebr's ethics policy can be downloaded from the link at the bottom of this page: https://cebr.com/about-cebr/our-approach/.

4. https://www.recode.net/2017/7/21/16008504/apple-amazon-google-record-lobby-trump-immigration-science-privacy.

5. See for example, just based on random googling, this link between working

for IBM and being a scoutmaster https://www.linkedin.com/in/kent-bruinsma
-2a275925/.

## Chapter 14

1. Roland Andersson and Bo Söderberg, 'Elimination of Rent Control in the Swedish Rental Housing Market: Why and How?', *Journal of Housing Research* 21, no. 2, 2012, pp. 159-82.

2. I am grateful to *The Guardian*, 19 August 2015, for much of this description. https://www.theguardian.com/world/2015/aug/19/why-stockholm-housing-rules-rent-control-flat.

3. This section draws heavily on analysis by Marginal Revolution. http://marginalrevolution.com/marginalrevolution/2015/07/rent-control.html.

4. http://www.bbc.com/capital/story/20160517-this-is-one-city-where-youll-never-find-a-home.

5. https://www.imf.org/en/News/Articles/2016/09/28/MS092916-Sweden-Concluding-Statement-of-IMF-Mission.

6. https://www.bloomberg.com/news/articles/2017-12-14/housing-slump-gathers-pace-in-sweden-with-buyers-losing-faith.

7. Bill Bryson, *The Road to Little Dribbling*, Doubleday, 2015.

8. The word was first coined by the marketing department of the estates department of the Metropolitan Railway in 1915!

9. 'Shaping the Nation', Confederation of British Industry and Royal Institute of Chartered Surveyors, Report of the Planning Task Force, CBI, RICS, 1992.

10. Review of Housing Supply Final Report – Recommendations http://news.bbc.co.uk/nol/shared/bsp/hi/pdfs/17_03_04_barker_review.pdf.

11. 'The Future Homes Commission: An Inquiry into the Design and Delivery of the UK's Future Homes', RIBA 2012 available at https://issuu.com /ribacomms /docs/futurehomecommissionhires2.

12. https://www.theguardian.com/money/2015/jul/16/tenants-in-england-spend-half-their-pay-on-rent.

13. Douglas McWilliams and Mark Pragnell, 'The Rich – Are they Different?', *Prospect*, 20 October 1995. http://www.prospectmagazine.co.uk/magazine/thericharethey-different-wealth-income -inequality-investment-tax.

14. Peter Ganong and Daniel Shoag, 'Why Has Regional Income Convergence in the U.S. Declined?', *Journal of Urban Economics*, January 2015. http://scholar.harvard.edu/files/shoag/files/why_has_regional_income_convergence_in_the_us_declined_01.pdf.

15. Douglas McWilliams, 'Will There Be a Shortage of Spending Power?', Gresham Professorial Lecture, 28 February 2013. http://www.gresham.ac.uk/lectures-and-events/will-there-be-a-shortage-of-spending-power.

16. For a flavour of the opposing view see Claudio Borio and Piti Disyatat, 'Global Imbalances and the Financial Crisis: Link or No Link?', *BIS Working Papers No. 346*, Bank for International Settlements.

17. See for example https://www.cityoflondon.gov.uk/business/economic-research-and-information/research-publications/Documents/Research-2015/Impact-of-Crossrail-briefing-paper.pdf.

18. http://www.ons.gov.uk/employmentandlabourmarket/peopleinwork /labour-productivity/bulletins/labourproductivity/2015-10-01).

19. https://www.ons.gov.uk/economy/economicoutputandproductivity/publicservices productivity/articles/publicservicesproductivityestimatestotalpublicservices/total publicservice2013.

Chapter 15

1. I dealt with the high cost of living in Western economies, particularly in Europe, in my Gresham professorial lecture of February 2013 'How to Make Western Economies More Competitive'. http://www.gresham.ac.uk/lectures-and-events/how-to-make-western-economies-more-competitive

2. Data from Bureau of Labour Statistics News Release Spending Patterns 2014/15, 30 August 2016. http://www.bls.gov/news.release/cesan.nr0.htm.

3. Author's calculations based on BLS statistics, notably the Spending Patterns 2014/15 data mentioned above and also http://www.bls.gov/opub/btn/volume-5/pdf /expenditures-on-celluar-phone-services-have-increased-significantly-since-2007.pdf.

4. Seán Healy, Michelle Murphy, Seán Ward and Brigid Reynolds, 'Basic Income – Why and How in Difficult Economic Times: Financing a BI in Ireland', Social Justice Ireland. http://www.bien2012.de/sites/default/files/paper_253_en.pdf

5. Source: International Telecommunications Union (Table 4.2 in the ITU's Measuring the Information Society 2015).

6. http://www.usgovernmentspending.com/social_security_spending_by _year.

7. http://uk.businessinsider.com/universal-basic-income-scheme-for-the-uk-2016-6.

8. By coincidence, my company Cebr was tasked with auditing this manifesto, though we did not audit the basic income proposals which were not spelt out sufficiently firmly to be audited.

9. https://static1.squarespace.com/static/56eddde762cd9413e151ac92/t/5a5f54ff 53450ae87509190a/1516197120863/Universal+Basic+Income.pdf.

10. https://www.whitehouse.gov/sites/default/files/docs/ERP_2016_Book_Complete %20JA.pdf.

11. David H. Autor, 'Why Are There Still So Many Jobs? The History and Future of Workplace Automation', Journal of Economic Perspectives, vol. 29, no. 3, Summer 2015, pp. 3-30.

12. https://www.gov.uk/government/statistics/taxi-and-private-hire-vehicles-statistics-england-2015.

13. http://www.alltrucking.com/faq/truck-drivers-in-the-usa/.

Chapter 17

1. 'Income Inequality and Growth: The Role of Taxes and Transfers', OECD Economics Department Policy Notes no. 9, January 2012.

2. https://www.ons.gov.uk/peoplepopulationandcommunity/personalandhouse-holdfinances/incomeandwealth/bulletins/theeffectsoftaxesandbenefitsonin-comeinequality/1977tofinancialyearending2015.

3. https://www.ifs.org.uk/publications/9178.

4. By far the most detailed report covering this is 'The Single Income Tax Final

Report of the 2020 Tax Commission' (421 pages), produced by the Taxpayers' Alliance. The author was a member of the Commission and personally wrote the part of the report dealing with the economic analysis of the impact of the proposals using the dynamic tax model developed by Cebr for the Taxpayers Alliance.

5. Stuart Ball, 'Baldwin, Stanley, first Earl Baldwin of Bewdley (1867-1947)', *Oxford Dictionary of National Biography*, Oxford University Press, September 2004; online edn, May 2008, retrieved 28 March 2009.

6. http://www.bbc.co.uk/news/uk-england-london-41468761.

7. http://www.telegraph.co.uk/news/uknews/12046438/true-and-fair-foundation-hornets-nest-charity-report.html.

8. See 'How winning the lottery makes you miserable' Melissa Chan, *Time Magazine*, 12 January 2016.

## Chapter 18

1. http://www.huffingtonpost.co.uk/entry/jeremy-corbyns-full-10-point-plan-to-rebuild-and-transform-britain_uk_57a30d8ce4b06c6e8dc6af2a.

2. https://berniesanders.com/issues/income-and-wealth-inequality/.

3. https://www.donaldjtrump.com/policies/economy.

4. https://www.cebr.com/reports/the-economic-impact-of-president-trump/.

5. 'How Preferential Trade Agreements Affect the U.S. Economy', Congress of the United States Congressional Budget Office, September 2016.

6. See, for example, Richard M. Alston, J.R. Kearl and Michael B. Vaughan, 'Is There a Consensus Among Economists in the 1990s?', *American Economic Review* 82, no. 2, May 1992, pp. 203-9; and Daniel B. Klein and Charlotta Stern, 'Economists' Views and Voting', *Public Choice* 126, March 2006, 331-42. More recently, a 2012 Initiative on Global Markets survey of prominent economists found that 94% of the respondents agreed with the statement, 'Freer trade improves productive efficiency and offers consumers better choices, and in the long run these gains are much larger than any effects on employment.' See Chicago Booth, 'Free Trade' (Initiative on Global Markets Forum, 13 March 2012, http://tinyurl.com/igm-chicago). Several of the respondents in that survey noted that society should do a better job compensating the workers and businesses that lose income as a result of trade.

7. https://www.donaldjtrump.com/policies/immigration.

8. See Douglas McWilliams, *The Flat White Economy*, Chapter 6.

9. *The Guardian*, 3 July 2017

10. The Conservative Party Manifesto 2017 https://www.conservatives.com/manifesto.

11. *The Flat White Economy: How the Digital Economy is Transforming London and Other Cities of the Future*, Duckworth, 2015 (updated paperback edition March 2016).

12. *The Flat White Economy*, updated paperback edition March 2016, p. 140.

13. Jonathan Portes and Giuseppe Forte, 'The Economic Impact of Brexit-induced Reductions in Migration to the UK', *Vox*, 5 January 2017 http://voxeu.org/article/economic-impact-brexit-induced-reductions-migration-uk.

14. C. Vargas-Silva, 'Potential Implications of Admission Criteria for EU Na-

tionals Coming to the UK', Migration Observatory report, COMPAS, University of Oxford, 2016.

15. Migration Watch, 'UK Immigration Policy Outside the EU', 2016 http://www .migrationwatchuk.org/briefing-paper/371.

16. E. Boubtane, J.C. Dumont and C. Rault, 'Immigration and Economic Growth in the OECD Countries 1986-2006', *CESifo Working Paper Series No. 5392*, 2015. Available at SSRN: https://ssrn.com/abstract=2622005.

17. The Migration Observatory, 'The Fiscal Impact of Immigration in the UK', Oxford University, 14 September 2016.

18. 'Migrants in the UK Labour Market: An Overview', 1 December 2016, Table 1, based on the 2015 Labour Force Survey.

19. 'Migrants in the UK Labour Market: An Overview', 1 December 2016, Table 2, based on the 2015 Labour Force Survey.

20. 'Migrants in the UK Labour Market: An Overview', 1 December 2016, Figure 3, based on the 2015 Labour Force Survey.

# INDEX

WITHDRAWN
AVON PUBLIC LIBRARY
BOX 977 / 200 BENCHMARK RD.
AVON, CO 81620